La Serre M-Ulili

THIS
BRIGHT LIGHT
OF OURS

Praise for *This Bright Light of Ours*

"*This Bright Light of Ours: Stories from the Voting Rights Fight* is a first-hand, from the front-lines report of the sixties southern voting rights movement in one of the most resistant counties in one of the most resistant states. This is a must read account of a less publicized aspect of the southern Civil Rights Movement, white volunteers risking life and limb to challenge white supremacy at its most brutal."
—Julian Bond, Chairman Emeritus, NAACP

"This is an important work about a neglected period of the Civil Rights Movement, the 1965 Voting Rights Movement. Gitin clearly communicates her commitment to civil rights and social justice by presenting us with the fresh voices of unheralded community leaders in Wilcox County, Alabama. Gitin's work adds wonderful new insight and texture to the story of how courageous Americans transformed their community and the country."
—Robert Michael Franklin, author of *Crisis in the Village: Restoring Hope in African American Communities*

"Gitin provides one of the most nuanced treatments of white involvement in the movement that I have read. She avoids many of the pitfalls that typically mar works treating the subject, most notably devaluing the role of outside organizers while simultaneously overstating the contributions they made."
—Hasan Kwame Jeffries, author of *Bloody Lowndes: Civil Rights and Black Power in Alabama's Black Belt*

"*This Bright Light of Ours*, shares important details of the experience of giving oneself to the country-changing work of the Civil Rights Movement. The Freedom Struggle in Alabama was seen and heard about around the world. Much credit is given to a select few whose names are often called as leaders of this powerful movement. But there would have been no freedom movement—certainly not of the breadth and scope to which it evolved—had it not been for movement volunteers like Maria Gitin and others she writes about. Because of their giving spirit, their willingness to suffer even, a cruel and unjust system that impacted the lives of all of us was changed."
—Dorothy Cotton, Director SCLC Citizenship Education Program and founder of the Dorothy Cotton Institute

"Maria Gitin's book is a unique blend of her own story and those of the local community members with whom she worked in Wilcox County in the exceptionally challenging struggle of the 1960's Civil Rights Movement. Very, very few books offer this kind of retrospective and prospective. Gitin's love for the people of Wilcox County shines through. The work reinforces an understanding of the courage of those times, the penalties exacted in real human lives and ways, the strength of the Black community, their openness and caring, and a brilliant documentation of how completely segregated the South—at least this corner of the South—remains. These are powerful stories profoundly relevant for our own times."

    —Bettina F. Aptheker, *Intimate Politics: How I Grew Up Red,*
       Fought for Free Speech, and Became a Feminist Rebel

"Bernard LaFayette and I worked together in Wilcox. In fact, the first Blacks to attempt to register since the fall of Reconstruction were from Wilcox County. We were introduced early to the violence of Sheriff L Jenkins and a county with more dead folk on the voter rolls than living. I am very proud to see that a Sister is out there telling the story from which at last hopefully soon a legacy of SNCC will emerge, a legacy that our young can use as bread from which to draw sustenance. We desperately need it."

    —Colia Liddell LaFayette Clark, SNCC field director, Freedom
       Flame Award recipient Selma Jubilee 2011

"Maria Gitin's lively and candid memoir-history answers the call for a grassroots rather than leader-centered account of the southern struggle against the Jim Crow system. *This Bright Light of Ours* helps readers understand how millions of black Southerners finally became American citizens."

    —Clayborne Carson, professor and director of the Martin
       Luther King Jr. Research and Education Institute

the MODERN ∫OUTH

series editors
Glenn Feldman & Kari Frederickson

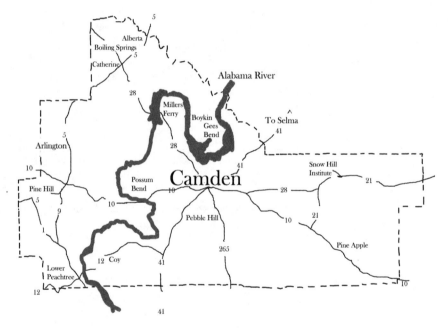

WILCOX COUNTY, ALABAMA

Frontispiece. Wilcox County, Alabama, 1965. (Copyright © 2012 by Samuel Torres Jr.)

THIS
BRIGHT LIGHT
OF OURS

Stories from the 1965
Voting Rights Fight

MARIA GITIN

THE UNIVERSITY OF ALABAMA PRESS
Tuscaloosa

Copyright © 2014
The University of Alabama Press
Tuscaloosa, Alabama 35487–0380
All rights reserved
Manufactured in the United States of America

Typeface: Caslon and Corbel

Cover photograph: Student demonstrators attacked with smoke bombs, Camden,
Alabama. (Bill Hudson photograph © Associated Press, March 31, 1965)

∞

The paper on which this book is printed meets the minimum requirements of American
National Standard for Information Sciences-Permanence of Paper for Printed Library
Materials, ANSI Z39.48–1984.

Cataloging-in-Publication data is available from the Library of Congress.
ISBN: 978-0-8173-1817-8

Dedicated to all of the courageous Wilcox County freedom fighters
and
to my beloved husband, Samuel Torres Jr.

Contents

Illustrations

Foreword

This book had its beginning in the actions of a nineteen-year-old, brave, intelligent, idealistic, and socially conscious white girl who volunteered to go to the heart of the so-called Alabama Black Belt during a critical period in the Civil Rights Movement. The girl's name was Joyce Brians (Maria Gitin), a college freshman from California, who worked with the Summer Community Organization and Political Education (SCOPE) project of the Southern Christian Leadership Conference (SCLC), the organization founded by Martin Luther King Jr. and other ministers to spearhead civil rights activities. The scene is Wilcox County and the time is the summer of 1965, when the struggle for the right to vote reached fever pitch. Brians (Gitin) is one of the few white participant-observers who were a part of the history-making events, and she re-creates what she observed, heard, felt, and did in those moments of amazing courage, sacrifice, and risk.

It is to Gitin's credit that she resisted the idea to write a simple personal memoir based on letters she wrote to family, friends, and supporters back home in California in 1965 and decided instead to tell both her story and the stories of her coworkers and acquaintances in the freedom cause. Drawing largely on letters, informal interviews, and oral histories obtained through her associations with the residents of Wilcox County and others over time, Gitin, with amazing scope and sharpness, provides a narrative commentary that sets the extraordinary eyewitness accounts and the diverse remembrances against the backdrop of the experiences and events she describes. The wide and diverse array of voices leaps from the pages of *This Bright Light of Ours* with stunning force. They are authentic voices, and the stories they share are dramatic, gripping, poignant, uplifting, and empowering. Reverberating as a central theme are the memories of Jim Crow in the rural Alabama Black Belt and of people determined, as a matter of conscience, to live out the fullness of their personalities. In short, this book speaks to the power of oral history to bring people and events to vivid life.

This Bright Light of Ours resonates with warm compassion and keen insight into what was occurring in the minds, hearts, and souls of the people who helped change the face of Wilcox County. Gitin is keenly aware of their concerns and motives. She also highlights the ways in which soul power came alive and found expression not only in the stories of these ordinary people but also in their songs, prayers, and sermons, which enlivened the quest for freedom. Culled from the memories of her everyday experiences, Gitin speaks of art elevated to a level that may never be matched, let alone transcended. Obviously, she was deeply inspired and profoundly transformed by these experiences—by people who tapped into their own personal and spiritual power to become shapers of a new order. Gitin's respect for these people and their artistic genius in the midst of struggle is not romanticized or patronizing but genuine and enduring, and she reflects on this with modesty and a keen sense of gratitude.

I actually grew up in Wilcox County, in the little town of Camden, and I remember so much of what occurred there in the 1960s. I experienced the injustices that black people routinely endured, and I will never forget the brutality visited upon white students like Maria Gitin who dared to take bold stands on our behalf. I knew and walked with many in that struggle and saw people beaten and verbally abused. The murder of brave civil rights soldiers, like David Colston, still haunts me to this day. Like so many others, I am the beneficiary of this fierce determination to defeat the forces of evil, injustice, and retrogression. This explains my deep appreciation for what Gitin shares on the pages of this rich, informative, and provocative book.

This is the very first book of its kind on this period of struggle in the history of black people in Wilcox County, Alabama. It records the voices and experiences of those who "talked the talk" and "walked the walk." In an era of anti-immigration hysteria, resurging racism, attempts at voter intimidation and suppression, attacks on affirmative action, and Occupy Wall Street activism, *This Bright Light of Ours* could not be more relevant and timely. It is here for social activists from the 1960s who wish to recall their struggles with pride and thanksgiving. It is available for today's agents of change, who look for some inspiration and direction from those who came before them. And perhaps more importantly, this book is accessible for youngsters, black and white, who seem to have little or no sense of what brought them to where they are today. Thanks to Maria Gitin, future generations will remember the names of many of those ordinary voices and agents of struggle who, up to this point, have been left out of the history books.

Lewis V. Baldwin, PhD

Acknowledgments

Deep gratitude and respect go to all of the courageous individuals who entrusted me with their stories. Special thanks to my dear SNCC friends Charles "Chuck" Bonner and Luke (Bob) Block for helping to re-create our summer as teenage civil rights workers. Wilcox County community leaders who opened doors and answered endless questions include: W. Kate Charley, Sheryl Threadgill, Alma King, Gloria Jean McDole, and John Matthews. Civil rights photographer Bob Fitch provided historic images that enrich this work immensely.

For generous encouragement, insight, and expert counsel over the years despite his own demanding publication schedule: Lewis V. Baldwin. For consistent fact checking, terminology, and political theory, thanks to Bruce Hartford, lay historian and web manager for the Civil Rights Veterans website. Scott E. Kirkland, curator of the History Museum of Mobile, played a vital role in the placement of this book. At the University of Alabama Press, acquisitions editor Donna Cox Baker embraced this project and ushered it through the publication process. Editor in chief Dan Waterman and the editorial board's commitment to the full history of the South is admirable.

For early encouragement, I am indebted to Kathy Nasstrom, Bettina Aptheker, and the late James Houston. Developmental editor Cassandra Shaylor helped shape the book. Historian Martha Jane Brazy of the University of South Alabama enthusiastically embraced the work and contributed to its readability, generously offering me graduate-student-level attention.

Thanks to my cousin Jeanne Hanks for her empathy during years of conversation about this project, and to Debbie Kogan and Esther Bass for friendship and practical assistance. Deep appreciation goes to Joy Crawford-Washington of BGC Communications for her tireless support and sisterly friendship.

Long ago, I wondered why people dedicated books to their spouses or partners, especially when the topic was unrelated to their relationship. Seven years later, the answer is clear. My spouse, Samuel Torres Jr., not only pro-vided me with the freedom to pursue this project, he also offered frequent and much-needed critiques, conducted research, tracked down copyright holders, proofread a dozen drafts, held my hand when I needed it, left me alone when that was best, and did my laundry. I could not have completed a work of this depth and complexity without his love and support.

Abbreviations

CEP	Citizenship Education Program
CORE	Congress on Racial Equality
CRA	1964 Civil Rights Act
HUAC	House Un-American Activities Committee
NAACP	National Association for the Advancement of Colored People
NCNW	National Council of Negro Women
SCLC	Southern Christian Leadership Conference
SCOPE	Summer Community Organization and Political Education
SNCC	Student Nonviolent Coordinating Committee
VEP	Voter Education Project
VRA	1965 Voting Rights Act
WPA	Works Progress Administration
YWCA	Young Women's Christian Association

THIS
BRIGHT LIGHT
OF OURS

Introduction

Through the hazy blue light of the Mt. Konocti Blues Club, one night in December 2005, Bettie Mae Fikes's deep contralto sang out "This Little Light of Mine" with as much passion as she had when she was a teenager with the SNCC Freedom Singers. As we sat around the table, my friends Charles "Chuck" Bonner and Luke (Bob) Block and I swapped tales about our arrests and close calls with Klansmen in the backwoods of Wilcox County, Alabama. Luke, Charles, and I hadn't seen each other in forty years. Later that night, Charles exclaimed, "We are so lucky that we all survived!" And Luke declared, "That's the truth! You know Maria, we should go back and find out what happened to those folks—Ethel Brooks, Dan and Juanita Harrell, the Crawfords, all of 'em."

Luke Block (then called Bob Block) and I (then called Joyce Brians) were among hundreds of white student civil rights workers who joined the voter registration movement during the Freedom Summer of 1965. When I met him, Luke had been working with Charles Bonner of the Student Nonviolent Coordinating Committee (SNCC) and Daniel Harrell of Southern Christian Leadership Conference (SCLC) for several months. Charles Bonner, a Selma native, had been demonstrating for equal rights since he was a child. That spring, as a nineteen-year-old San Francisco State College freshman, I responded to Dr. King's call for voter registration volunteers by signing up for the SCLC Summer Community Organization and Political Education (SCOPE) project, which conducted the last large integrated voter registration drive prior to the passage of the 1965 Voting Rights Act in August. Luke and Charles befriended me soon after I arrived at my assignment in Wilcox County. For over ten years before our reunion at Clear Lake, I had been working on a memoir based on letters I wrote home to my supporters and family in 1965, trying to recapture the emotional truth of that time.

After our forty-year reunion, I knew it couldn't be just my story—not even just our story. I had to rediscover and include the incredible freedom fighters of Wilcox County who invited us to share their struggle.

In 2008, three years after our first reunion, Luke and I returned to Wilcox County together. One of our first stops was the site of the old Camden, Alabama, jail where we had been briefly incarcerated. As we stared at the empty red dirt lot, being there in safety felt almost surreal. A sheriff's deputy smiled as he drove by without questioning us. Luke said, "I guess all the officers are black now, so we likely won't be arrested today."

Luke came for healing; I came with questions. *What difference did the movement make? Did we cause more harm than good? What did the community hold dear from those days and what part of the dream was still unfulfilled?* As I sought out people we had known, I rediscovered an extended family of those who risked their lives for the right to vote, a right that had been denied black citizens in the South for nearly one hundred years after passage of the Fifteenth Amendment. Few recalled me by name; more recalled Luke. I was but a flicker through their lives and a brief partner in their struggle, welcome but temporary extra help in the long freedom fight. Nearly everyone I contacted was generous with their time, their stories, and their acceptance of my small role in their historic battle for the right to vote.

This book has three primary aims. Foremost is to honor the courageous civil rights activists of Wilcox County, Alabama, by creating a venue in which they can tell their own stories, in their own words. Second is to document that local black activists were both the leaders and the backbone of the Civil Rights Movement. SCLC and SNCC recruited volunteers to add arms and legs to their ongoing freedom fight, not to take charge of local organizing efforts. Third, by describing in detail my youthful civil rights experience, I hope to inspire others to consider their role in ending poverty and prejudice.

This memoir and work of creative nonfiction is written from the cheerfully biased point of view of a civil rights activist. Unlike purely sociological or historical accounts of the Civil Rights Movement, these participant-witness accounts are subjective interpretations of events where we had (and may still have) partial, even conflicting information.

This Bright Light of Ours is divided into two parts. Part I is a memoir, my personal account of coming of age in the midst of the last battle of the Civil War: states' right to maintain segregation versus the federal right to vote. While my stories are highly personal, similar ones could be told by many of the hundreds of youth who worked with SCLC or SNCC. I was fortunate to be trained by and work with both organizations. My own early story is that of an idealistic, judgmental, and painfully naive young woman. I deliberately retained my misunderstandings and biased comments from that time. My misadventures are included because there is no way to write honestly about being a teenage civil rights worker without writing about the fact that youths often break rules during heady and dramatic times. It is important for students and others to realize that experiments with sex and drinking were products of our age and of the times, not of our project.

Part II is testimony: these personal stories were gathered from more than forty people who lived, worked, and were committed to the movement and/or are related to people I worked with in Wilcox County. Throughout the book, I use natural language as much as possible while reducing dialect that could be interpreted as discounting the intelligence of the speaker. African American is used in reference to places and events. While some living individuals prefer the term "Black" be capitalized and there is some scholarly debate around the issue, for conformity the word "black" will appear lowercase throughout the book. The term of respect in 1965 was "Negro" and is used in archival materials.

I did not conduct formal interviews. Originally, I had a set list of questions, but few respondents answered them completely or sequentially. Soon, I just listened to what people told me was important for others to know. Some conversations were recorded and transcribed but most were re-created from notes, which were jotted down during telephone calls, corrected, and augmented by follow-up communication. The result is a collection of voices speaking of their lives during the freedom fight.

While all events and names are factual, I reorganized my 1965 letters and stories as well as the sequence of events during my return visits to make the book more compelling. Actual conversations and interview dates are included in endnotes and in the bibliography. My closest friends from that summer, Luke (Bob) Block and Charles "Chuck" Bonner, reviewed my re-creation of our conversations, and numerous former and current Wilcox County residents added to my memories. Where necessary, these stories were then backed by focused archival research, and lastly to other published works.

My perspective is grounded in what I experienced in 1965 and the insights I have gained since then, but the book was shaped by what the Wilcox County natives told me was most important to them. Other than my stories and those of two white coworkers and one lay historian, all stories are told by black people and from black perspectives.

With regard to the SCOPE project, historians have virtually ignored it, and most press accounts at the time were inaccurate. Based upon my own papers from the period as well as the testimony of other participants, this book fills a void and begins to illuminate the significance of the SCOPE project. To date, this is the only published narrative by a participant in the Atlanta SCOPE orientation. In my notes from that time, I attempted to paraphrase the words of famous and soon to become famous civil rights leaders, including Martin Luther King Jr., Hosea Williams, James Lawson, Andrew Young, and James Bevel. I augmented the letters I wrote to my family and supporters with materials given to us at the orientation as well as documents reproduced in *The SCOPE of Freedom*, edited by Willy Siegel Leventhal. While I belonged to and worked with SNCC as well as SCLC's SCOPE, I offer more description of the relatively unknown SCOPE.

The Civil Rights Movement not only changed laws and practices in the South but also changed forever those of us who joined in the freedom fight. Rev. Hosea L. Williams's daughter, Barbara Williams Emerson, recently told me, "The movement was transformative. Even those of us who lived most of our lives in the struggle were surprised to learn how other civil rights workers, even those who were involved briefly, reported that it changed them. For so many their lives, their educational choices, and their career paths were redirected toward activism for a whole range of other social justice issues."

There is no *one* story about the Civil Rights Movement; within the movement, within each community, in each decade of the movement, there were layers of complexity and a rich variety of experience forming a giant patchwork quilt of incredible beauty and strength. The single binding thread was our absolute commitment to racial equality, even when our experience varied by organization, location, and duration or by differences of background, race, and faith.

I was one of the smallest foot soldiers in a nonviolent army led by black activists who fought vitriolic racism with determination and optimism. My purpose in sharing intimate stories of my life as a teenage civil rights worker and of gathering the stories of some of my personal heroes is to help others realize that even when faced with violence and confusion, personal limitations need not stand in the way of righting wrongs and of building community. The freedom fighters of Wilcox County taught me to live with courage, compassion, and even humor in the face of danger and discouragement. I hope that I have been able to live up to even a small part of their example. Together, may our stories shine a light for the next generation to carry on the struggle for economic, educational, and racial justice in Wilcox County, and beyond.

I
MY FREEDOM SUMMER 1965

1

The Call to Action

It was after 4:00 A.M. when we heard truck doors slam as booted feet quickly surrounded Antioch Baptist Church where our exhausted group of newly trained civil rights recruits was trying to get some sleep. "Get down and stay down till I say," shouted our leader, Major Johns. Then there were shots—unmistakable shotgun shots. I moved closer to Bob, a fellow civil rights field worker I had met only ten hours earlier. "They won't kill us tonight," he whispered as I shivered in fear. "Not likely anyway. I've only been cattle prodded once and never been arrested yet. Welcome to Wilcox County, Alabama, that's all." I held my breath and prayed.

How could white men who called themselves Christians come onto this sacred ground with the intent to scare us away when we were only here to help ensure that all Americans had the right to vote? How dare they? Well, I'll show them, I thought to myself. I won't be afraid. After a while they stopped shooting. My heart was racing as I heard the sound of heavy boots retreating to trucks that roared off down the dark tree-lined highway.

It was the summer of 1965. I had joined hundreds of other college students in a voter education and registration drive aimed at supporting disenfranchised black people in segregated counties across the Deep South in their long struggle to register to vote. The Fifteenth Amendment to the US Constitution, ratified in 1870, gave all citizens the right to vote, regardless of race or creed. The Civil Rights Act of 1964 augmented this right by requiring equal application procedures for all voters. However, lawmakers and law enforcers in the South not only ignored these rights, they also fought them with every legal and illegal weapon in their vast racist arsenal.

I had just turned nineteen and was full of optimism. We student civil rights volunteers believed we could make a difference, force the law to work for instead of against the people, and maybe change some minds, too. Despite excellent briefings in Berkeley and orientation in Atlanta, I had only a vague idea of what awaited us until that first fearful night as I crouched on the hardwood floor of historic Antioch Baptist Church in Camden, Alabama.

San Francisco, California, and Selma, Alabama

In the spring semester of 1965, I was a freshman at San Francisco State College. On March 8, I saw Dr. Martin Luther King Jr. on television for the first time. In my youthful imagination I believed he pointed his finger directly at me and said: "We need you to come down and join our nonviolent struggle, become part of the movement and help our people fight for our rights."

In an era when there were only three channels, the images on the small black-and-white TV at my friend Jeff Freed's parents' house were grainy, but unforgettable. Jeff tried to explain the political situation, but I could only watch in horror as masses of white Alabama state troopers and Selma policemen attacked unarmed peaceful protesters from the safety of their horses. They launched tear gas canisters from huge guns, and troopers beat hundreds of people, including young children as they scrambled for safety, just because they had tried to march to Montgomery for voting rights. Dr. Martin Luther King Jr. was not among the marchers on that Sunday, March 7, when the unprovoked attack took place, but he rapidly responded with a compelling national call to nonviolent arms.

What I had witnessed became known as Bloody Sunday. The series of attempted marches and an ultimately successful march commonly referred to as the Selma to Montgomery March actually began a month earlier. In Marion, some thirty miles from Selma, Alabama, a white state policeman shot and killed twenty-six-year-old Jimmy Lee Jackson who was trying to protect his mother and grandfather from being attacked by state police during a peaceful voting rights march.

Jimmy Lee Jackson's murder inspired the first attempted march from Selma to Montgomery. That Sunday, March 7, march was organized and led by Student Nonviolent Coordinating Committee (SNCC) chairman John Lewis and Southern Christian Leadership Conference (SCLC) project director Hosea Williams and others. More than five hundred peaceful protesters assembled with plans to walk the fifty-four miles from Selma to the state capitol in Montgomery to protest Jackson's murder, to demand the right to vote, and to demand federal protection from attacks on voting rights activists by Alabama state troopers and their volunteer posse, local white men who were deputized to brutalize civil rights activists in communities throughout the South.

But before the marchers left Selma, they were attacked by state troopers and city police and brutally beaten back across the Edmund Pettus Bridge. SNCC leader John Lewis (later Congressman John Lewis) suffered a fractured skull, and many others were severely beaten and jailed.

As I watched the televised replay of this violent attack on peaceful people marching for their lawful rights, everything converged for me—from the Quaker values of my grandmother to my childhood identification with oppressed people to years of Sunday School in our small farming community to our high school debate club where we questioned why the federal government didn't intervene more in the segregated US South. When I heard Dr. King's call to nonviolent arms, I decided right there and then, "I can do that. I have to go!"

Rural Childhood and Early Progressive Influences

Although I grew up in Penngrove, a small farming community about forty-five miles north of San Francisco, my family was more progressive than many. My mother's family descended from Quakers, some of whom had been active in the Underground Railroad, a network of abolitionists who helped fugitive slaves escape to the North and to Canada in the years leading up to the Civil War. My five aunts on my mother's side were considerably more liberal than my father's ten brothers and sisters. There were forty-eight first cousins between the two sides of my family, and most of them lived within twenty miles of us.

I adored my maternal grandmother who we lived with at her Cotati chicken ranch from my birth in April 1946 until we moved to Penngrove, five miles away, on my first birthday. We lived in a two-bedroom 1904 house built for farmhands on a tenth of an acre attached to my father's parents' farm. I missed my maternal grandma Brookover's big lap and easy laughter. My paternal grandparents were not fond of children. When I toddled over to Grandpa and Grandma's house, they sent me home with a note that said "keep this child at home" pinned to my top. Stern Grandfather Brians spanked me if I was caught with stained hands in his raspberry patch. He scolded me every time he saw me, even if I was just swinging on the swing hanging from his big acacia tree. My mother's family was loving and more concerned with what was happening in the world, but they didn't live nearby. My Brookover city cousins recall liking to come to our place in the country to pick wildflowers, make hay forts in the barn, and pick vegetables from our garden to take back to Oakland and San Francisco.

My political consciousness was forged early when my beautiful, auburn-haired Aunt Ruth took me to my first political demonstration when I was about seven years old in 1953. I was scared but proud as we stood outside the San Francisco Market Street Macy's store at Christmastime with signs that said "No War Toys." The protest was organized by Women's International League for Peace and Freedom (WILPF) in an effort to make parents stop and think before they purchased gifts of guns and toy soldiers for their young children. As I stood in the cold fog in my thin coat, my older cousin Bob took my hand when people yelled at us "Communist!" It was then that I learned that you might suffer for doing the right thing, but you also got the rewards of belonging. Aunt Ruth took us out for Chinese food afterward, so my first political protest left a good taste.

During my youth in the 1940–60s, rural northern California was mostly white and Protestant. We joked that tiny Penngrove had a population of two hundred, counting cows and chickens, but at least 25 percent of the kids in my elementary school had parents who were born outside the United States and many more had immigrant grandparents. Our tiny kindergarten through sixth grade elementary school was a melting pot of Jewish, Russian, German, Polish, Portuguese, Azorean, Japanese, Italian, Irish, and other ethnic groups, but there were no African American families.

We were the first wave of post–World War II baby boomers. My closest elementary school friends were Jewish except for my cousin Michael, who was Catholic. Some of my classmates said that the pope told their Catholic parents how to vote. I heard stories of prejudice and persecution from my earliest years, including one about a Jewish man who was literally tarred and feathered for attending a Socialist Party meeting in Santa Rosa, the county seat.

I learned from a young age that religion could divide people, especially in a small town. I also learned that faith could bring people together, like when I joined my best friend, Jackie Goldstein, trick or treating for money to plant trees in the new state of Israel. We were given money, Halloween candy, and praise from the adults whose doors we knocked on in nearby Petaluma. Afterward, we all danced and sang with an Israeli folksinger at the Jewish Community Center.

Jackie and I are still friends today. We look back in amazement at how serious we were. In second grade, we pored over *Life Magazine* photos of bodies piled in the Nazi gas chambers as Jackie explained that she could have relatives among them. I led her to the secret Indian graveyard in the hills behind my uncle Ben's property where entire families were wiped out by smallpox contracted from white settlers in the 1800s. We whispered made-up Indian blessings as we put daisies on the broken-up granite gravestones that had no names, just "Indian child. Age 10."

My father teased my mother about her Indian blood, which her sisters denied. Even after I learned that my great-grandmother was born on a Potawatomi Indian reservation in Indiana, they said she was likely the daughter of a Quaker teacher at the Indian school. After World War II, northern white people talked about a new melting pot America. They didn't want to talk about separate heritage, although our teachers taught us that white Spanish missionaries had enslaved and slaughtered Indians, and they even mentioned "Negro" slavery. But they said it was long ago, in the distant past, and that everyone was the same now. I wasn't so sure about that.

My Japanese classmates had been born within months of their families' release from federal internment camps where those born in Japan and Americans of Japanese descent alike were incarcerated during World War II. People did not add "American" onto ethnic designations in those days, even though most Japanese people in California referred to themselves both as Japanese and as loyal Americans. Many Japanese families returned from the internment camps to find their houses and farms stolen through false paperwork or destroyed by those who had agreed to watch over them while they were away.

Returning internee parents and grandparents watched warily as their Americanized kids played with white classmates. Once while visiting my Sunday School teacher Shirley Nakagawa's home, her parents shooed us away from their beautiful Shinto shrine where their ancestors' photos were displayed. Some adults, like my Italian Aunt Liz, were openly biased and used slang like "Jap" and "Portugee," while in other homes I heard that same aunt called "Wop."

It was easy for me to identify with those who were considered "other." Although we didn't look different, our nonfarming yet not-really-professional father, our tiny house on a tenth of an acre, and me wearing glasses from the age of three, were unusual in that era. My father's siblings lived on large farms all around us yet there was very little socializing. At rare Brians family gatherings I overheard his brothers talk about my slightly built father. "Never had what it takes to be a farmer; thinks he's better than us with his slacks and shirts. Doesn't make enough clerking at that hardware store to support all those girls," they said. My father was short, wiry, but strong for his size. He could repair anything and worked long hours after his regular job to improve our home and property. As the oldest girl, I often helped him with painting and yard work.

My mother gifted me with little sisters, one after another five years apart:

auburn-haired, brown-eyed, brainy Sylvia; cute, creative, sandy-blond Alberta; and then adorable, little blue-eyed, blond Cindy. My mother was a pretty, petite, dark brunette, a talented gardener, seamstress, singer, and cook, but she was insecure, and emotionally unstable. Her family left Oklahoma when she was only four and a half, after her father failed at farming. They spent a year and a half as migrant workers picking fruit and cotton living out of a tarp-covered truck. During those formative years, my mother must have felt insecure. Like my mother, I had to wear glasses from an early age and sometimes mean boys called me "four eyes." I developed into a sensitive child in the midst of a community of hardy, hard-working farm kids, many of them my first cousins on the Brians side. Sometimes kids called me "fraidy-cat," although I was inquisitive and adventurous enough to get in trouble at school and home as often as any child. In the creek I captured tadpoles that turned into frogs hopping around the house, and I sneaked bouquets of allergy-producing acacia branches into the room I shared with my sisters.

Rural kids were expected to do a lot of hard work, and my parents took that tradition to extremes. As the oldest girl I was responsible for dishes, laundry, ironing, cooking, cleaning up the kitchen after dinner, weeding the garden, feeding the chickens, and taking care of my sisters. Housework consumed most of my after-school and weekend time. When I was still in elementary school, I sprained my neck while helping my father shovel sand into the cement mixer to install a sidewalk around our house. The country doctor yelled at my father, "You are working this child like a slave!" That admonition stayed in my mind for a long time, although my parents continued to work me just as hard as before.

From earliest memory, regular attendance at Penngrove Community Church and its summer Camp Cazadero were my refuge from home and primary source of social consciousness. The church was Congregational, a progressive Protestant denomination later called the United Church of Christ. We were taught acceptance of all races and to believe in world peace. Some members of our church organized an early peace march before the United States formally entered the war in Vietnam. My parents' faith didn't ease the constant conflicts between them, arguments that seeped from under their bedroom door into my sensitive, inquisitive ears. Although my parents were nondrinkers, they were both given to unexpected fits of rage, at each other and sometimes at me, often over money. My father kept a ledger where he itemized every penny spent on each child. I was deemed expensive due to my need for glasses and orthopedic shoes. From a young age, I longed for my parents' approval but always felt like a failure in their eyes despite my decent enough grades and starring role in school musicals. I was eager to get away from home.

Nearly every summer, I attended Camp Cazadero where I learned new songs about peace and justice, including "Kumbaya," an African hymn that I would later sing in Georgia with other civil rights volunteers. In the redwood forests that covered the hills of northern Sonoma County, about fifty miles from my flat farmland home, we hiked, swam, and sang as well as listened to talks about world problems. At Camp Cazadero I learned the importance of putting faith into action. I met a minister who visited death row inmates and organized demonstrations against the death sentence at San Quentin Prison, despite his neighbors in wealthy Marin County threatening his life in anonymous letters. Another church leader told us of going to Africa, not to convert black people to Christianity, but to work on race relations between black and white churches there.

During the summer of 1959 I met a person of African heritage for the first time. Our church's student minister from the Berkeley Theological Seminary pulled up with a very dark man in a white starched shirt in the backseat of his 1952 Chevy. Rev. Barton conferred with my father for a few minutes and then drove away, leaving the man and his small brown suitcase. Rev. Enriche Sucquaqueche was a distinguished African minister who was stranded in the United States because the Angolan war of independence from Britain broke out while he was making the rounds of Congregational churches and summer camps. I was grinning ear to ear as he shook my hand and he said, "You can call me Henry." He settled into a quickly made up half room off of the garage. My father warned me, "Don't even think about going out there and don't bother him at all; understand?"

At school my cousin, Rita, reported that her folks thought my parents had gone off the deep end, letting a "Negro" stay in a home with four young girls. I was appalled at such open prejudice. My mother's relatives were all for Henry's visit and so was I. That summer I read *Cry the Beloved Country*, in which a poor black parson and the father of a murdered white antiapartheid activist share an uneasy alliance in an effort to save the black farming community and commemorate the death of the murdered man. I was weeping over apartheid in Africa while ongoing racial strife in my own country was almost invisible to me because we did not watch television or follow national news. During Henry's short stay, I quizzed him at meals and followed him around the yard when he emerged from his room looking sad and thoughtful. One day Rev. Barton came and took him away as suddenly as he arrived. I heard my father tell my mother that he had moved to Oakland, where "he'll fit in better." Tragically, he was never able to return to his homeland and family.

Even though our family had little time or money to spare, my mother taught me from an early age that the smallest actions of goodwill and kindness could make a difference, from taking meals to poor shut-in elders in our area to sending our used clothes to the children flooded out on the Russian River during the winter rains. The lesson of the importance of taking direct action, however small, was one of the greatest gifts of my upbringing.

By the time I was in junior high, I became ill from trying to juggle longer school days, increased homework with housework responsibilities and babysitting my newest sister, Cindy. After I developed migraines, I was examined at the University of California Medical Center in San Francisco. The doctors couldn't find anything to explain my headaches except stress and told my parents to ease up on me a bit, so they did. By then, Sylvia was old enough to do housework, my father got a raise at the hardware store, and my mother began to make decorated cakes to sell from home. My life began to improve.

Between eighth and ninth grade I received a scholarship to attend youth music camp at the College of the Pacific in Stockton. There, in the stifling heat of California's Central Valley summer, I joined two hundred other students to learn from Jester Hairston, a classically trained composer who someone told me appeared on the *Amos and Andy* show, where he played a mockingly dignified character, Henry Van Porter. Never having seen that show, I only saw a distinguished sixty-something-year-old, tall, thin black man with such conducting talent that I believed he could have coaxed music out of a chair. He was patient but firm as he kept us practicing his later-to-become famous song, "Amen," over and over and over. This man had magic in his hands. When we gave our final concert, I felt part of something bigger and more beautiful than I ever had before. The next year in Glee Club I was awarded the solo at my junior high graduation. I sang "Somewhere Over the Rainbow," a song that still makes me cry.

By the time I entered high school in Petaluma in 1961, I was committed to social change, like many of my generation. My cousin Michael and I formed the Limbo Club, a debate club that we convinced our history teacher, Mr. Tuck, to sponsor if we promised not to get too controversial. We debated whether or not what was then called Red China should be admitted to the United Nations. A group of geeky intellectual kids, "the brains," we prepared our material from the limited resources of our small school library, encyclopedias, and the local newspaper. We debated the merits of the US two-party political system and whether our educational system really respected the separation of church and state.

It wasn't long before conservative civics teacher Mrs. Schofield convinced our high school principal that Mr. Tuck was allowing us to talk about Communists as if they were human beings instead of the monsters she was certain they were, so he shut down our club. I wondered if the teachers and administration knew that some of my classmates' parents still quietly attended Communist and Socialist Party meetings, but I knew better than to say anything. Sometimes I worried that one of my friends might suddenly disappear, like I had heard about during Stalin's time when Russian Jews were persecuted and fled to the United States. It was already becoming clear to me that governments do bad things to people who disagree with their policies and that the government doesn't always represent all the people.

My friends and I were passionate about justice. Even though none of us cared about cruising around town during the lunch hour and few of us smoked cigarettes, we supported a walkout and a parking lot sit-in staged by students we considered tough, and who wanted an open campus during lunchtime. I participated in this first political action of Petaluma High School students in spring 1963 by walking out to the parking lot, but only at noon. I was too scared to leave class like the others—but it was a start. After three days of threats and negotiations, the rules were modified to allow leaving campus at noon again, and a smokers' bench for seniors only was designated on the campus quad. The walkout leaders were suspended for a few weeks, and everyone else returned to class with extra assignments. We called it a victory.

By my senior year I set my sights on getting away from home by going to college in San Francisco even though my guidance counselor had pegged me as only suited for community college due to my poor math grades and my low-income family. I led my high school graduating class in singing "We Will Have These Moments to Remember," but I could hardly wait to begin forgetting my old life. My only regret was leaving behind my three sisters, whom I loved dearly.

My parents refused to offer financial support if I left home, and they truly had little to offer. That summer, my aunt Dorothea helped me get a job as a live-in maid for a family with five children under age seven in Mill Valley, just across the Golden Gate Bridge from the city of my dreams, San Francisco. My summer responsibilities included cooking, cleaning, and eight- to ten-hours-daily child care, for which they paid me $25 a week plus room and board. It was hard work, made worse by children who were allowed to treat me like a servant and by their psychiatrist father who groped me whenever he got the chance. I gritted my teeth and saved enough money to live on for my first semester of college.

Convinced that I'd soon be begging to come home, my father drove me to San Francisco, my big blue Samsonite suitcase bouncing around the back of the ancient station wagon along with a used Smith Corona typewriter. When Dad dropped me off at my cousin Jeanne's apartment on Irving Street I felt like my real life began. His final stern lecture was lost on me, but I recall my father's small shoulders slumped as he gripped the wheel and blew his nose before he drove away. I ran upstairs to join my new housemates, not looking back.

San Francisco State and Selma, Alabama

In spring 1965, I was in the second semester of my freshman year of college. The political scene at San Francisco State was exciting. Buffy St. Marie, Joan Baez, Huey P. Newton, and other activists frequented campus, supplementing the political awareness I was developing in Dr. Weinstein's American Institutions and Ideals class. Dr. Weinstein showed us two films on the House Un-American Activities Committee (HUAC) hearings; one made by the government called *Operation Abolition* and another called *The House Committee on Un-American Activities* that questioned the government's prolonged investigation of its own citizens who were suspected of being Communists.

My friend Jeff Freed reminded me that the McCarthy hearings had taken place in 1954 while I was in elementary school.[1] The investigations that destroyed the lives of hundreds of social activists had a tremendous influence on US national consciousness and on mine. Jeff's parents had been investigated but refused to testify. In a slow dawn, I realized that some of my childhood friends' parents must have been fearful of being called before McCarthy's HUAC and that was why we weren't supposed to say anything about their secret party meetings. When Sen. Joe McCarthy was finally discredited as the fanatical bigot he was, Americans became divided between those who vowed never again to allow extremist elected officials to break the laws in the name of preventing Communism or any other political belief and those who looked for a "Commie" behind every pillar. Although I had always questioned world events, these films were my first graphic lesson in the uses of propaganda and an introduction to point of view versus differences of beliefs and opinion. There isn't just one set of facts. After all, I had already been called a Communist while standing innocently on the street with my aunt Ruth in her Women's International League for Peace and Freedom boycott, and my high school civics teacher thought I was a "pinko" for even wanting to debate political viewpoints.

In the weeks following Bloody Sunday, that first attempted march from Selma to Montgomery, I sought out civil rights news from other students because I did not have a television. I pieced together what I heard from my professors and fellow students. Over the next two months, I became much more aware of the history being made in the South than the history I was supposed to be studying in my textbooks. Fortunately, I was at liberal San Francisco State, so my professors discussed current events. They quickly drew comparisons between past uprisings against injustice and this new wave of the Civil Rights Movement. I wanted to be part of this great social change, in whatever small way I could. Despite the initial fanfare accompanying the passage of the 1964 Civil Rights Act, which reinforced some federal laws guaranteeing all citizens the right to vote, in reality, racist segregation was both law and practice in the Deep South. Alabama's Governor Wallace spoke for most southern politicians and law enforcement officials with his belligerent commitment to state-sanctioned segregation.

The second attempted march from Selma to Montgomery began on March 9. Despite a court injunction prohibiting this march, several thousand people gathered at Brown Chapel in response to Dr. King's call. In a move still debated by movement veterans, Dr. Martin Luther King Jr. and other SCLC and SNCC leaders led the marchers over the Edmund Pettus Bridge up to the point where they would cross the city limits and violate Judge Johnson's order. State troopers again blocked their way with billy clubs, rifles, and tear gas canister guns at the ready. Against the wishes of many of the younger leaders, Dr. King asked the marchers to kneel and pray, then turn around and return to Brown Chapel, a church in the heart of the poorest black neighborhood in Selma. This curtailed march became known as "Turn Around Tuesday," and it increased the split between SCLC and SNCC—between the strategies of nonviolent attempts at justice and a move toward more militant confrontation—a conflict that had been brewing ever since the younger SNCC group organized. I thought both groups had good points; I just hoped the violence would stop and that the voting rights marchers would be protected. At that time, I was unaware that a Selma voter registration campaign led by local leaders and SNCC organizers had been going on for years. While they welcomed the resources that King and SCLC brought, they did not appreciate the media lionizing King for beatings they had been taking for a long time.

Tensions continued to mount in Selma. On the evening of Turn Around Tuesday, forty-five-year-old Rev. James Reeb from Wichita, Kansas, and two other white Unitarian ministers who had come to support the voting-rights campaign were attacked and savagely beaten by white men while they were walking toward the Selma SCLC and SNCC offices on Franklin Street after dinner at Walker's Café on Washington Street. Rev. Reeb suffered life-threatening injuries and was taken to a Birmingham hospital where he died a few days later.

This murder of a white civil rights worker captured international attention unlike the earlier murder of Jimmy Lee Jackson, a fact that pained and angered black activists. In an era when newspapers were still the primary source of information, suddenly every headline was about the marches and voting rights. The *San Francisco Chronicle* dedicated the front page to demonstrations in the South. In San Francisco, young African American pastor Rev. Cecil Williams, who had been attacked on Bloody Sunday, spoke strongly at his Tenderloin district community church, Glide Memorial, about black voting rights and the importance of people of all races supporting the struggle, as did white Episcopal Bishop Pike at elegant Grace Cathedral high up on Nob Hill. These and many other religious leaders called for a national response to continued denial of fundamental rights for blacks.

After hundreds of hours of meetings, legal filings, and negotiations, SNCC and SCLC prepared to organize a third march designed to draw mass participation and maximum media attention—a march that would have federal protection. Hosea Williams, James Bevel, Diane Nash, James Orange, Andrew Young, and John Lewis were among the prime organizers. Celebrity participants included singers Joan Baez, Tony Bennett, and Pete Seeger, and actors Dick Gregory and Sidney Poitier. And, of course, Dr. King and his wife, Coretta, were at the front of the march. Student marchers flooded out of college campuses. Going to march was not a real consideration for me. I needed to study for midterms, but I followed events as best I could.

On Sunday, March 21, upwards of 1,500 marchers set out to walk the fifty-four miles from Selma to Montgomery, walking twelve or more miles a day, much of the time in driving rain. They slept in makeshift camps in fields where actors and singers entertained them. By the time they reached the capitol on March 25, the march had grown to nearly 3,200 participants, black, white, young, and old. The crowd that greeted their triumph was estimated to have been as many as 25,000.

Among the marchers were some who would become my dearest friends. My future coworker and first love, Bob Block, was among the white students who responded to the call from Dr. King. He walked the entire five alternately hot and rainy days, and then stayed to work with SNCC in Selma.

1. Rev. Hosea L. Williams addresses the crowd on the final day of the Selma
to Montgomery March, May 25, 1965. Others on the platform include James
Baldwin, Bayard Rustin, A. Phillip Randolph, John Lewis, Coretta Scott King,
Martin Luther King Jr., Bernard Lee, Ralph Abernathy, Roy Wilkins, Fred
Shuttlesworth, Ralph Bunche, and Whitney Young. Montgomery, Alabama.
(Courtesy of Barbara Williams Emerson and the Hosea Project, Inc., at Auburn
Avenue Research Library on African American Culture and History, Atlanta-
Fulton Public Library System.)

A large contingent of my soon-to-become Wilcox County friends met the
marchers in Montgomery, enjoying one day of celebration before returning to their own unheralded, unprotected marches in Camden, more than
seventy-three miles away. Although local activists Amelia Boynton, J. L.
Chestnut, Marie Foster, Charles Bonner, Cleophus Hobbs, Terry Shaw, and
many others had been organizing in Selma for years, SNCC's and SCLC's
organization of and Dr. King's participation in the big march turned that
small city into the new epicenter of the Civil Rights Movement.

My education at San Francisco State was giving me the grounding I
needed to better understand what I believed in my heart: that nonviolent
protests and the daily work of grassroots politics—voter registration, adult

literacy programs, and antipoverty work, along with high-profile equal justice lawsuits against segregated school districts—were all necessary for social justice, which meant social change.

Soon after Dr. King's first call for volunteers, I headed to the SNCC office on campus because I had heard that their effective Mississippi Freedom Summer got the 1964 Civil Rights Act passed. A young man there told me that I could join Friends of SNCC, the white support group that shared their office, so I joined that and began to get some instruction in the role of whites in the freedom movement. My Protestant roots easily intertwined with the political education I absorbed in San Francisco. Everything I was learning from the books I read and from activists on campus fit right into my liberal childhood faith and continued to do so when I converted to progressive Reform Judaism a few years later.

My main hangout while at San Francisco State was the Ecumenical House across from campus on Holloway Avenue. The place buzzed with activists. Dubbed the "Ec House," it was where I made friends with my future roommate, Jeanne Searight, and with Methodist Rev. Al Dale, a crew-cut former marine chaplain who offered practical assistance in my getting to the South. Most of the students who gathered and ministers who worked at the Ec House were white, but there were a few Asian and black students, including Ruben Greenberg, who became one of the earliest black deputy sheriffs in California and later served as chief of police of Charleston, South Carolina, for many years.

Introduction to the SCOPE Project

That spring, while I was trying to figure out what I could do to respond to Dr. King's call for action, in Atlanta SCLC's Rev. Hosea Williams and SNCC chairman John Lewis, who was also an SCLC board member, were planning the ambitious voter education and political organization program named the Summer Community Organization and Political Education (SCOPE) project, spearheaded by SCLC.

The 1965 Voting Rights Act (1965 VRA), which was supposed to fix remaining voter exclusion loopholes, was making its way through Congress. The SCOPE project was timed to coincide with what SCLC strategists had good reason to believe would be the first summer that the new Voting Rights Act would be available as a tool. The 1965 VRA was expected to become law before the project began in June.

I learned that the most important new provisions contained in the 1965 Voting Rights Act provided for checks on practices that continued to con-

spire to deny blacks their right to vote. One section required states and local jurisdictions with a documented history of discriminatory voting practices to obtain prior federal approval or "preclearance" of planned changes
in their election laws or procedures. Communities with concentrations of
US citizens who were not yet fully literate in English had to provide those
voters with assistance when they registered, including informing them of
the details of the elections and clarifying how to cast their ballots. The bill
also provided the Department of Justice with the authority to appoint independent federal observers and examiners to monitor elections to ensure
that they were conducted fairly.

Existing federal civil rights laws were not enforced in the South. Segregationist voting officials conspired with white supremacists to deny voting
rights to black citizens, most egregiously in Alabama and Mississippi. For
example, Wilcox County, Alabama, had a more than 70 percent majority
African American population and years of largely unsuccessful voting rights
efforts and lawsuits. Documents Hosea Williams filed to support the Selma
to Montgomery March state that although white people of voting age were
outnumbered two to one by blacks of voting age in Wilcox County, no eligible black voter had ever been registered. White voter registration was 113
percent of eligible voters (possible because of a practice of registering dead
people to increase the rolls) and "Negro" registration was .09 percent, according to the federal voting records on file at SCLC in spring 1965.[2] Due
to this flagrant injustice, Wilcox County, where I would soon be assigned,
was selected as one of the Alabama counties for the SCLC-SCOPE voting
rights campaign and for continued filings in federal courts.

While the Department of Justice processed civil rights violation complaints that were primarily filed by the National Association for the Advancement of Colored People (NAACP), federal law enforcement did nothing to
intervene in what was considered a states' rights issue by representatives from
the Deep South who carried tremendous political and financial weight in
Congress. Thousands of eligible black voters were denied the right to register, making it impossible to get black candidates elected to any office, even
to local offices such as school board trustee. Even if a potential voter managed to get through the arduous and federally illegal voting requirements
in Alabama, their registration applications were deemed incomplete or inaccurate and denied. Voting rights activists and their families were often
threatened with fabricated crimes for which they were arrested, fired from
jobs, and evicted from housing. Many suffered threats and physical assaults.

SCOPE training materials said that this project planned to meet three
objectives: voter registration, political education, and recruitment of potential

elected officials from the black community. SCOPE activities were expected to build on grassroots community organizations that had been carrying the burden for a long time, bringing in fresh student troops who would hopefully return summer after summer to volunteer in school integration efforts, the new federal War on Poverty initiative, and to support the education and election of new black leaders.

The project would result in over 1,200 SCOPE workers, including 650 college students from across the nation; 150 SCLC staff members, mostly scarcely paid field workers ($5–25 a week stipend); and 400 local volunteers who together worked in six southern states to organize, educate, and assist black citizens in registering to vote.[3] As soon as I heard about the project from SNCC and got more information at the Ec House, I signed up.

In order to join the project, I had to raise $200 for my travel and living expenses—a huge sum of money for me in those days—get my parent's permission, and attend intensive briefing sessions in Berkeley every Saturday for a month. I raised the money two ways: first, I wrote to the leaders of youth groups I knew through Camp Cazadero and asked them to raise money for my trip. My home church contributed $25, and Ben and Millie Young, youth group leaders in Mill Valley, sent $50. Most of the money came from selling textbooks that Dr. Weinstein in the Sociology Department collected from his colleagues; in fact, I exceeded my goal.

Since I was under twenty-one, I had to convince my father to sign an affidavit swearing that he wouldn't sue SCLC if I were injured or killed, which I did by telling him that I would forge his signature if he would not sign. My parents knew they had already lost what little control they had over me by not supporting me financially through college.

After I signed up for SCOPE, I walked around campus through the dripping, swirling San Francisco fog, feeling alive and part of the change taking place in the world. At one briefing in Berkeley, I volunteered to recruit more students for SCOPE since firm commitments were slow in coming. I checked in with SNCC on campus to make sure they wouldn't have a problem with a white girl recruiting, and they said it was no problem as long as I made it clear that we were not working in competition with SNCC; in fact, they sponsored what the Berkeley leaders optimistically called the San Francisco State Chapter of SCOPE. I continued to cheerfully chat up the black SNCC members, despite their head shaking at my naive enthusiasm for going south. I paid scant attention to my year-end exams.

Despite sitting out at the quad several foggy noontimes drawing much interest and having many stimulating conversations, when it came time to

SNCC sponsors SCLC's SCOPE

An organization called SCO-PE, directed and sponsored by Martin Luther King's Southern Christian Leadership Conference (SCLC) will be on campus for the remainder of the semester recruiting students for summer projects.

SCOPE will set up an information booth in front of the Commons between 9 and 11 a.m. and between noon and 2 p.m. daily.

"We are being sponsored by the SF State Friends of SNCC, because we're not trying to start another on-campus organization, we're just recruiting," according to Joyce Brians of SCOPE.

The SCOPE effort will be launched in 120 counties of six Southern states, Miss Brians said.

SCOPE volunteers accepted for the summer will work in voter registration, political education and community organization projects for ten week projects.

Volunteers will receive orientation in the particular locality to which they are assigned, as well as training by SCLC staff members in Atlanta from June 14 to 18.

Forensics Union undefeated in Washington meet

Three debate teams from the Forensics Union succeeded in winning the two top trophies at a tournament in Washington last week.

In the competition, five Western college teams debated whether civil disobedience is justified as a means of obtaining civil rights.

Two teams from SF State were undefeated. They consisted of Tom Bettis, Dave Allen, Frank Carmody and Gordon Johnson.

Golden Gater

Volume 89, Number 61   Tuesday, May 18, 1965

Editorial Office HLL 207   Phone JU 4-0443, or Ext. 570

Editor: Geoffrey Link
Managing Editor: Tom Carter
City Editor: George Boardman

Published daily during the regular academic year, weekly during the summer by the Board of Publications for the Associated Students of San Francisco State College, 1600 Holloway Ave., San Francisco, Calif. Entered at Daly City Post Office as third class matter. Subscription rate: $5.00 per year, 10 cents per copy. Represented by National Advertising Service, Inc., 420 Madison Ave., New York 17, New York.

2. San Francisco State College SNCC announces SCOPE project, May 1965.

arrange transportation, I wasn't aware of anyone else from my college going to volunteer on this ten-week project, although there may have been.[4]

The Saturday SCOPE briefings emphasized history and nonviolent theory along with updates on current events in the southern Civil Rights Movement. The instruction we received from professors, ministers, and activists was based in a genuine belief in strict nonviolence and the benefits of integration. We were informed that SCOPE was the brainchild of brilliant civil rights strategist Rev. Hosea Williams, an SCLC program director who had been a primary organizer of the Selma to Montgomery marches. One presenter read us the qualifications to be a student civil rights worker: "Working on civil rights in the South requires dedication, courage, and maturity; however these qualities can and have been acquired by many seemingly dilettante young college students. Any person old enough to go to college is old enough to work on voter registration."[5] I knew I was committed and brave but I wasn't sure about the dilettante part. If that word meant anything like debutante, I was pretty sure I wasn't one. I hadn't been one of those girls with the big party at age sixteen. I was without a clue, but it seemed like everything would be explained at the necessary time so I trusted the adults who I imagined had all the answers.

Although SCOPE was an SCLC project, SNCC activists whose names I regrettably did not record also spoke to us during those Saturdays in Berkeley. SNCC—the newer group of mostly college-aged students—seemed very exciting to me, based as it was in love of all humanity. "We affirm the philosophical or religious ideal of nonviolence as the foundation of our purpose, the presupposition of our faith and the manner of our action. Nonviolence as it grows from the Judaic-Christian traditions seeks a social order of justice permeated by love. Integration of human endeavor represents the crucial first step towards such a society," stated SNCC's founding purpose statement written in May 1960.[6]

SNCC was born with these stated ideals, however, a rapidly emerging philosophy of self-determination and black liberation was permeating the organization as I already understood from being denied membership in the "real" SNCC on campus. SCLC leaders were staunchly pro-integration and believed that we mostly white SCOPE student volunteers would bring media, money, and perhaps safety, although the increasing violence toward whites and blacks working together in the South did not auger well for that outcome. Some SNCC leaders anticipated that we would bring more violence because racists go crazy when they see white women with black men. They also accurately anticipated that we would bring superior attitudes that disrespected their sacrifices and achievements. Dr. King believed strongly that integration of all races and faiths would result in equal justice and opportunity for all. I took careful notes and wondered what it would be like in the trenches, how things would play out in the county I was assigned.

SCOPE was conceived of as an ongoing project, a summer Peace Corps here in the United States where, we were told, things were as bad for black people in the South as in any third-world country. During the year, we students could influence our colleges, families, and communities to get active in civil rights and, hopefully, send money to support the year-round southern movement. The briefing leaders were open about the fact that most disenfranchised black people would be more apt to listen to a white college student than to one of their own youth. They aimed to use bias as a tool to overcome prejudice. We went in understanding that this was a temporary thing, that we were to help raise up the the the "Oppressed Negro," which was a term used in SCLC talks and literature. It didn't strike me at the time that objectifying poor black people who were denied decent jobs and education might be contributing to the problem. This was the common language of the day, just as the sole use of the pronoun "he" meant a person; no one said or wrote "she."

I eagerly looked forward to the briefing sessions during which the speakers tried to teach us the entire history of segregation, the status of past and pending civil rights legislation, how the movement worked, how to control our own unconscious bias, what to expect, and how to behave when we went south. Much of it was a blur, but I remember feeling that it was a great turning point for me and for the United States. The leaders made it very clear that we were to be white allies to an entirely black-led organization, which was just fine with me.

The person who stands out most clearly from the briefing sessions was Rev. Cecil Williams, the dynamic young black preacher from San Francisco's Glide Memorial Methodist Church, who exhorted us to make black voter registration safer with our young, white, eminently newsworthy, federally protectable bodies. One fact that stood out in my mind was that we could be killed, but worse—girls could and had been raped by jail guards and Ku Klux Klan members.

We reviewed footage of the beatings and tear gas canisters fired at marchers during Bloody Sunday in which Rev. Williams himself had been injured. We listened to stories from people who had been on the big successful Selma to Montgomery March and learned more about the recent murders of Jimmy Lee Jackson, Viola Luizzo, and James Reeb in Alabama as well as the summer of 1964 assassinations of James Chaney, Michael Schwerner, and Andrew Goodman while they were working with SNCC to establish Freedom Schools in Mississippi. The message I got was that this was risky business; the stakes were high but the cry for justice was more important than any of our lives.

We were given sketchy written materials, including a flyer that said "Help me find the key to freedom" next to a drawing of a very dark black man in chains. The briefing leaders taught us to think of ourselves as heroic temporary workers—disposable perhaps—but absolutely essential right now. Our leaders' continual use of the term "The Negro" seemed to objectify a group of people facing a serious sociological problem that we who had more economic and educational privilege could help them overcome if we all worked together. This appealed tremendously to idealistic college students like me who wanted to tackle tough social issues head on.

We were given a required reading list for student volunteers. It included: *Freedom Road*, Howard Fast's study of Reconstruction; *The People Who Walk in Darkness*, a black history book by Schulte Nordhootle; V. O. Key's *Southern Politics*; and COPE AFL-CIO's *How to Win*, to give us an idea of grassroots activism. Films of civil rights workers being attacked and inspirational stories added to my strong impression of how important this movement was. I compared *Up from Slavery* by Booker T. Washington, which my professors labeled reactionary, with *The Souls of Black Folk* by W. E. B. Du Bois. Frantz Fanon's *The Wretched of the Earth* was the most upsetting book I read. According to Fanon, I was an oppressor without even knowing it. But then I reasoned there was just one solution to that. If people who look like me have messed up the South, then people who look like me ought to go fix it. I read most of these books in one month, taking even more time away from what should have been preparation for my final exams.

Final Preparations

During the ride to our last briefing in Berkeley, I peppered Rev. Cecil Williams with questions like, what was the appropriate way to address adults in the South. He smiled at my naïveté and kindly answered without condescension, "Mr. and Mrs., pronounced *Miz*, is preferred because since slave times we have been called first names and wrong names by those to try to make us feel inferior." Rev. Williams continued, "If you look at the movement now, you can see that trying to make us feel lesser hasn't really worked, but you be sure to show respect to adults, especially our elderly."

Originally, I had hoped to catch a ride with other San Francisco State students. After the second briefing, it seemed that I was the only student from my college still going, so I had to throw my lot in with some white University of California–Berkeley boys who probably would not have considered ride sharing with me except that kindly Rev. Al Dale guaranteed the rental car if they took me. I couldn't drive because I was too young. I was disappointed because I had hoped to travel with an integrated group from my college, even though it had been explained that traveling in integrated cars through the South was suicidal.

Back in San Francisco, Rev. Al Dale helped us with logistics. He sug-

3. Maria Gitin (Joyce Brians) (bottom left) with sisters Alberta (bottom right) Cindy (top), and Sylvia (inset) at family home in Penngrove, California, spring 1965. (Courtesy of the author.)

gested that we keep to a northern route for as long as possible and that we drive straight through without staying overnight anywhere. There had been incidents of harassment of civil rights workers from California who had gone to the Selma march, and we wanted to minimize risk until we got where it would make a difference.

As I prepared for this eventful journey, my parents behaved with typical inconsistency: telling me all the trouble I'd likely get into at the same time they were telling everyone at church how proud they were of me. I went home once before I left to see my little sisters: five-year-old Cindy, ten-year-old Alberta, and fourteen-year-old Sylvia. On Sunday, Rev. Ron Barton proudly introduced me to the Penngrove Church congregation as one of the students going south. Just three years before, he had counseled me during a deep adolescent depression. He didn't know anything about counseling, so he had loaned me the theology and philosophy books he was reading at seminary in Berkeley. Inspiring writers like Viktor Frankel fueled my desire to make a difference. I felt heroic, like Joan of Arc, as I prepared to put my life in danger for "The Good." I was eager to meet the challenge, to show how much faith I had.

In San Francisco, close to the time of departure, Rev. Dale took me aside for a well-rehearsed lecture on how tragic it would be if I became pregnant over the summer. I assured him that I intended to remain a virgin until I married. He asked how I would feel if I got pregnant from rape by a white southern man and warned me again that there had been stories of Klansmen attacking civil rights workers and of police raping women while they were in jail. I didn't question his counsel at the time but later guessed that he and his wife, Dottie, who was on the Planned Parenthood board of directors in San Francisco, must have predicted what would happen when students like me were thrown into the violent immediacy of the civil rights struggle at the same time we were coming of age, many of us unsupervised by adults for the first time in our lives. His tactic avoided questioning my virtue and at the same time gave me the protection he and his wife anticipated I might need.

At Planned Parenthood in downtown San Francisco, the male doctor who examined me questioned my request: "Why do you want to start the pill so young? You're still a virgin. Are you getting married?" When I explained that I was leaving for the southern freedom movement in a few weeks, he nodded, wrote the prescription, and wished me good luck.

When the receptionist handed me the brown paper bag she said, "Take one a day every day for twenty-three days and then stop for five like it says on the instructions. No charge, you're doing this for all of us." I felt confident that I wasn't going to need the pills, but they seemed like part of a well-prepared civil rights kit and made me feel more grown up.

Although I was headed south for the summer and already felt deeply committed to the Civil Rights Movement, I planned to return to finish college and become a social worker. I'd had that dream since elementary school. There seemed to be so much cruelty and prejudice in the world that I struggled to understand and wanted to change.

I continued reading theologians Martin Buber, Günther Bornkamm, and Paul Tillich, who I was familiar with from Rev. Barton, and I began reading contemporary Beat and New York poetry. My mind was spinning all of the time as I tried to synthesize so many new concepts. What stuck out for me was this: everyone has inherent dignity and it's up to all of us to help our fellow man. As I read, I began to notice that women's beliefs and feelings were often not mentioned as being different from men's. But feminism was far from my own consciousness at the time.

From that evening when I saw my first images of policemen beating innocent marchers and heard Dr. King's call to action, up until the time of my departure for Alabama, where I quite literally put my life on the line, I tried to integrate what I read, what I heard, and what I felt into some kind of personal philosophy. The philosophy of nonviolence made perfect sense to me. "Go love the Hell out of Alabama," Rev. Andrew Young was quoted as saying. It sounded like Alabama needed a lot of love, although I didn't know that I was going to be assigned to Alabama until the last day of orientation in Atlanta.

While I was in class, I became aware that history was being made, not only in the South, but also right outside my classroom. Students gathered on the quad for something called free speech. A young long-haired Berkeley student with a high-pitched voice spoke through a megaphone. I paused for a few minutes to listen to her impassioned plea for support of the Berkeley students' anti–Vietnam War and pro-hotel-worker protests in San Francisco. I remembered her name, Bettina Aptheker, the first woman student leader I ever heard give a speech. I couldn't imagine doing what she was doing, standing on top of police cars and organizing thousands of students, but I sure admired her courage. I had never even traveled outside of California, but I was ready to live what I was learning. I was inexperienced and scared, but I was ready.

2

The Journey Begins

A week before we left in early June, I sang the "Ode to Joy" from Beethoven's Ninth Symphony with the San Francisco State College Choral Union and the San Francisco Symphony. The performance was my final exam for my Choral Union class. We sang under the direction of famed, stern conductor Josef Krips in the elegant War Memorial Opera House. Although we sang in German I felt the words translated to the mission I was about to embark upon:

> Joy, daughter of Elysium
> Thy magic reunites those whom stern custom has parted;
> All men will become brothers under thy gentle wing.
> Be embraced millions!
> This kiss for all the world![1]

That's what I wanted to do: kiss the world and be brothers with everyone. I wanted to help others and to be loved and seen for who I was. My parents' love was conditional and confusing, based on meeting strict expectations, not on nurturing differences or aspirations. I felt that I continued to disappoint them with my illnesses, my rebellious spirit, and my average grades. I made an effort to gain approval from others through my singing and community service. Underlying this urgent need to be seen as special was my belief that I was not as good as others—an inferiority complex they called it then. Although I wasn't conscious of it at the time, when I was called to become part of the voter registration project, I felt that there was a whole group of people saying, "We'll accept you; just come and help us." I would risk my life for love and acceptance. It would be even better if I could be part of a movement that would change the world.

The symphony hall was so beautiful inside with its marble foyer, vaulted ceilings, and gilded columns. High on the risers it felt very warm. Our voices filled the hall with passionate energy. I felt like I was flying until I began to faint on the final high note of the chorus. As the curtain closed, a classmate helped me down. The chilling San Francisco fog cleared my head as I waited for the streetcar to carry me back across town to pack the handful of belongings we were allowed to bring. Singing that great music with a world famous conductor seemed like the perfect, dramatic send-off for the summer ahead.

The Journey South

On June 10, the University of California–Berkeley guys, with a bottle of tequila and a lemon in hand, came to pick me up. Asking for salt, they did some kind of ritual drinking. One guy was blond and distant. The other guy, I think his nickname was Carlos, seemed friendlier. I couldn't manage to swallow the harsh tequila so I spit it in the sink. Although teetotalers had raised me, by now I had been around enough people who drank without becoming totally crazed rapists (which was my biggest fear) that I pushed any concern to the back of my mind.

As I locked the apartment door for the last time, I was glad I had already moved my belongings to the new house around the corner, which I would be sharing with three other girls when I returned in August. I told myself everything would be fine. After all, we believe in God, equality, and Martin Luther King. Amen. I wanted to begin the trip with prayer rather than tequila, but I didn't say anything. I got in the backseat and was glad when Carlos, the friendliest of the three, took the wheel for the first leg of our journey.

On our way out of the Bay Area, we stopped in Carmel to pick up another volunteer who was older than the others. As Larry Metcalf kissed a weeping woman and got into the car with a full cup of coffee in hand, I tried to focus on the biblical story of Ruth. I had never been out of California before and didn't realize how big the country was. I couldn't imagine making it to Atlanta in three days. My companions talked mostly among themselves. My observations on the passing landscape and attempts to initiate political discussion were ignored by all but Carlos, who deigned to speak to me sometimes.

I was wracked with worry as we drove, thinking that the guys must be irritated because I was too young to legally take a turn behind the wheel of the rental car. They stopped frequently to get beer. Although they were not very friendly, they didn't mind helping themselves to the food and Kool-Aid

I had packed for the first leg of the journey or letting me pick up the tab for soft drinks with some of the funds I had raised.

The ride was long, hot, and uncomfortable. In the middle of the second night, I awoke suddenly to a lack of motion. It was dark, the car was still, and there was no sound except cicadas. Two of my traveling companions were leaning over the hood holding a flashlight and arguing over the map. It seemed that while three of us slept, the driver had taken a two-hundred-mile wrong turn, and we were in Illinois instead of Indiana. After that, I was assigned the task of checking the map and road signs to make sure we were headed in the right direction.

After this delay, I was afraid we would be late and miss some of the SCOPE orientation. Famous and soon-to-become-famous civil rights leaders would be giving us an intensive six-day-long training before we were sent to our counties, and I didn't want to miss a second of it. So I stayed awake, chatting up the rotating drivers for the next twenty-four hours.

We had been told at the Bay Area briefings to keep north as long as we could and then to avoid white areas once we crossed the Mason-Dixon Line. When we crossed over the wide, shockingly muddy Mississippi into East Saint Louis, the pavement ended. Raggedy kids ran in the muddy streets. Old folks with hopeless eyes stared from rickety rockers on collapsing porches. Men in undershirts stood smoking, staring as we passed. The slums were beyond anything I had seen in the Fillmore district and Hunters Point, black neighborhoods in San Francisco. Imagine a city where the pavement, garbage collection, lighting, and every public service simply stops; that's what these all-black neighborhoods looked like. The buildings seemed old and ugly compared to San Francisco's marble and Victorian splendor. From then on, we drove through towns like that, starkly divided between black and white.

We didn't use the word "ghetto" then. We said "poor section" or "Negro neighborhood." We aimed to eliminate these poor neighborhoods by implementing the 1964 Civil Rights Act and passing the 1965 Voting Rights Act. We didn't dream there would still be use for the terms "ghetto" or "barrio" decades later. Back then, I still believed we would join the forces of The Good, God, and Martin Luther King and throw off the oppressor, get black folks elected, create jobs, integrate schools, and educate the poor and rich alike. We would teach the whole nation the principles of nonviolence, win the War on Poverty, and probably end the war in Vietnam at the same time.

We student activists believed that our thoughts and feelings were identical to those of the disenfranchised poor, and that black and white together we could lay our bodies down and become the bridge to social justice. What would happen to all the hatred, bigotry, and violence? My image was that it would be something like what happened to the evil witch in the Wizard of Oz. In the face of the Truth, the Bad would auto-destruct from the force of our overpowering righteous conviction and just melt away.

Atlanta SCOPE Orientation

When we finally arrived in Atlanta on June 13, my first impression of Morris Brown College was how different it was from the modern, utilitarian, cement buildings that constituted the San Francisco State College campus. The wooden and brick dormitory assigned to white women during my stay was weathered and in need of repair. A student proudly told me that it was Gaines Hall, over a hundred years old, where some of the first freed slaves attended college. When I heard that W. E. B Du Bois had taught there, I felt like I was already becoming part of history.

The dignified white-haired dorm matron let me know the rules in short order. "This dorm is for white girls only," she said sternly. "The door will be locked every night at 10:00 P.M. There is no smoking inside. If you have been drinking, we will call Rev. Williams, the project director, and you'll be sent home. We don't want any trouble, and we'll thank you not to bring any here."

With that, I was left to find my room. Ann Nesbitt, a college junior from somewhere in the North, had already chosen the bed next to the window, so I took the other. After testing the bouncy bare bedsprings, I tossed the lumpy mattress on the floor. This room would be my home for the next six days. Ann was a little plump, with medium-length brown hair and pale skin. She was quiet and I was buzzing with excitement, so we spent very little time together. Because I didn't want to miss a second of the official or unofficial orientation activities, I usually came in long after she was asleep.

After I put my things in my dorm room that Sunday morning, I found a couple of guys from California with a car who were going to hear Rev. Martin Luther King Sr., who was known as "Daddy King," preach at historic Ebenezer Baptist Church. Tired as I was, I came alive at the news. This was something I couldn't miss. Sitting there with the church ladies, wearing their Sunday hats and best dresses, waving paper fans, sweating in the heat, and calling out "Amen! Yes Lord! Yes Lord! Preach! Tell it like it is!" was a dream come true. We were young and naive, old and wise, black and white together, and we were working toward one cause: *Freedom Now!* I believed that this summer could either end my life or begin my life as a real adult. At that moment, with passionate praise songs shaking the rafters, either outcome would have been fine with me.

The formal schedule called for five days of fourteen-hour sessions plus a halfday on Saturday before we headed out to our assigned counties. By the time of the first informal Sunday evening session, I had not slept in over twenty-four hours. I was not used to the ninety-degree temperature, especially with steamy humidity. During our first friendship circle with arms crossed over each other, holding hands on both sides, during the last chorus of "We Shall Overcome," I fainted and was taken to a nearby segregated hospital. I was embarrassed to cause a fuss. After they moved me to the front of the line of black patients filling the hallway of the emergency room, the doctor admonished me to drink more water and sent me back with the SCOPE staffer who brought me in. Not one day into the project and already I felt like I was more of a liability than a help to the movement.

The plenary speakers as well as workshop leaders hammered into us how dangerous this work was and how badly we would harm the movement if we failed to keep a calm, clear head at all times. Early on, each of us had to take something that seemed to be a shortened version of the Minnesota Multiphasic Personality Inventory—in use at the time to diagnose mental illness—that I had taken when I was treated for migraine headaches four years earlier at UC Medical Center. Did they want to see if we were stable enough to face the challenges ahead? Years later I heard that there were psychiatrists hired to spot unstable volunteers in the orientation and that other forms that I thought were tests were actually questionnaires, part of a research project by sociologists from the University of Wisconsin.[2]

Early in the week, my name was called out as one of six who were told to stay behind after the morning session ended. I was worried. Was it because I fainted in the auditorium after a three-day nonstop drive, or was it more serious? As I walked toward a small cluster of students on the grass outside the auditorium where I had been summoned, I saw that the handsome SCLC executive director, Rev. Andrew Young, wanted to speak to *me*. Only here a few days and I had already been branded as someone who might not be able to hold up under the strain. I was determined to be both charming and forthcoming so that I could convince him that I was as prepared as anyone else.

Rev. Young seemed friendly; he wanted to know where I was from and what church I attended. When I answered San Francisco and the Congregational denomination, he seemed to warm even more. Did I know Ben and Millie Young, youth leaders in Mill Valley? Talk about a small world. Did I know them? They were practically like parents to me. I had been in their summer camp workshops; I had been to their house—they knew how dedicated I was. I asked Rev. Young if he was related to them. Rev. Young laughed and said they were good friends, good people. He then said I could stay but that I would need to obey all rules and to keep my emotions in check. My dorm matron had reported that I came in late two times, and I would have to demonstrate that I was serious if I wanted to work in the movement. I gave Rev. Young my most winning smile and said I wasn't about to let anything send me back home. Hiding my discomfort, I reassured him that I couldn't wait to get started educating voters.

The next day, after being threatened with expulsion, I volunteered to blanket the area around campus with flyers announcing Julian Bond's first run for the Georgia state legislature.[3] As I walked through the West Side, a poor neighborhood that surrounded the college, we handful of white students were greeted with interest, amusement, or indifference by black youth and head-shaking adults who were uncomfortable with integrated groups of civil rights workers in their neighborhood.

At the end of our first official evening session, well after 10:00 P.M., we began to learn the freedom songs that were essential to keeping up hope. Mrs. Septima Clark, SCLC Citizenship Education Program (CEP) leader, who at age sixty-nine was easily the oldest person in the room, led what was billed as a late-night songfest. She taught us northerners to drop the "g" on the ending of words and instead sing "tryin'" and "cryin'." She patiently peered through her wire-framed glasses as she exhorted us to embrace the passionate religiosity so essential to the movement. Mrs. Clark was already famous for working to establish citizenship schools throughout the Deep South. She was brave, strong, and a real lady. Tired as we were, she got us to lift our voices and sing our hearts out.

We were given mimeographed song sheets. As Mrs. Clark introduced each song I made notes about what she said on the back on my song sheet. My comments reflect how I immediately identified with people who had been and would be in the trenches far longer than we summer workers.

From my June 1965 notes:
"I Love Everybody" is sung often, "I love everybody, Oh! I love everybody in my heart." In spite of bad housing, no tap water, poor clothes, people sing and really mean this song. Great love for mankind. Verses include the names of governors and of sheriffs who were beating and killing civil rights workers.

"Oh Freedom!" Inspires courage, reminds us of the ugly history of slave times, People are still treated like slaves. They want freedom now.

"Oh Wallace or You Never Can Jail Us All" is a long, ever changing lyric song to the tune of pop hit Kidnapper—It can have endless verses. We sing it on long drives and in jail. Many pop tunes are taken over by civil rights workers and words changed.

"This Little Light of Mine" is my favorite song of all. I know it from summer camp. I want my little light to "Shine, shine, shine all the time."

"We Shall Overcome," the Movement anthem, is sung over, and over and over, but it always makes my spine tingle.

I may have left San Francisco singing Beethoven's Ninth Symphony, but I soon memorized "Lift Every Voice and Sing," which to this day is the theme song of the NAACP:

Sing a song, full of the faith that the dark past has taught us.
Sing a song, full of the hope that the present has bought us.

We closed every evening of orientation with a huge friendship circle, singing the movement anthem "We Shall Overcome." Looking around at brown and white hands clasped together made my spine tingle. I just knew that we could change the world with the force of nonviolent love.

Every night during that whirlwind week in Atlanta, I collected my detailed notes into long handwritten letters that I mailed to my roommate Jeanne Searight with the plan that she would type them, make mimeographed copies, and mail them to a list of about a dozen people who had made financial contributions to support me. My family received copies of these letters in addition to a few that I wrote only to them. Even though I had just arrived, I immediately identified myself as a civil rights worker and freedom fighter and used the term "we" to include everyone there as well as all of the people I expected to meet and work with.

Excerpt from my first letter, June 1965:

Monday, June 14, really began the intensive weeklong session. Rev. Ralph D. Abernathy, VP at large and treasurer of SCLC, told us the history of SCLC beginning with the famous day when Mrs. Rosa Parks refused to sit in the back of the bus any longer.

Hosea Williams, SCOPE project director, then gave us a long and fine talk on "Why We are Here." He made us see our responsibility and our obligation. As has been said so many times, "none of us are free until all of us are free."

We had a discussion and general announcements and then adjourned for lunch. Food in the South is something else. My stomach is beginning to adjust to grits, collard greens, okra, and black-eyed peas. We have little meat or milk and no desserts or fresh fruit.

I quickly accepted the label of "northerner" rather than the western identity I had grown up with. In the South, there were just two designations for whites (southerner or northerner), and they depended solely on whether or not your family had fought for the South during the Civil War.

Letter excerpt continued:

In the afternoon we heard the history of the whole civil rights movement from SCLC staff member, Bayard Rustin. Following that we broke up into discussion groups and two or three staff members sat in on them.

After dinner Dr. King was scheduled to speak, but he wasn't able to come. However, Joseph Ruah, counsel for Leadership Council on Civil Rights gave an informative presentation on the Civil Rights Act of 1964. He said the only reason the bill was passed was because Martin Luther King dramatized the need for it. Mr. Ruah went over each section of the bill with us in great detail, both its provisions and its shortcomings.[4]

Tuesday the 15th was nonviolence day. This was one of the most fascinating subjects to me. I talked to men, women, and children—black and white—who have had their "heads whipped" by state troopers and who can still honestly sing "I Love Everybody."

Rev. James Lawson, Director of Nonviolent Education said, "Violence is a man-made force. But nonviolence can also be a force. Nonviolence is the courage to be—to insist on one's own existence. There should be compassion and solidarity between all persons. Every man is me—even my enemy. When you love people you enable them to become human. Nonviolence is contagious and it does work."[5] He urged us to back all boycotts. "Civil disobedience forces people to take a new look at their policies. They will accept the responsibility if we just act as though we expect them to."

Rev. Andrew Young, a handsome dynamic leader in the field of civil rights, gave us some more inspiration and understanding about nonviolence. Kids who had been beaten and whipped told us that it doesn't really hurt that much when you know you have a reason for taking the beating.

In the afternoon C. Vann Woodward of Yale University addressed us about "The Relationship of Southern History to the Negro Revolt." He said the South has a separate history from the rest of the nation. Secession, Civil War, and Reconstruction occurred only in the South. We must learn from past history.[6]

Woodward then went on to explain that every federal program from Reconstruction to the 1964 Civil Rights Act was blocked from reaching southern black citizens by state and local legislation, by racist attitudes, and by a lack of understanding by whites that their own interests in a prosperous South were and always will be intertwined with those of blacks.

Letter excerpt continued:

We sang freedom songs that night as we did whenever we had free time. I began to feel what they call "soul" in the songs. The freedom songs are the heartbeat of the Movement. When we are joyous we sing "Freedom is a Comin'" and when we're tired we sing "Hold On." For every occasion there is a song to express our feeling.

By Wednesday, June 16, we were beginning to get pretty tired. Long evening discussions, parties, and little food are standard in The Movement. It's strange but true that the tireder and the hungrier we got, the more sure we were that it was worth it. Never have I learned so much in such a short time.

James Bevel, SCLC Director of Direct Action told us, "Negroes all over the country have been prevented from sharing in the accumulated knowledge of society. They have been exploited and their humanity has been destroyed. We haven't been able to end segregation by integration; we have been tricked. Busing New York kids to white schools doesn't give them equal education. Segregation is a smoke screen. The Civil Rights Bill of 1964 says that Negroes are human but the white folks won't admit it. The Negroes don't even want to vote, they have been so humiliated. We must ask them to work with what they have. That is how The Movement started and that is how it gets its strength. The money, the power is in the hands of the federal government and we must demand our power from them."[7]

We heard a lengthy talk by Michael Harrington, author of *The Other America*, who explained in detail how the Civil Rights Movement was breaking up the Dixiecrat-GOP (Republican) coalition. He said that from 1938 until recently, the segregationist southern politicians really ran the country. Harrington went on to explain that President Johnson's War on Poverty was likely only to reach the cream of the poor unless we got the 1965 Voting Rights Act passed.

Excerpt from letter continued:

Our county assignments were made and a person from each county gave a short talk. Randolph Blackwell, Program Director for SCLC, talked about community organizing. My paraphrase of his talk is: There will be leaders and organizations in every community we will be working in. Be sensitive to the leadership. Don't base your analysis on education or economics. In the Negro community leadership is determined differently. Don't have preconceived notions about who can and cannot be involved in voter registration. Senior citizens bring their backgrounds with them. They think they are radical, but they really aren't. Don't offend them by implying they are out of focus. The young adult segment will be the best trained. They will feel they have a right to determine policy in the community. Beware of taking part in something that will alienate the rest of the community.

Youth leaders (16–23 years) are desirable, energetic, and capable. Identify with this group but be careful you don't get caught up in believing that the ends justify the means. If there are community organizations, work with them. The key to success is working with sensitivity with them. Stay out of arguments. You do not have to defend SCLC. You have not come to confront the white community. We are justified if our project is carried on in a fashion that will bring the Negro community through this experience intact.[8]

Mr. Albert Turner, an SCLC field director from Marion, Alabama (where Jimmy Lee Jackson's murder that launched the march from Selma to Montgomery took place), told us how to organize a civic meeting.[9] Mr. Turner was almost formal in his instruction to us and didn't dramatize the work the way some of the younger speakers did. "Big Lester" Hankerson, who lived up to his name in both size and strength, was introduced as a "specialist in street-corner registration." He said that he just had one thing to say: "Don't give up when you are turned away. Get them to register!!"[10]

Excerpt from letter continued:

Golden Frinks, a nonviolent leader from North Carolina told us about mobilization of the community for direct action. Find out who the white leaders are and who the Negro leaders are and who the minister is. Find the kids and play with them. See what needs to be done in a particular area. Learn a lot about the county. Create confidence but don't act like you know it all.[11]

Our project leader, Hosea Williams, spoke specifically about SCOPE: "You are a representative of SCLC. Be careful how you say what you say. No matter how bad the local leadership is, don't degrade them. Build confidence in the local leaders so when we leave we don't leave them alone. Talk to them on their level. Know a little theology, talk religion. Forget yourself and become an instrument of the local people."[12]

Rev. Dan Harrell, the SCLC field director from my county, spoke last. He reiterated what the others had said and added, "It is important not to create conflicts. We are all working for one goal . . . voter registration!"[13]

I tried to hang on to every word, writing in my notebooks, on the back of the agendas, and on napkins at times. Lofty rhetoric was combined with graphic descriptions of jail conditions and the pathetically slow pace of the federal government as it was being dragged into the biggest states' rights issue of all time, using federal enforcement to guarantee the right of all citizens to vote. Sharecroppers who had risen to leadership stood in overalls side by side with divinity school students wearing short sleeve dress shirts and slacks. This was democracy all right.

Most of the civil rights field workers had experienced terrifying violence but also reported significant successes in turnout at mass meetings and marches to courthouses. They eagerly shared their stories from the front in hopes that we could learn from their injuries, setbacks, and victories.

We were instructed how to organize mass meetings and canvass communities for unregistered voters, and how to provide people with the information and transportation they needed to register. We were told to support existing political education workshops and literacy classes and to begin new ones only if necessary. This was a get registered, get out the vote campaign designed to interface with existing local actions.

At the time, how SCOPE was organized was not entirely clear to me. From what I read later, many records on file with SCLC didn't reflect what actually happened on the ground, so I am only including what I wrote down at the time and what I clearly remember. Two of the most important things were to listen to our SCLC county directors and to local leaders when we reached our assigned counties, but also to accept leadership when assigned.

Jimmy Webb, a Nashville activist, emphasized that although we were being trained to become community organizers, we must respect local leaders. "Remember," he said, "they know more about their community than you ever will." Vernon Jordan, then working for the US Office of Economic Opportunity in Atlanta and who later became an advisor to President Bill Clinton, told us about the new federal War on Poverty. Dr. John Hope Franklin of the University of Chicago spoke on "Negro History" to help us realize that this was not a new movement, that there had been continuous achievements as well as struggles for civil rights ever since Reconstruction. Mrs. Septima Clark instructed us in how to organize adult citizenship and literacy classes that would not make a black man (she and most older speakers used the term "The Negro") feel ashamed of his lack of opportunity to attend good schools.

We heard over and over the importance of avoiding any tendency to take over, even if the local people encouraged us to do so. At the same time, we were told to use our whiteness to advantage by telling potential voters something along these lines: "I know you've been told by the white man that you don't deserve the vote. But that man is an ignorant white supremacist. I am an educated student here to tell you that you have the right to vote, and that Martin Luther King Jr. backs me up." Or at least that is how I heard the message. It resonated with what I had heard at the Berkeley briefings.

We heard conflicting messages on the topic of "going black," meaning adopting the clothes, language, and manners of locals who had less education and income due to centuries of violently enforced segregation. Some felt it was a good idea to try to fit in, others said that was mockery. SCLC reinforced the concept of using whiteness as an advantage to call meetings and to move people to action. At the same time, they told us to respect local leaders who may not have had the opportunity to finish high school. We absorbed all this and were told to try to tell which way our county was leaning once we got there. My assignment, Wilcox County, Alabama, turned out to be firmly in the "act like who you are and don't try to pretend you are anything else" camp, despite which I quickly picked up slang and points of view from local students already influenced by SNCC during their demonstrations in the months before we arrived.

A workshop on how to respond nonviolently to attacks was separated into two groups by gender. A civil rights worker told our women's group about her rape by cattle prod. I believe she tried to tell us how to cope, but my mind glued on the image of what she had endured and stuck there so I didn't catch the instructions. At the time, I did not consider the extra layer of oppression that black women labored under as targets of both sexual and racial violence. The men's session apparently focused on brutality against white men in jail and against black men outside of jail. They were warned that it was common to put white male civil rights workers into cells with violent white criminals who needed little encouragement to beat the white "agitators." Prisoners were promised preferential treatment for brutalizing white activists. Black men could be jumped and beaten anywhere, anytime, and they were. Since all jails were segregated, black men were almost never in the same cell with the white men. The ones deemed troublemakers were often taken down to bull pens (isolation cells) to be beaten in a place where all the other prisoners could hear their cries.

I tried to block out my fears, a habit developed in a home where there was a lot of tension and fear of the unknown. My sense was that there would be safety in numbers and that we would always stick together. I drew confidence from the fact that all these brave speakers had survived. Besides, I figured that they wanted to frighten us so that we would follow the rules.

We were instructed to stay out of jail if possible. While filling the jails had been a strategy in past campaigns, our job was to educate and register voters and support, or create if necessary, local organizing groups that would identify and recruit new leaders to run for elected office as soon as possible.

One of the most intense workshops was on relationships between whites and blacks and men and women in the field. It seemed that the best strategy for girls was to mind your own business, avoid parties, and try to get along with everybody. If you were drawing too much attention, date a man of your own race as protection.

I wondered if attractive girls were more at risk or if it would be easier for them. I was just beginning to sort out whether my parents, who never praised my looks, or the men of all ages who looked at me with interest were right. I was petite and delicate looking. My hair was glossy medium brown, my eyes bright blue, and I tanned easily. A photo from that summer shows me with full, unpainted lips in a half smile and downcast eyes, shy, slightly mysterious. I was five foot two and weighed 102 pounds at the beginning of the summer. Between the birth control pills, cornbread, gravy and biscuits, grits and hash browns, collards with fatback, mayonnaise and bologna sandwiches, Coca Cola, and endless cups of coffee with cream and sugar, I gained ten pounds before I returned, even though we were often short on food.

I didn't particularly notice sexism or discrimination against women in the movement. It was ever present but it was hardly the exclusive realm of the black male leaders—it was just how it was back then, everywhere. It would be another decade before I became fully conscious of gender inequity. Because of my mindset at the time and because few women were leaders at the orientation, I didn't seek out and have conversations with the incredible women who were there. Beautiful, dynamic Dorothy Cotton, SCLC's educational director and Citizenship Education Program (CEP) program director, was the highest-ranking female in SCLC and was the only woman

4. Maria Gitin (Joyce Brians), San Francisco, California, 1965. (Courtesy of the author.)

5. SCLC Citizenship Education Project leaders Dorothy Cotton and Septima Clark, Annemanie, Wilcox County, Alabama. (Copyright © 1966 by Bob Fitch.)

I recall hearing speaking from the podium besides Septima Clark. Cotton served as a commentator on several evening panels and co-led the women's workshop on responding to violence and on interpersonal relationships. Tall, painfully thin Anelle Ponder, who had been brutally beaten by police while in jail for civil rights in Mississippi two years earlier and now worked with SCLC's CEP, co-led one of the breakout sessions.

I always had been, and expected to remain, a "good girl." It wasn't until I was in Atlanta where I saw other girls like my roommate, Ann, diligently preparing for the travails of the summer by turning in early, staying away from the parties, and ignoring the storm of sexual heat unleashed among four hundred steaming black and white student bodies that I considered maybe I was missing out on something.

Late one night I piled into a car full of white guys and girls who were older than I was, and ended up in an upper-middle-class home filled with well-dressed black people. Our hosts had a wood-paneled basement lounge complete with lava lamps, a stereo playing soul music, and a full bar with leather stools. They were serving something called Manhattans, which looked pretty with a maraschino cherry in the glass. Soon I was doing the Twist and Watusi with who knows whom. The ride back to Morris Brown College was hazy. When they dropped me at my dorm, I lurched up the path toward the dormitory door. Unbeknownst to me, a couple of nonmovement men were waiting behind bushes and must have noticed that I was obviously drunk.

The next day, Benet Luchion, a wiry, big-haired, flute-playing SCLC staff member from New Orleans, told me of my narrow escape. First, he thoroughly chewed me out for making myself vulnerable as I staggered up the steps. He had intervened between a knife-wielding man and me. I hadn't seen any men, let alone a knife. Second, Benet cautioned me that since I did not appear to have the sense I was born with, but did appear to be a nice girl, that I should hook up with some white boy as soon as I got to my county assignment and get myself some protection. He explained that with few exceptions, it was generally accepted that a movement guy didn't hit on someone else's girl. "Oh," I told him, "that's just like back home."

Rev. Dr. Martin Luther King Jr.

From a letter to supporters, June 1965:

Thursday the event we had all been waiting for occurred. Dr. King came into town. He rode in a parade, sitting on the back of a powder blue convertible headed by a band of small boys beating drums. Wherever he goes hoards of people follow him. He is indeed the leader of

The Movement. When he rose to speak a hush fell over the audience. He didn't yell and he didn't shout but what he said gripped our hearts, and our souls and our minds. This is part of what he said: History is being made here. It is the students who are making history now. People have reached the end of their patience. With nonviolence we found a new ally for freedom that black and white together can use. New York has abolished the death penalty and taken strong civil rights measures because of student nonviolent pressure. SCLC believes in the value of student groups and for this reason has organized SCOPE. We are here because we are humanitarians and patriots. The depreciation of the Negro has affected our nation drastically. The older generation is lost because it hasn't achieved democracy.

We are the Hopeful Generation because we can face the racists in Montgomery. The 1965 Voting Rights Bill will give government sanction to "outsiders." The Supreme Court and Washington, DC are outsiders. People say it is sacrilege to use churches for civil rights meetings, but Thomas Paine and Paul Revere used churches. SCOPE workers are wanted and needed by the community. If people say you are crazy—maybe they are right . . . but it is "creative maladjustment." Don't be satisfied with less than Freedom.

After King left, shouts and cheers ringing in his ears, we saw the (30 minute) film *Right Now*, made by the United Church of Christ, which tells the story of voter registration. "Big Lester," [Lester Hankerson, SCLC field organizer] a 250-pound SCLC field director, was the hero of the movie and was also sitting with us in the audience. He said a few words and I could tell that he has a heart as big as he is and he is going to love everyone right into freedom.

Shortly after that session ended, more than one hundred of us snuck into a pitch-dark theater around 11:00 P.M. to see a new Hollywood film, *Nothing But a Man*, before the police arrived to break up this integrated gathering off campus. It seemed like we were in a commercial theater, but we came in a back alley entrance so I didn't see the marquee. I was thrilled and a little bit scared, too.

The final Friday night session didn't end until after 10:00 P.M., and although I believe it was chaired by Dr. King himself, I didn't write down a word of it, such was my exhaustion. At the end of that evening, we gathered in a huge friendship circle to sing "We Shall Overcome" for the last time before we set out to our forty-nine separate counties in six states. I stood not far from Dr. King. Because of years of voice training, my high soprano rang out among the many strong voices in that circle. Dr. King leaned forward and said softly, "You have a beautiful voice, darlin'." Those were the only words the great man ever spoke to me. I went to sleep floating on air but kept quiet about this for decades, to protect the memory.

I described the excitement of our departure in a letter: "We got up early Saturday morning and said our farewells but ended up sitting around most of the day waiting to leave. In civil rights the concept of time is totally unlike anything I have experienced before. We have a song that goes 'I'm gonna do what the Spirit says do' . . . well they not only do *what* the Spirit says do, they do it *when* the Spirit says do!!!"

When we finally crammed ourselves into one of three beige VW vans, Benet Luchion peered into the middle seat where I was squished between Charles Nettles, an irreverent, skinny, and shrewd teenager from Camden, and Bob Block, a short, muscular, white eighteen-year-old who had been working in Wilcox County since the Selma March. John Golden, a sandy-haired, pale California seminary student in his thirties, was behind the wheel. My orientation roommate, Ann, was in the last seat with some other white kids. Benet was worried about us being in an integrated car with Charles Nettles, but we would be traveling mostly after dark. Benet's last words were directed to me, "Now, when you get tired and need to lean your head on someone's shoulder, lean on Bob, not Charles." Since Benet had saved me from possibly being assaulted, I took his advice, and after all, they had warned us to steer clear of interracial relationships. Besides, Bob was kind of attractive to me with his tan skin, golden eyes, and thick mop of black hair. He had the movement look—blue work shirt, jeans that had been worn so many times they could stand up on their own, and broken-down sandals that spoke of many miles of canvassing. I hoped to learn from his experience so I could be a good worker too.

The three vans formed a convoy filled with excited, sweaty civil rights workers headed toward Montgomery just before dusk on Saturday evening. We didn't have water or food and scarcely had room to breathe, but our minds were set on freedom. We pulled out in a cloud of dust, windows down, singing at the top of our lungs "Ain't Gonna Let Nobody Turn Me 'Round," with Benet playing his flute and a handful of SCOPE workers assigned to remain in Atlanta waving wildly. We sang dozens of choruses of that song, which carried us across Georgia and deep into Alabama.

After midnight, somewhere outside Montgomery, we stopped for a few minutes to eat baloney sandwiches on the floor of an empty Freedom House and to do our business in the bushes. A single flashlight pointed upward lit the ceiling of the windowless, doorless shack. The men took turns standing guard. We ate in near silence while the electric buzz of cicadas served as our dinner music. We returned to the vans and caravanned through the dark night another two hours to Camden, the county seat of Wilcox County, Alabama, where I would spend my summer.

3

The Wilcox County Voting Rights Fight

In the mid-1960s, outsiders easily could have been lulled into thinking that gradualism, a favored philosophy of liberal southern whites, was working. The 1955–56 Montgomery Bus Boycott, organized by the Montgomery Improvement Association with Rosa Parks as a test case, forced that city to integrate public transportation, although other forms of discrimination—especially barriers to voter registration—continued. The student sit-in movement that swept the South in the early 1960s resulted in stiffer federal laws against segregation in public accommodations. Although the activists protested the lack of compliance with federal laws, the federal government seldom defended any civil rights activities unless forced to do so by public opinion and political pressure.

In 1961, Freedom Riders who tested federal laws requiring integrated seating on national bus lines were violently attacked and then jailed in Anniston, Birmingham, and Montgomery, Alabama, and other cities. News of attacks on the activists forced the federal government to sue states that refused to comply with interstate transportation laws and inspired a new wave of civil rights action across the South. In May of 1963, King convinced local and SCLC leaders to recruit children for demonstrations in Birmingham. The "Children's Crusade" brought greater media and federal attention and was considered a success both in Birmingham and throughout Alabama.[1] On August 28, 1963, before a large integrated crowd assembled in front of the Lincoln Memorial in Washington, DC, Martin Luther King Jr. gave his famous "I Have a Dream" speech. Jubilation turned to grief and anger on September 15, 1963, when the Sixteenth Street Baptist Church was bombed, leaving four little girls dead. During the Mississippi Freedom Summer of 1964, activists throughout the South stepped up their fight against the prevailing pathology of segregation. The vast majority of freedom fighters were students and young adults. Cracks began to show in the foundation of white supremacy, but the system continued to stand as long as black people could not vote, could not change policy, and could not participate in civic life outside of their own segregated communities.

The 1964 Civil Rights Act overturned generations of state-sanctioned segregation in public accommodations and in employment. It passed only after years of vicious police brutality, arrests, and attacks on nonviolent protesters and the accompanying litigation. The murder of young civil rights workers Cheney, Schwerner, and Goodman in Mississippi in June of that year is widely credited with speeding the signing of the act in July.

But the 1964 Civil Rights Act did not fully address challenges to voting rights in the South. As summarized by civil rights veteran and lay historian Bruce Hartford, "The Act had little effect on voting rights. It did not eliminate literacy tests, one of the main methods used to exclude Black voters in the South, nor did it address economic retaliation, police repression, or physical violence against nonwhite voters. The Act also failed to address the pernicious notion of voter qualification—the idea that citizenship does not confer an automatic right to vote, but rather that voters must meet some arbitrary standard beyond citizenship."[2]

SNCC had been working with grassroots organizers on voting rights since 1963, but it was not until the highly publicized violence of Bloody Sunday in March 1965 that the nation was forced to recognize that voting rights suppression would continue until there was a new, stronger federal bill. The average white northerner had no clue that almost all black citizens in the Deep South were prevented from registering to vote. SCLC, SNCC, and NAACP believed that ongoing legal intervention coupled with massive political organization would be required to enforce the provisions of this new bill as well as other existing but continuously violated civil rights laws.

Black activists did not wait for the government to take action; they organized to change the system. In small communities throughout the South, local leaders organized in churches and schools. In rural areas, organizers developed secret communication networks with word passed by children on school buses, farmers on mules, and preachers with cars. Wilcox County activists intensified their protests, increased their demands, and traveled to Selma, Montgomery, and Atlanta to be trained in nonviolent action by SCLC and SNCC. Each demonstration and protest was counted as progress on the road to freedom. Many participants recalled their marches, even their arrests, with enthusiasm for the next battle. "Ain't Gonna Let Nobody Turn Me 'Round" echoed through rural churches during mass meetings. But the use of traditional tactics of physical terror and legalistic obstacles to

equality continued unabated. The minority white population in rural counties like Wilcox was terrified that if the majority of voters were black then
that would surely lead to an end to the white southern way of life and loss
of political power.

Seventy-three miles from the state capitol in Montgomery, Alabama,
Wilcox County is in a region known as the Black Belt. Its rich, dark farmland is capable of producing high-quality cotton and acres of pine trees for
lumber. The twisting Alabama River runs through Wilcox County and is
so wide in places it looks like a lake. The county seat of Camden is located
thirty-seven miles from Selma, which had become a center for training, inspiration, and support of the Alabama voting rights fight. Camden is inter-
sected by State Highways 10, 28, 41, and 64 and by Federal Highways 164,
221, and 265, but few people stopped in the small town when they could
push on to Montgomery or Selma where there were hotels and restaurants.
In 1965, despite the constant pass-through of logging and cotton-hauling
trucks, Camden was as segregated as it had been since it was founded in
1842. But the Wilcox County freedom fight was well underway long before we arrived.

Despite grinding poverty and prejudice, Wilcox County locals had been
engaged in a struggle for their civil rights ever since the failure of Reconstruction to deliver on its promises. As early as the 1940s, Wilcox County
World War II veteran John Davis went all the way to the White House to
ask President Roosevelt himself to overturn Alabama's discriminatory voting regulations.[3]

The fact that activists filed cases as early as the 1950s is documented by
legislation passed by the Alabama state legislature to restrain the NAACP
from collecting dues and organizing legal cases in Marengo County in 1956.
Included in this legislation was a similar regulation, applying only to Wilcox
County. It required any organization soliciting membership in the county
to pay a $100 licensing fee, plus $5 for every member who joined. Its sponsor candidly explained the necessity for the bill: "Without such a proposal
it would be very easy for the NAACP to slip into Wilcox County and teach
the Negroes undesirable ideas." Governor Folsom took a different view and
vetoed the bill as "unjust, unfair, and undemocratic," but the legislature over-
rode the veto and passed the act into law.[4]

Even with a historically black majority, whites controlled Wilcox County
economically and politically. Back in 1900, the black population of Wilcox
County was 28,652, or 81 percent out of a total population of 35,431, with
6,779 whites forming only 19 percent of the population. Our SCLC leaders
told us that by the 1960 census, Wilcox County had lost over one-third of

its total population. By 1965 there were a total of 18,739 residents, 78 percent black and 22 percent white. Despite the overwhelming majority black population, it was nearly impossible for these families to earn money and accumulate wealth. With the exception of funeral homes and a few small stores, whites continued to own the majority of businesses. Whites owned much of the valuable land, which was mostly worked by tenant farmers and sharecroppers who lived in perpetual financial servitude to the landowners.

One area where black land ownership was more common was Gees Bend, a former plantation that took more than an hour to reach from Camden after local officials removed ferry service to punish the community's voting rights activists in 1962. As far back as Roosevelt's New Deal administration, federal officials identified the community as one of the poorest in the United States. They gave them land and "government built" homes through the Farm Security Administration (FSA). By 1965 many of the farmers had become independent, giving them greater political freedom, but they continued to be locked out of the white economic system by county and state officials. Farm loans were unavailable to them, and they could not get elected to the powerful county agricultural committee. Gees Bend farmers and preachers became leaders in the local Civil Rights Movement, particularly around issues of voting rights.

Whites had used the southern states' legal systems to systematically, yet legally, retard the ability of black people to exercise their full rights as citizens.[5] Time and again dozens of persistent Alabama residents managed to complete registration forms but then were told they "didn't pass the test." The Pulitzer Prize–winning *Slavery by Another Name: The Re-Enslavement of Black Americans from the Civil War to World War II* by Douglas A. Blackmon fastidiously documents the advantages whites gained through their use of corrupt legal systems.[6]

Fortunately, by the 1960s the US Department of Justice and outside legal groups such as the NAACP pressed cases on behalf of Wilcox County residents. Martin Luther King visited Gees Bend in 1963, where he stayed with farmer Willie Quill Pettway's family and encouraged other farmers, led by Rev. Lonnie Brown and World War II veteran Monroe Pettway, in their fight for the right to vote. Prompted by these civil rights activists, the federal Department of Justice filed a suit against the Wilcox County registrar.

When we first met him in Atlanta, one of our Wilcox County SCOPE field directors, Daniel Harrell, gave us a snapshot of what had gone on before our arrival and what we were likely to encounter. He told us that the community was completely segregated except for black people working for whites in their homes and in other subservient jobs. Children attended seg-

6. Rev. Daniel Harrell, SCLC SCOPE field director, Antioch Baptist Church, Camden, Alabama. (Copyright © 1966 by Bob Fitch.)

regated schools; churches were either all white or all black. Limited association took place in stores and other public venues where it was always made clear to blacks that they were considered "less than" whites. Just that spring, the mayor of Camden publicly beat a thirteen-year-old boy, two families were chased out of town, and a white reporter had his head split open while photographing a student demonstration. Harrell told us there were forty-nine black residents on the Wilcox County voting roll in spring 1965, but due to intimidation and illegal tactics by the registrar, no black people had voted or held office since Reconstruction.

Wilcox County students, some as young as elementary school age, were fed up with substandard segregated school buildings, tattered used textbooks, and watching school buses pass them by as they trudged along miles of muddy roads in search of an education that could lead to a better life. Dozens of these students were recruited by Dan Harrell and local leader Ethel Brooks to join in the January 1965 Selma children's youth rally and march for their parents' voting rights. Young Camden Academy students returned home fired up and began their own walkouts from school on a nearly daily basis during the winter and spring of 1965.

Although Camden Academy was originally a Presbyterian mission school owned by the church, the Wilcox Board of Education funded teachers' salaries in order to maintain segregated schools while claiming to provide equal education for all students. The student actions attracted both seasoned and novice civil rights workers from Selma and beyond. SCLC stationed two experienced field workers who had worked together in Louisiana to support local Wilcox County organizers. Dan Harrell was mostly raised in Union City, Alabama, and our other project leader, Major Johns, hailed from Plaquemines, Louisiana. Both men had served in the military, Harrell in the air force and Johns as a conscientious objector in the army. Before being assigned to Wilcox County, the two had organized for SCLC in Shreveport, Louisiana.

Legal challenges were being decided in the federal courts around the time we arrived in Wilcox County. After the Bloody Sunday assault on peaceful voting rights marchers in adjacent Dallas County, Hosea Williams, John Lewis, and Amelia Boynton sought a federal injunction to protect their constitutional rights to peacefully assemble and to recruit voters to register. The court ruled that police were required to protect the rights of voting rights marchers and issued an injunction that protected the big march to Montgomery a few weeks later. The litigants cited Wilcox County as one of the most egregious examples of the difficulties African Americans faced in their effort to register to vote. The court opinion stated: "In Wilcox County as of December, 1963, where Negro citizens of voting age outnumber white citizens two to one, 0% of the Negro citizens were registered to vote as contrasted with the registration of 100% of the white citizens of voting age in this county."[7]

Long after it was illegal to do so, Gov. Wallace authorized voting officials to continue to require a so-called literacy test, administered only to black applicants. The officials also required a registered voter to act as a voucher for the good character of the person attempting to register, and since no African Americans were registered voters, no one could get a voucher. Like many others, Wilcox County imposed an illegal poll tax long after other areas of the South had given it up. The main provisions of the 1965 Voting Rights Act addressed these three issues and authorized outside federal examiners to oversee and overrule local voting officials, which was why its passage was so important to our registration efforts.

Previous registration efforts in Wilcox County had been futile. In addition to the Gees Bend voting rights case brought by Monroe Pettway and others, local movement leader Rev. Lonnie Brown had initiated a complaint with the Department of Justice alleging threats, intimidation, and coercion interfering with the abilities of blacks to register and vote based on his being arrested for trespass when he attempted to inform his insurance clients of their voting rights. Several of his policy holders lived on land owned by white people, and despite the fact that he had visited the properties in question numerous times in a professional capacity, he had been arrested for trespassing when he attempted to talk with them about their right to vote. The federal government initiated a federal complaint under the Civil Rights Act of 1957 that prohibited intimidation, threats, and coercion to interfere with the right of a person to vote. However, the federal district court in Montgomery dismissed the complaint and ruled that Wilcox County property owners had the right to exclude Brown as a trespasser from their private properties. To comply, Brown would have had to leave the area, to move away from his home county, to continue employment. Instead, he stayed and fought on. The appellate court later reversed the district court's decision.[8] The Justice Department suit against the Wilcox County voting registrar was finally won in April 1965 when the Federal Court of Appeals in the Fifth District ruled that the use of a supporting witness (voucher) requirement was discriminatory.[9] However, discrimination due to illiteracy and an illegal poll tax continued until after passage of the 1965 VRA.

While Wilcox County was unique—in its proximity to Selma, in its deep, direct connection to Martin Luther King Jr., through King's friendship with community leader Rev. Threadgill, and because of the strength of the Gees Bend community—it was also typical of majority-black counties at that time. The fierce, unheralded, local resistance to white supremacy that built the backbone of the movement was met with death threats, firebombing, incarceration, and assassination of African Americans who were seeking freedom and equality. Alabama is steeped in the blood of martyrs who have never made the history books, but they were heroes to us. Their courage inspired me to try to manage my own mounting fear as threats escalated around us that summer. The fact that death was a potential price to be paid by freedom fighters was always on our minds. We were in awe of our local leaders who knew that inviting outside civil rights workers could make things worse, yet kept their eyes on the prize of the ballot box.

It is not an exaggeration to state that the environment that civil rights workers stepped into in the Freedom Summer of 1965 was murderous and violent. Recent civil rights murders committed not far from Camden were on our minds.

On February 26, 1965, in Marion, Alabama, just fifty-seven miles from Camden, twenty-six-year-old Jimmy Lee Jackson's death became the rallying event for the Selma to Montgomery March. Because he was murdered by police, no case was opened. In nearby Selma, Rev. James Reeb died March

11 after he and other white ministers were severely beaten. An all-white jury acquitted the four Selma murderers.

The evening of March 25, Viola Luizzo, a forty-year-old white mother of five from Detroit, was shot to death on her way to retrieve more marchers on a second round-trip from Montgomery to Selma after the Montgomery march. Klansmen, including an undercover agent for the Federal Bureau of Investigation (FBI), shot at Mrs. Luizzo and nineteen-year-old black activist Leroy Moton. Mrs. Luizzo died instantly. Much later, two of the murderers served light sentences, and the FBI agent went into a witness protection program. Camden residents recalled this event as particularly traumatic because they had just returned from celebrating the successful march on Montgomery. They thought: If they will kill northern whites, will the violence against us ever stop?

While we were in Wilcox that summer, word came that Willy Lee Brewster, age thirty-eight, a black foundry worker, was shot and killed by white men on his way home from work in Anniston 185 miles from Camden in a community that was active in the Alabama voter registration drive. The attackers belonged to the National States Rights Party, a violent neo-Nazi group whose members had been involved in church bombings and other murders. No one was convicted.

Few civil rights leaders suffered more death threats than Dr. Martin Luther King Jr., and no one provided greater inspiration than he. His friend and fellow Morehouse alumni, Rev. Thomas Threadgill, who was chaplain at Camden Academy, called King's attention to opportunities to inspire Wilcox County organizers. Whenever he could fit it into his increasingly frenetic schedule, King came to Wilcox to encourage local activists in their marches and demands for the right to vote.

On Monday, March 1, 1965, King joined a march in progress from Antioch Baptist to the courthouse in Camden. He spoke to a crowd of about two hundred people attempting to register in the pouring rain. Some residents speculate that he got out of Camden alive because there were state troopers assigned to his security that day.

This is the day when King famously confronted Sheriff Lummie Jenkins asking him to "vouch" for the registrants who still had to: (1) Pass a literacy test; (2) Prove citizenship; and (3) Have an already registered voter vouch for their good character. King gave a rousing speech to encourage the people to keep on going. "Doncha get weary chillun" was his frequent exhortation. Although the sheriff refused, eyewitnesses said that the sheriff appeared a little bit intimidated by King, which made everyone feel proud and reinspired to press on. Ten people were allowed to register that day. King's participation in the march, his nonviolent confrontation with the sheriff, and the success of the new voters would be celebrated by the community in story and ceremony from that day forward, forever accompanied by a reminder that King marched in Camden before Bloody Sunday and before he led the march to Montgomery later that month.

While King's visits thrilled and inspired the students and adult leaders alike, they knew that when he was gone they were on their own. Soon I would meet and work with several of the heroes of the Wilcox County freedom fight.

4

Welcome to Wilcox County

For some of the dozen or more of us who participated in the SCLC SCOPE orientation in Atlanta and then jammed into three VW vans for an eight-hour drive, Camden was just a stop on the way to another county. For me, this was going to be home for the rest of the summer. On wobbly legs, we crept into Antioch Baptist Church at 2:30 A.M., using as little light as possible. The fragrance of old hymnals, candle wax, mildew, and damp wood combined in a familiar smell that comforted me a bit after our long drive from Atlanta. A back injury I suffered in high school had flared up and I felt a little feverish, too.

Major Johns, a short, dark, solidly built thirty-year-old who was one of our two SCLC field directors, greeted and hushed us. On the way down, Bob Block had told me that Major (that was his first name, not a title), who led the walkouts and sit-ins for the Congress of Racial Equality (CORE) in Baton Rouge, had been beaten and arrested lots of times and even served his military draft as a conscientious objector. Major's movement commitment was iron strong and he'd survived some tough times, so we needed to heed his direction. We got so quiet I could hear the cicadas again. Everything about Major said no nonsense. He surveyed us with stern eyes and took a deep breath. "Y'all gonna have to sleep here tonight. A certain local who was gonna take some of you was visited by Sheriff Jenkins and had his mind changed. Now get some sleep." There was no question and answer period. Apparently our orientation was no longer going to be theoretical.

We made ourselves as comfortable as we could on the wooden pews. Major shut out all the lights. I had slept in churches with my youth group when we did service work, but usually we had sleeping bags and pillows. Bob offered to go get my pillow from the van. On the long trip from Atlanta, I enjoyed his stories of outwitting racists and getting folks excited about voter registration. He had survived the march from Selma to Montgomery and several marches to the Wilcox County Courthouse without getting beaten too badly, which made me think he could keep me safe. Despite being sweaty and unshaven, he was good looking. In a little while I could hear lots of snoring. I whispered to Bob, "You awake?" No, he was leading the snore symphony of lucky good sleepers.

As I was wondering where we would sleep tomorrow night and hoping it would be more comfortable, I heard truck doors slam and booted feet outside the church. Major shouted in a low voice, "Get down and stay down till I say." Bob and I rolled under the same pew and squeezed together.

"What's going on?"

"Oh probably some crackers out there trying to scare us."

"It's working on me," I said, trying not to think about the men outside. Then there were shots. I clung to Bob who didn't seem to mind our sudden closeness.

He was whispering, "They won't kill us tonight. Welcome to Wilcox County, that's all." I held my breath and prayed.

We were here only to ensure that all Americans had the right to vote. How dare they try to scare us away! Well, I'll show them; I won't be afraid, that's what I told myself. After a while the shots stopped, boots retreated to trucks that roared off down the dark tree-lined highway.

When Major Johns said it was safe to come out, some of the workers left for another county and others crawled back up onto the pews. I thought the floor was just as comfortable as any old wooden pew so I stayed down there, and Bob did, too. He and some others went back to sleep for a while as I lay thinking about those men with guns and their history of using them on "outside agitators" like us.

A few hours later I stood in the hot morning sun on the steps of Antioch Baptist greeting children and ladies coming for service. I hoped I had cleaned up well enough in the church washroom. We SCOPE girls had been told to wear dresses, not pants, all summer. We were supposed to be role models for young black women, but glancing around it looked to me as if most were modeling themselves on white women, at least when it came to flat-ironed hair. In contrast, most of the little girls had neatly braided plaits, sticking out all over, some tied with ribbons. I thought the children were adorable with their many shades of chocolate, tan, and olive skin and their big brown eyes. How dare anyone try to make these beautiful children feel bad about their looks!

Although the children inspired me, I was skeptical about their parents and their future, as this excerpt from an early June letter indicates: "In the morning, I got dressed and went to the church service. There were only a few people there—lots of children and a few ladies, no men. After church I talked to the children who gathered round me and asked them to help me canvass for voters. They told me their parents wouldn't register because they just don't care anymore. The children are beautiful—they still have hope. There is hardly anyone in Camden between 18 and 35 years old. There is nothing here for youth—no jobs, no schools, no social life—no opportunity for advancement."

Antioch Baptist Church, a small, whitewashed clapboard building with simple white and blue frosted glass windows, had been serving as the area's movement central before we arrived. It would be impossible to overstate the importance of this historic church to the movement in Wilcox County. Antioch had been the rallying ground for the demonstrations that had taken place between February and May of that year. Voting rights demonstrations were planned here, and most marches either began or ended at the church. Its clapboard walls seemed thin, but the one-hundred-year-old church was a true sanctuary for civil rights workers. The church sat on a plain dirt lot near downtown on the edge of a black section called simply "the Quarters" on Highway 41 (Claiborne Street) near Highways 28 and 10. These roads ran out to the areas where I would work most of the summer: Arlington, Coy, Boiling Springs, and Gees Bend. Rev. Samuel J. Freeman and the deacons allowed us to use this church as our SCOPE project headquarters, which added fuel to the fury of the segregationists, as if they needed any excuse to attack Camden's strong core of movement activists.

I couldn't help but look around the sanctuary, hoping I wasn't staring rudely. The church people were all black, which was unfamiliar to me. Some of the adults smiled and welcomed us, some looked away, some looked anxious. The ladies fanned themselves with paper fans from Brownlee's Funeral Parlor with Bible verses printed on one side. I'm sure Rev. Freeman gave a wonderful sermon, but I could scarcely keep my eyes open in the hot humid sanctuary where I had spent a sleepless night. Kids were all over us before and after services. "Where y'all from? Do you know Dr. King? Why is your hair like that [straight]? Are you comin' to our house?"

"Yes, Dr. King sent me. That's right, I hope to visit your family. Are your parents registered?" I tried to remember what we'd been told to say, but when it came to my hair, I just offered, "Would you like to touch it?"

Two little girls stroked my long, straight brown hair, and one said, "Oooh it's soft!"

I had read about the study that was used in *Brown v. Board of Education* in which the black children preferred white dolls to ones that looked like them, so I quickly and sincerely said, "Well, I like yours more. It keeps its shape better in this heat."

Camden Academy

In the wee hours of the morning, Major Johns had assured us he would have housing for us before nightfall, and he was as good as his word. He convinced the chaplain, Rev. Thomas Threadgill, to let us white girls stay in the boys' dormitory at the Presbyterian Church–owned Camden Academy where two white ministerial students had been staying for a few weeks. When Major drove us there, I realized that Antioch Baptist and Camden Academy were only a few blocks from each other, and I wondered why we hadn't walked to save gas.

The Freedmen's Board of the United Presbyterian Church of North America had founded six Presbyterian mission schools in Wilcox County by 1894. Although founded by the northern church board, by the 1960s they were accredited under the Wilcox County School Board in order to maintain segregation. The Camden Academy campus, which housed the elementary, junior high, and high school, was considered the crown jewel of this system, even though the students received tattered books and broken equipment discarded by the white public schools. A strong cadre of teachers committed to teaching religion, ethics, civic responsibility, and African American culture along with academic subjects instilled pride and optimism in youth who might otherwise have been ground down by living in a community where almost no power and very little money was in the hands of people who looked like them.

Camden Academy students represented the future hopes of the community. As a church school, religion, morals, and manners were taught along with grammar, math, and history. We had been told to speak simply but to use good English. Mission schools like Camden Academy were doing all they could to prepare their students to speak Standard English because they were expected to become professionals and community leaders after they went on to college in larger communities like Tuscaloosa, Montgomery, and Atlanta. However, all of the students and adults we met, including our project leaders, used black southern English that was poetically ungrammatical and deeply infectious. By my second letter home I wrote my parents, "I am sure it sounds funny but I have picked up a [black] southern accent and the expressive grammar that 'go with it'!"

Camden Academy campus was up a steep drive just a short distance from downtown. There was a flat area at the crest of the hill with several long, two-story wood frame buildings, a chapel, and the principal's and chaplain's homes, all painted white. The boys' dormitory had broad upper and lower porches. There was a half-circle drive and a huge pecan tree out front. We were told this housing was temporary but to go ahead and take any empty room, so I chose one closest to the bathroom and put my meager belongings in the small wooden chest beside the narrow bed. The dormitory was nicer than the one I stayed in at my church summer camp, Cazadero, and I was surprised when one of the other girls said this was "really roughing it." She must have come from a nicer home than I did. I rinsed out my underwear and dirty dress and hung them on a hanger in the open window to dry while I luxuriated in my first shower in two days.

Downstairs in the large front room there were two white student ministers we came to call "the Revs," and two white girls, Connie Turner, who had been there before us, and Ann Nesbitt, my orientation roommate. We met two white SCOPE boys, Mike and Bill, who were staying somewhere else. Soon after, we met Judy and Sherry, two northern white girls who didn't seem to identify with our project but who worked with us sometimes. They were staying with Charles Nettles and his father, across from the church. We called everyone under age of twenty-one "girls," "boys," or just "kids." At first I thought the two seminarians were in charge of us because one immediately started telling us what to do, and they were at least five years older than we were, but when the dignified and well-dressed Rev. Thomas L. Threadgill arrived, it was clear who had real seniority.

As school chaplain, Rev. Threadgill aided the students with their protests and stood up for them to Mr. Hobbs, the principal who objected to the disruption of classes. Rev. Threadgill not only defended the students who left school to march and participate in boycotts, he even went with them. Both his livelihood and his housing depended on his position at the school as chaplain and teacher, so standing with the students over the administration took true courage. Rev. Threadgill's leadership of the Camden Academy student body and its handful of other brave teachers, his articulation and powerful oratory, and his fearless stands before the white authorities made him the most respected local leader I met during the time I served as field worker.

Prior to returning to the community of his father and grandfather, Rev. Threadgill had graduated from the prestigious all-black, all-male Morehouse College in Atlanta and from the Pittsburgh Theological Seminary. After serving in a combat unit of the US Army in World War II, he returned, like many veterans, with an increased sense of commitment to ending the oppression of his own people. The family's commitment to civil rights spanned generations. Mrs. Mildred Threadgill's maternal grandmother, Rosie Hunter-Steele, had recently risked her life by opening her farm to the Selma to Montgomery marchers as a place to sleep on the second night of the march.

The Threadgill children were already active in the boycotts and marches although their oldest child, Sheryl, was barely in her teens.

Seminarian John Golden was friendly and very earnest. He seemed to feel responsible for us because he was older. John Williams, on the other hand, was a square-faced, crew cut, self-righteous fellow who immediately offended almost everyone he interacted with due to his constant expressions of white male entitlement. He seemed to find the SCOPE workers an annoyance, and as the summer wore on, his bias against integration completed his alienation from our group and hastened his departure.

John Golden told us that he and John Williams were studying at the San Francisco Bay Area Theological Seminary. They had been working for a few weeks with Rev. Threadgill to try to improve race relations, although we didn't see any evidence of that. Integration was not part of the SCOPE mission. Our purpose was strictly to canvass for unregistered voters, educate them as needed, and get them to register. I never spoke to a local white person all summer except in the course of being arrested. And I never heard of any aid or assistance being given to our voter education and registration project by local whites.

Personally, I thought there were an awful lot of "Reverends" around there, but it was the custom for both black and white seminarians to be called Reverend, and in the black community, preachers who were "schooled" (been to graduate school and ordained) as well as those who were "called" (moved by the Spirit) were addressed as "Reverend." It seemed that many were called.

Rev. Threadgill was both called and ordained. He was a dark handsome man, a powerful speaker, and that afternoon, highly agitated. His family had hoped for a more peaceful summer after a spring filled with marches and demonstrations. Many marches originated right on this campus where some of the students boarded when school was in session and where we white field workers were now staying. Students had been tear gassed, beaten, and jailed. Some families sent their children away this summer, predicting that racist violence would get even worse with us there. Others always sent their children away during the summer to relatives in Chicago, New York, and elsewhere so they could get a glimpse of life beyond their small hometown. Particularly missing were young women, especially teenage girls. Rev. Threadgill's own twelve-year-old daughter was spending the summer with an aunt, away from tumultuous Camden.

My mind wandered as I listened to Rev. Threadgill's instructions, but I clearly heard his rules against smoking and male-female relationships in the dormitory. Those prohibitions stood out in my mind as I thought about the fact that I had started smoking cigarettes during the last semester. That shouldn't create a problem; most of the young men smoked and at least half of the women did, too. From what I observed, all of the adult leaders smoked cigarettes. But my mind was wandering to thoughts of Bob Block and when I would see him again. Along with others who lingered in Selma after the march to Montgomery, Bob had come to Camden to join the voting rights marchers who were being tear gassed and violently attacked in early April. He had worked in the rural county ever since. Bob had been very warm toward me from the time we met, offering his shoulder for me to rest on during our long drive the night before.

The Quarters

After meeting with Rev. Threadgill, some of us walked from Camden Academy back to the other side of town by way of Water Street to avoid downtown as instructed, so we could get a taste of areas where we would be working. In a hollow near Antioch Baptist Church sat a large all-black area called Wilson's Quarter or simply "the Quarters." Former slave shacks sat side by side, a few had space for a vegetable garden out back. Some of the bigger places had a good size patch of dirt in front so the kids could play safely, away from the nearby streets of white Camden. Down in another hollow was the Sawmill Quarter where the mill employees lived in company-owned housing; this is where I was told I would be assigned.

No amount of orientation could have prepared me for my first glimpse of this contemporary version of slave housing with unpainted, warped wooden shacks, no glass in the windows, broken screen doors, or no screen doors at all. We kicked up dust with every step. Even with all the rain there was little grass in the red dirt yards, where an occasional chicken was pecking. The contrast between the green grass and weeds, trees and vegetable gardens, and the red, red soil was pretty, but the most beautiful sight was the collection of curious children who came up to say hello. They seemed to know that white people who came from the church were different from the ones their parents told them to be polite to or to stay away from entirely. They flocked to me immediately, and I loved them right back. This would be an area that was nearly impossible to canvass, but we were instructed to try.

My First Mass Meeting

Our first night in Camden, John Golden drove some of us out to Little Zion Baptist Church in Coy to a mass meeting led by Rev. Daniel Harrell, our SCOPE field director. Harrell was a stocky, good-looking, medium brown, medium height man in his early thirties with a stylish pencil moustache and a conservatively short haircut. He told us to call him Dan. His light-skinned, delicate wife, Juanita, offered us a warm welcome and much appreciated hugs. The couple seemed more accessible than either Major Johns or Rev. Threadgill, men who had intimidated me at first.

Before he was assigned to Wilcox County to direct community organizing, literacy, and voter registration for SCLC, Dan Harrell had worked with Major Johns on public accommodations integration and voter registration in Louisiana. Dan's wife, Juanita Daniels Harrell, was also considered SCOPE staff. Juanita worked as hard as anyone in the county, although it soon became obvious to me that she was not completely accepted by the local ladies who had worked at great risk without recognition or remuneration for so many years.

Dan and Major were in charge of our work, so I paid close attention to what they said. Despite being exhausted, I was on the edge of my pew for two hours while first Dan and then Major preached to a full house about getting out the vote, taking the next step to freedom. Major exhorted the crowd, "Don't be waitin' for the Promised Land. You can be in the Promised Land tomorrow. You can fulfill that promise: You can be a free man, free to vote! Get yourself registered. We need volunteers to carry folks into town, to help organize others, to take in some of our summer workers. You can sign up tonight with Mrs. Angion in the back. But get yourself registered first, that's the first thing. You wanna *be* in that number! These students come all the way from Atlanta and California just to help us so we gotta show them we can help ourselves." I thought that Major Johns preached just as well as Dr. King. Major wasn't ordained at the time, but he'd been called since youth and he was a natural. The cadence of the ministers' voices sounded like music to me, although I wondered if they used non-Standard English because they hadn't been able to attend good schools or as a technique to bond with the locals. At the end of the meeting, Dan had us stand while people applauded and cheered. Then we sang "We Shall Overcome." I liked it out in Coy; I liked it a lot.

Late that night, I started coughing. I felt a fever coming on, but before I could rest, I had to complete my first letter to my friends and supporters back home in California, which Jeanne Searight, my college roommate and secretary at the Ec House, would type, mimeograph, and mail to the list I left for her. Some supporters sent me small checks or $20 bills folded in a letter, which really helped when it emerged that there was no plan for our food after the families who were supposed to host us backed out.

From my first letter, June 1965:

Dear Family and Friends:

This is another world. It's a world where I, a 19-year-old white north-ern woman, am not free. I am not free to go into the white section of Camden, Alabama with a Negro.[1] I am not free to work in civil rights and still relate to the Southern whites. I can't go out after dark or go on a single date or swim in a public pool all summer. You people think you are free. When I was in San Francisco I thought I was free. But, we're not free. I'm not down here fighting so any Negro can vote; I'm fighting for my rights—my human right to choose my friends as I please, to work with whoever I want, to worship with all peoples.

There is a Movement going on. God is acting in history. It's God, not Martin Luther King, or James Bevel or Hosea Williams that is leading this movement. It's faith that enables people to endure with one meal a day, four hours sleep, and one change of clothes. And they can still sing and shout praises.

When I finally crawled into bed, worried and scared about a hun-dred things, sick from the local croup, tired from the long meeting, I had a hope in my heart. It's a hope I found in the midst of these people who live in the midst of hatred and degradation; I found it in the faces of the young Negro children and I found it in the voices of my fellow SCOPE workers. This hope is that We Shall Overcome.

I want to thank all of you who are making my summer possible by your contributions, your encouragement, and your prayers. I need all three in order to continue the work. If any of you want to be of fur-ther help to the Movement write your Congressman about the Vot-ing Rights Bill, insist that it be passed now. It is a good bill and will greatly implement our efforts.

We have one great need in Camden which some of you might like to meet. There are no doctors or drugstores that will serve Negroes or civil rights workers. We need alcohol, Lysol, antibacterial soaps, and vitamin pills desperately.

Again, I want to thank you for your support. Anyone who wishes to contact me should write in care of: Camden Academy, Camden, Alabama. Please register your letter if it is important, because all our mail is opened and read.

After I began the work in Camden, I started to look at myself differently. That second night, after I washed my face in the communal bathroom where a long mirror hung over the basins, all I could think was: I look too white. I remembered how my mother always dabbed Esoterica bleaching cream on her dark pigmentation that she blamed on Indian blood in her family, and now here I was, wishing I were darker. Since I didn't bring any hats, I figured I'd tan quickly, but not enough to blend in the way Bob could. Ever since the Selma march he'd been telling people that he was Hawaiian. With his dark Semitic looks, he looked like he could have been. I wondered where he was sleeping that night.

Ann, who planned to work in the new Head Start program and seemed a natural for that with her patience and quiet ways, chose a room down the hall. Pretty, blond, blue-eyed Connie from Marin County, who was about my age, already had a room across the hall from mine. She had some connection with the white seminarians; I never did find out what it was, but I had not seen her at orientation. By her manners and dress, I guessed that Connie was from an upper-middle-class family. She was energetic, friendly, and seemed to think the project was a grand adventure. We all said goodnight and I took some aspirin for my aching back.

I fell asleep thinking about the words to the hymn someone was playing on the piano downstairs: "The Church's One Foundation . . . though there be those who hate her, and false sons in her pale, against both foe or traitor, she ever shall prevail." Surely we'll be safe here with the Revs downstairs and Rev. Threadgill watching out for us just across campus. But thoughts of being a target of the Ku Klux Klan, along with a persistent cough, kept me from deep sleep most of another night.

5

They Were Ready for Us

From my second June 1965 letter to supporters:

Dear Friends—

On Monday we began our voter registration program. The second & fourth Mondays are registration days in Alabama. There are 6,000 Negroes and only 1,000 Whites (of voting age) in Wilcox County. White voter registration is 110% & Negro registration is less than 2%.[1]

Our SCOPE people began going from door to door encouraging everyone to get out to register. The little kids in the community showed us where the likely people lived.

Five of our workers went down to the Quarter (a piece of property owned by white people where Negro people live) & were promptly arrested. One Negro boy was beaten and sent to the hospital in Selma.

It seems the white folks in Wilcox County prepared well for our arrival. Armaments were purchased by state troopers and distributed to the white citizens. Last night they spent several hours shooting around the church.

We are trying to move everyone out of a centralized location. I don't know how long I can stay at the Academy. Yesterday morning before I came to Good Samaritan Hospital I was staying at the Academy by myself [because I was sick in bed]. Two white men drove in and around the dormitory for almost 1 1/2 hrs. One of them got out and stood on the porch for a while. I just kept on with my reading and writing but I was terribly afraid. At last they drove away and the phone rang. It was one of the white ministers. I could tell the line was tapped so I just said we had some company. Luckily, he got the message and within 10 minutes one of the local Movement workers was up to get me. A

Negro man was driving the car but when I got in, he just said, "Get out!" He wouldn't drive through Camden with me in the car.

So I walked with Bob Block, an 18 yr old native San Franciscan and one of the best workers we have, through Camden, out to the church. As we walked, we stopped people in the streets and told them to get out to register. When I got to the church, they made the decision that I should go to the hospital.

Every one of the local youth working with us that summer had stories of mistreatment by whites that fueled their commitment to civil rights. One young man told me that his parents taught him to use his hands as an ashtray if there were white people around while he was smoking because if you were black, you could be arrested for flicking your ashes on the streets in Camden. Another said, "You think that's bad. One cracker made me hold out my hands to use as an ashtray for *his* cigarette. He would've killed me if I hadn't, and I don't even smoke."

Good-looking, well-spoken Academy student Robert Powell was three years my junior but at age sixteen was very much my senior in understanding the pathology of racism. He explained how cruel some whites were, even to young children who "forgot their place." "When I was younger, maybe ten or eleven years old, my friend and I picked blackberries to sell to the white people," he said. "In order to make the sale you have to go to the back door. One day my friend forgot, and he went to the front door. The lady turned bright red and said, 'Nigger,[2] what you thinkin' coming to my front door, get your black ass to the back door where you belong.' He went around to the back and then she yelled at him, 'Hell no I'm not buying anything from you nigger,' and chased him away. We were just kids trying to make some money. They were so mean to us, for no reason at all."[3]

Black people had been arrested for failing to step off the sidewalk or lower their eyes for a white person or even for taking an open parking space if a white person arrived at the same time. That's why we shouldn't be surprised some folks were not ready to attempt to register until they had federal protection, but it was our job to try to convince them to trek to the courthouse anyway. Dan Harrell inspired us by telling again the story of a handful of residents from Gees Bend, led by Rev. Lonnie Brown and farmer Monroe Pettway, who had attempted to register in 1963 and succeeded in filling out the registration forms but were denied on the basis of the Alabama requirement that new voters be vouched for by an already registered voter from this county. As we knew from orientation, no whites would sign the supporting witness declaration, so all of their applications were denied. But, Dan explained, their case was pending in an appellate court and they were sure to win by next year. That's why we had to educate and register voters now, so that they would continue to pressure the registrar until the Voting Rights Act passed, which would finally ensure their right to vote.

During the winter and spring of 1965, things had heated up; there were student walkouts protesting lack of voting rights and employment opportunities for their parents, and student demands for their own decent textbooks and supplies. Hundreds of students had been tear gassed, some were beaten or shocked with cattle prods, some had been jailed in Selma and the state prison farm, Camp Camden. Student marchers assembled at the Academy and went straight to white-dominated downtown. Adult and youth marches began in front of Antioch Baptist Church. Marchers always had the same destination, the courthouse in the town square where they were being denied rights that had been guaranteed since 1870 by the Fifteenth Amendment to the US Constitution. Camden barely had six blocks of businesses and public buildings, but armed white men and local police defended them like a fortress against civil rights activities. The local authorities and racists who had joined them always had the same goal: to block the progress of the marchers by any means possible, including beating, tear gas, and arrest. When Dr. King came to support local actions, there was an even greater police presence, but also greater restraint since the national press traveled with the civil rights leader.

Wilcox activists worked in other counties as well. Dan Harrell and local leaders had taken dozens of students to Selma for the SCLC Children's March in January. More than one hundred students and adults traveled to Selma to participate in what turned into the Bloody Sunday march, and some walked in the already legendary Selma to Montgomery March. Despite being far from the media spotlight, having few civil rights field workers in residence for long, and no federal protections, Wilcox County leaders had already organized hundreds of potential voters.

As field workers, our main message to young and old alike was, "Some white folks believe that black folks' place is by our sides and as leaders of your own communities. We aren't here to start anything but to support what you already have going on." I was relieved that our leaders' messages here were the same as they had been at orientation in Atlanta.

Campaign of Fear and Intimidation

Law enforcement officials—the sheriff, the Camden police chief, Alabama state troopers, and as it turned out the FBI—kept a list of all of our names.

The notoriously cruel Wilcox County sheriff, P. C. "Lummie" Jenkins, and his posse, as well as the local white supremacist Klan, were well prepared for our arrival. The sheriff had distributed firearms to an experienced bunch of vitriolic racists and swore them in as his posse. He could count on the federal agents from Montgomery to do nothing if we filed complaints. Camden did not get federal injunctions like Selma did. Everyone living here and working in the movement risked his or her life daily and knew it. Although we had been given an overview of potential dangers at orientation, in this tiny rural town I began feeling that we had crossed over into another land; this could not be the United States of America. Klan members went to their jobs or worked their farms by day, terrorized movement folks by night, and went to church on Sundays. Local leaders told us that the Wilcox County Klan was headed by the Lane brothers, whose business, Lane Butane, was the chief source of cooking and heating fuel for most of the county. Seeing one of the big Lane Butane trucks anywhere near movement activities was a sure sign of trouble. Major explained that the Ku Klux Klan was no longer a joke in scary movies. We were to hide or run away the minute we saw one of their trucks. This was a challenge since all white men had gun racks that carried loaded guns. They stared at us with such hatred that everyone looked like a potential attacker. There were timber and cotton plantation owners who designated some of their men to represent them in the local KKK. Besides well-known families, many businessmen and small farmers joined the Klan or supported them by covering up their hateful activities. The Wilcox County Klan had the full support of Alabama state troopers and local police; they could harass, shoot at, and conduct illegal searches of movement activists. These men made little attempt to hide their activities or their hatred of civil rights workers, especially white ones. They figured that if they lashed out against us after we left, they could intimidate the black community back into submission, as they believed they had done in the past. The racists were furious because they were having much less success since the spring protests, and the arrival of reinforcements from SCLC and SNCC had emboldened the community. Bandy-legged, homely sheriff Lummie Jenkins actively endorsed and enforced efforts to keep segregation firmly in place, all the while shaking hands, patting black children's heads, and talking like a good old boy as he strutted around town.

Most local leaders welcomed our extra legs and voices in the slow process of individual recruitment of new voters in an area where homes were often miles apart. Tiny outlying communities organized at churches and local cooperatives, with leaders like the Smiths in Lower Peachtree, the Crawfords in Pine Apple, and the Brooks in Coy taking charge. We supported their efforts and brought the aura of Dr. King and the North, even if we did bring additional danger; the racists went wild over our integrated meetings and housing arrangements. Dan and Major worked tirelessly trying to get us to where we were needed to work and away from where we were most likely to be harassed. I wondered if Major felt removed from the action, having to babysit inexperienced civil rights workers in this backcountry far from the urban Baton Rouge and Shreveport movements. Or did the fact that he was a student when he was attacked himself make him more empathetic? In any case, he was as diligent as a parent and just as fierce if we messed up.

We worked under the assumption that federal registrars would arrive as soon as President Johnson signed the Voting Rights Act, whenever that was going to be. Until Washington, DC, sent registrars and examiners from outside the state of Alabama, obstructionist tactics were likely to continue to be used.

Wilcox County racists wanted to make sure that locals knew that no one, especially no outside civil rights workers, could offer protection from their swift retribution. Intimidation included firing people from their jobs, closing down schools and churches, and demeaning those standing in line to register, just for starters. If folks didn't "stay in their place," they lived with certain fear of arrest, unwitnessed beatings, shots in the dark ringing out near their homes, and in cases of severe resistance, homes burned to the ground.

Teachers and preachers, who clearly understood the need for a voting majority, were fiercely divided into those who risked their professional livelihoods in direct action and those who worked quietly in the background or did not come forward at all, believing they could achieve more by educating people to better themselves over time. It was Booker T. Washington confronts Malcolm X, sometimes all in the same family. Most preachers were also teachers, farmers, or millworkers. Some worked all three jobs since few pastors could support a family solely on contributions from tiny congregations, which had shrunk along with the county's population.

The county registrar of voters office was only open two days a month. Although there may have been a federal court ruling stating that they were required to register a minimum of one hundred new voters each day that they were open, there was no one to enforce it. People who wanted to register to vote had to take time off from work or away from their farms and then stand in line behind the red brick courthouse in the center of town where everyone could see them and know who to harass afterward. Many applications were still being denied on technicalities.

Consequently, we ended up recruiting mostly people who owned their own land, determined and fearless older folks, and those who did not work for others. As part of a legacy of humiliation, blacks were forced to go to a courthouse annex that had been the former jail rather than be allowed to go to the historic white-columned courthouse where whites could register without meeting literacy or other qualifications.

One of our target groups was supposed to be people who could become community leaders and run for office someday. We did get a good turnout of those folks at mass meetings, but most of them were waiting until the federal registrars arrived after the Voting Rights Bill passed. After the entire nation watched the beating, tear gassing, and arrests of peaceful protesters in Selma, I couldn't comprehend how it was possible for Congress and President Johnson to drag their feet all summer on this potentially life-saving legislation. Now that my own little life was at risk, I took this failure of our federal government quite personally.

Camden was the county seat and the only town recognizable to a northerner. It also had the highest concentration of white residents. Our efforts to organize and register voters in Camden's segregated all black areas—Wilson's Quarter and the company-owned Sawmill Quarter—were frustrated from the start and finally abandoned. Our group was arrested every time we tried to register in either quarter.

I was supposed to be in charge of registration in the Sawmill Quarter, but after getting run off by the sheriff's posse a few times, our leaders pulled me out of Camden and kept me in more rural areas. The white men didn't actually need to approach us. They would drive their trucks around the area where my local companions and I were canvassing. When we saw them coming, we would high tail it out of there as we had been instructed. We were not there to force confrontations.

The Sawmill Quarter was a company-owned area down in a hollow some folks called "the Bottom," across the railroad tracks off of Highway 28. Workers lived in peonage-like conditions despite laws that prohibited these practices. Families lived in former slave shacks and were paid in housing, accounts at the company store, and other "services" with virtually no cash salary. Men worked at hard, dangerous labor and had nothing to show for it at the end of the day—or even the end of the year—so that most of the women went out to work as maids for white families. Despite this oppression, or maybe because of it, many of the youth who lived there were active in the movement, at great risk to themselves and their families.

The shacks in the Sawmill Quarter were tiny, unpainted wood cabins with no window glass and sat right on the road where logging trucks passed daily, leaving piles of wood pulp by the side of the road; the dust coated everything inside the cabins, including the people themselves.

Although the poverty was the first thing that struck me about the Sawmill Quarter, what stayed in my mind just as strongly was how folks looked out for each other, the sense of community they had even with the disagreements that naturally arise when folks are beset with hardship. I admired the activists of Wilcox County even as I failed to respect the poor white folks of my farming community back home, or the poor white folks of Wilcox County for that matter. They were invisible to me at the time. I only had eyes for potential voters and my comrades in the struggle.

The day I was sent to Selma, when the local man refused to let me get in his car even though I was seriously ill, I realized why Major hadn't let us walk the short distance through Camden when we came to the Academy that first Sunday. Some of the most violent white reactions to the movement were triggered when the segregationists saw blacks and whites acting like equals. Major reminded us that Chaney, Goodman, and Schwerner, who were shot off the road and buried in a riverbank in Mississippi the previous summer, were targeted for traveling in an integrated car.

Bob Block told me to hold my head up high as we walked quickly down Depot Hill then out to the church by way of Water Street. As we walked, Bob told me how much he admired Dan Harrell. "Dan has a plan to get this new War on Poverty money from Washington, buy land, build a textile factory, some kind of a co-op that can sell produce, raise money to loan folks to build houses. Then they can build their own community center and become self-sufficient."

"Wow, that would be really something, but wouldn't they only need to do that if integration fails? Isn't everything people need to live well already here and just needs to be shared fairly?" I asked.

Bob shook his head as if he were reassessing my intelligence and changed the subject. He told me he was staying across the street from the church at the Nettles home for a few days. Bob didn't like being that close to the sheriff and his goons, as he called them. Sixteen-year-old Charles Nettles, who had been to orientation with us, lived right across the highway from Antioch Baptist Church with his father, Sylvester, who was the custodian at Camden Academy. The other Nettles children lived nearby with their mother, Mattie. Their parents may have been separated, but the whole family was active in the movement.

I didn't like Bob staying at the Nettles's with those two northern white girls, Judy and Sherry, but he let me know he didn't care much about them as he smiled and moved closer to me. The connection between us seemed to be blossoming.

Despite my excitement about this growing romance, it is not surprising that I caught pneumonia; I was run down after the cross-country trip, a week of day and night activities in Atlanta, and then the long drive to Camden. Little sleep, a strange diet of mostly starch and sugar, extreme heat and intense concentration as I tried to absorb every word that could make me more helpful to the movement had depleted the resources of this nineteen-year-old girl. It had been seventy-two hours since I'd had any real sleep and weeks since I had rested. Once we arrived in Wilcox County, stress-free hours were few and far between. The whole county felt like a ticking bomb that could blow up at any moment. Our job was to act and speak nonviolently, no matter what we encountered, which actually wasn't as hard as one might imagine because I totally believed in nonviolence. I wanted to be part of this historic fight for justice, but I really didn't want to die. Right now I was coughing so hard that I thought I just might, so I gave in to the wisdom of my elders and let Major drive me to see Dr. Maddox, a black doctor in Selma who treated white civil rights workers, breaking a state segregation law. At his small home office, I was diagnosed with pneumonia and ordered to Good Samaritan Hospital.

6

Selma and SNCC

Excerpt from a June 1965 letter to supporters:

I'm still in the hospital. My cough is dying down & my temp has returned to normal so I hope to get out of here soon.

Everyone in the hospital has been in to see me, from the janitor to the supervisor. When other patients have visitors, they always send them in to see me. And I tell them all the same thing. "I wouldn't be in here if you would register to vote. If you got people in office who would give you street lights & running water & decent jobs & new homes & edible food—I wouldn't be here."

Selma is a battle-scarred city & the residents are tired. The improvements after The March have only been token, although Negro bargaining power has been strengthened. Now they just have to use it.

One nurse said she'd love to go bowling at a new alley across town but she knows she'd get killed if she went alone. I suggested she get other nurses to go with her but she says—no, they're all afraid. And who can blame them? They saw their brothers lying bleeding in the streets while townsmen rode horses over them, just a month ago.

We are trying, without drawing attention to ourselves, to get local folks to have courage. It doesn't do The Movement any good for Negroes to come into my room & tell me they wish they had my courage. It only does good if they can see what I am trying to do with the very little courage I have & then summon a greater strength from within themselves.

During the first twelve hours of my illness I was delirious and remember little more than bright white light and gentle dark hands. When the penicillin kicked in and my fever went down, I woke to find myself in a bright, nearly empty room that seemed larger than it should be for one patient. It appeared that other beds had been removed. The sheets, the window blinds, the blanket, my hands lying on the covers—everything was white except the kind staff women who popped in frequently. I tried to remember how I ended up here, in a segregated Catholic hospital in Selma, Alabama, far from my life as a college student in Northern California. When I realized I was ill instead of injured, I felt restless and guilty. Major Johns came to check on me once. Other people came and went but I wasn't conscious until the second day, and I was released after less than seventy-two hours in the hospital. It was dangerous to keep white patients there but there was no white hospital that would admit civil rights workers of any color.

I was ashamed to be sick while others went to jail for working in my assigned area, the dreaded Sawmill Quarter. Major told me that one of our local youth had been beaten while canvassing there, so that there were two of us in the hospital from Wilcox County. The young man from Camden was released before I was strong enough to walk down the hall to visit him.

As soon as I could walk, a nurse took me to meet a white boy who had been hospitalized after a severe beating by state troopers. His head was beaten so badly he couldn't be moved. He had blond hair, blue eyes, and a wide bandage wrapped around his head. When I entered the men's ward in my cotton hospital robe, a cheer went up from the men. They assumed that any white person here had been injured in the movement. I visited a few minutes with the white man who smiled faintly as he told me his parents wouldn't come get him; they had disowned him for going to Selma without permission. I spoke with other youths who had been beaten until someone alerted the nurse that a supervisor was coming so she hustled me away. I smiled and waved, called out "Freedom Now!" and left feeling silly, but also liking the attention.

The day before I returned to Camden, my favorite nurse poked her head in to see if I was awake. She smiled and announced, "You got company." In loped a tall, thin, handsome dark man my age with a big smile and the high, squared-off haircut called a high top that was in style before full-on Afros. With him was a pale white woman with golden brown eyes, glossy brown hair, and a face like an angel. Charles "Chuck" Bonner and Janet Baker were a beautiful couple who had met during the Selma marches. Jan had been a novice at a Catholic convent. After leaving the nunnery, she became a student at the University of Illinois at Urbana-Champaign and came down South with other white students for the Selma march. Chuck was a Selma native, expelled by Selma University for leading a protest. Many school administrators were fearful of the retribution that would come from student protests, while others didn't think that marches were the appropriate way to achieve equality.

Chuck said that he had been active in the movement since tenth grade at Hudson High School, along with his close friend Cleophus Hobbs. They were trained in nonviolence by SNCC organizers Bernard Lafayette and Worth Long. "Cleophus and I were the first students Bernard trained to organize. Bernard is the man; he can organize! We've been walking out of class, demonstrating, marching, getting arrested for more than three years. I've been jailed dozens of times. I was kicked out of Selma U, and now they aren't going to let me back into any college down here."

"But isn't Selma University a black college?" I asked.

"That's just the thing, man—because of the SNCC training, I've always been active and tried to get students from other areas who came into Selma for college to get involved, but participating in voting rights action is foreign to most of them," he responded. "So I challenged the university policy about us not participating in the movement, even though we are the major black college in this whole area. At secret meetings, I told the students we have to take action; we have to be leaders in this. So forty of us organized a walk out during chapel.

"You should've been there that day, man, there was a lot of tension in the room; everyone knew something was up. When the minister got to the climax of his sermon we filed out of that big auditorium. You could hear our footsteps on that old wooden floor, echoing against the emptying wooden pews. After that, we sat in and integrated everything—libraries, theaters, restaurants—every place where they had never let us go before.

"When we got arrested, we heard word that our straight-haired, wire-rim-glasses wearing, light-as-a-paper-bag president of the college was going to expel all of us. The parents, including my mom, protested and the president let thirty-nine of us back into the school, all except for me. I was the leader that they wanted to get rid of."

At first, Chuck and Jan lived together with some other SNCC kids in the Selma Kids for Community Development (SKCD) house. Jan and Chuck organized this house not only for locals like Chuck, but also for white kids who had come down for the big march and wanted to stay and work with SNCC on voter registration. The SKCD (pronounced "skid") house is where Bob briefly stayed after the march. That's how Bob and Chuck met. Chuck explained that they had come to the hospital to see me not only because Bob wanted them to but also because Chuck was responsible for SNCC voter registration efforts in Wilcox. Chuck wanted to count me as one of his field workers.

Chuck was the first person who really explained to me the difference between SCLC and SNCC. Chuck said that when Ella Baker took on the role of adult advisor during the formation of SNCC, Dr. King and Rev. Ralph Abernathy hoped it would stay within SCLC, but Miss Baker encouraged the students to launch an entirely new youth organization.

"You see, Joyce,"—Chuck drawled out my (former) name so it cascaded into two syllables "Joy-ous" and sounded much prettier than I'd heard it before—"the thing is that SCLC is history, the past, and SNCC is now, the future. This nonviolence thing isn't going to work. Whites ain't never gonna do right unless they're forced to, at gunpoint if necessary. That's what Malcolm was talking about; that's why they killed him." I was ashamed to admit that I barely knew anything about Malcolm X, who had been killed a few months earlier—the papers said by one of his own followers. It didn't get much coverage in San Francisco, but I could tell it was important to Chuck so I listened up.

"This 'kumbaya' Dr. King stuff is all right for a transition, to get the black man off his feet and into some action, but we have to press forward. We don't have time for evolution; it's getting to be time for revolution." Chuck was saying "the black man," not "the Negro." I wondered if there would be any place in this revolution for whites. He mused, "I don't know. Malcolm didn't think so, but I see that some of y'all could be useful in some support way, like you are right now. Anyway, don't worry 'bout that now. Here's the book you need to read to help you understand where we're comin' from." He handed me a battered copy of Fanon's *Wretched of the Earth* with the Selma SNCC office address on Franklin Street written inside. When I told Chuck I had read Fanon before I came, he grinned, "How 'bout that. That's all right then."

At some point, Jan had moved in with a woman who lived in an almost middle-class black neighborhood, but she still did clerical work in the SNCC office. I admired Jan's boldness, and Chuck was immediately like a brother to me—warm, funny, and ready to take on my SNCC indoctrination. Although I had met SNCC members and joined Friends of SNCC in San Francisco, Chuck and Jan were my first real SNCC friends.

Chuck immediately began filling me in on the Selma scene, "Like I said, Bernard Lafayette got me into SNCC; you met him yet?"

Jan interjected, "And Colia Liddell, don't forget her; she's more than just his woman, you know."

"Anyway," Chuck continued, "Bernard is one brave guy. We're organizing students in Selma and running literacy classes, registration drives, helping get folks registered. Then the marches happen. Mrs. Amelia Boynton, they told you about her, right? She and Bernard (okay, and Colia) from SNCC organized this whole city. It was all organized before SCLC arrived. Then 'De Lawd' [Dr. King], he comes in and takes over like he's the head of the march. Over a thousand Snickers [nickname for SNCC members] come from Mississippi, Tennessee and all over to help with the Alabama protests but the Slickers [SCLC participants] shut them out. You know this is my hometown so I didn't get into it. I just want to work where the action is, where the work is getting done. Right now, that's mostly with SNCC but this SCOPE project could be a good thing if it turns out. We don't need it over here. We got this city completely organized, but man they can use just about every kind of help over to Wilcox. That is one *baaad* county over there."

Chuck said he'd be coming to Wilcox soon, along with his high school buddy Amos Snell and another SNCC worker Eric P. Jones. At this early point in my involvement with the movement, I thought that SCLC had the dynamic leaders but that SNCC was more egalitarian. SNCC, with its younger leaders, decentralized power structure, and outspoken anti-white-oppression stance, also seemed much hipper, an important factor to impressionable students like me.

Later that afternoon, Jan returned alone with a single white calla lily. When I reached for my water glass to use for a vase, she said, "No, it's for an ashtray" and flicked her cigarette into the beautiful flower's center. Jan was so white she was almost translucent. She had large brown eyes that reflected a mixture of sadness, anger, and defiance that I never really understood. After three months of living and working in Selma, she was ready to leave, except for her attachment to charming Chuck.

When he thought I was well enough, Major Johns came to the hospital to deliver a stern message from SCLC program director, Rev. Randolph T. Blackwell, "You are costin' us a lot. You were on the list from Atlanta of those students we need to keep an eye on, and here you are runnin' up another hospital bill. We could use this money a whole lot better elsewhere." In the short time I'd known him, I had come to respect Major not only as our leader but also as my temporary guardian. I hated making his job harder. Tears spilled over as I begged him, "Please tell Rev. Blackwell that I raised my own money to come and that I'll pay back anything that I can at the end of the summer if he'll just let me stay."

"That's all right. You're ours now, so just get well and get out of here, you hear?" He smiled but didn't touch me; none of the black men ever did except Dr. Maddox.

"Yes Major," I said eagerly. "I promise I won't cause a problem, ever again. Honest!"

Before I left the hospital, Chuck and Jan came to say good-bye. Chuck handed me a chain with a beautiful silver medallion of the SNCC logo, two clasped hands inside a circle. As I placed it around my thin neck I said, "I don't deserve this yet, but I'll wear it proudly." Chuck replied, "Don't worry, before the summer is over you will have earned it. Just coming here, you already belong to SNCC. I put your name on our list of workers in Wilcox."

Excerpt from a June 1965 letter to my family:
Dear Family,

I am sorry I haven't been able to get in touch sooner. I have only received *one* letter since I got here & that was from Mom. No other mail has reached me. Has anything else been sent yet? While I'm thinking of it—let me know if this letter appears to have been opened. I will tape it shut.

I was in Good Samaritan Hospital in Selma for a few days with a touch of pneumonia. Don't worry about it. I am fine now & they have me doing secretarial work indoors until I get my strength back.

They've jailed 7 people so far but all were treated well & released promptly. One boy has been beaten and that was by a white man. We got 150 people registered Monday so I think it's well worth our efforts.

There is a lot of tension among people here—trying to be brave when they are living in constant fear. I refuse to be afraid all the time. If I am, then the enemy wins. If I am not afraid—then I win the victory. After all, what can they do to me?

Thank God things aren't this bad in the rest of the South. This is a backwards county. There are no industries or big businesses or healthy farms. The irony of it is that the land is beautiful & fertile. If black & white would just work together, I know they could make Wilcox a rich county.

I think of you all & pray for you. When I was in the hospital, I kept dreaming I saw little Cindy walking in my room with a bouquet of flowers. She was so beautiful it made me cry.

We had stepped into an entrenched system of racial segregation and violent discrimination that was firmly protected by the government and the Klan. Tension between the races had increased dramatically in the months before we arrived. Although many credited the increased action to the appearance of Dr. King. and his confrontation with sheriff Lummie Jenkins when he asked him to vouch for the voters that day, the local students we worked with said it was they who continued to demonstrate day after day, they who continued to be chased and tear gassed, and they who called for support from Selma SNCC workers like Bob and Charles.

But fleeting moments of pride from successful demonstrations and a handful of effective voter registrations were tempered with the reality that as soon as voters registered, they and those who helped them were harassed, fired from jobs, and even shot at. The racists wanted to make it clear that every move made toward equal rights put all our lives in danger. My statement, "they were treated well and released promptly," was uninformed and part of early instructions that we should try to downplay reports of violence. When I was arrested myself, I got to witness this "good treatment." Wilcox County was far from alone in resistance and violence toward the inevitable change that we were fighting to bring about. Similar scenes played out in countless communities throughout the South that summer.

After Dan Harrell explained to me that I had misunderstood and that SCLC *did* want us to write our hometown papers about violence without using local names, I wrote home as many details as possible in hopes that my parents would forward my letters to the press, but they did not. They were conflicted, both proud and worried about my activities, so they didn't talk about me except at church. My sisters were not told much about what I was doing. I had been a primary caregiver for the two youngest girls until I went away to college. I missed them terribly and hoped my parents weren't being too hard on them. Now I realized that our modest country life was pure luxury compared to the lives of the folks I was living with this summer. My parents had only high school educations and lived within a few miles of where they were raised. My insecure mother could be loving one day and lash out irrationally the next, which upset the little ones in a way that affected them all their lives. My father could be alternately stern and distant or fun loving. He undermined my mother in front of us kids, mocking her family for being Oklahoma Dust Bowl refugees, "Oakies," even though the Brookovers actually came to California before that terrible drought. Neither of my parents nor any of my father's siblings continued their education, but on my mother's side, she was the only one of her five sisters who did not hold a college diploma. When I was young, education was not emphasized as important for girls. On the positive side, my parents had taught me to share what I had with others, to be creative with limited resources, and to appreciate the cycles of nature, components of my childhood that served me well in rural Wilcox, along with my childhood faith.

As soon I was released from the hospital, I went to the SCOPE office in Rev. Freeman's study at Antioch Baptist Church. I typed up reports of abuse of recently registered voters and my jailed coworkers. We were told to document all incidents for SCLC, so that they could file voter registration complaints with the US Attorney General. We also prepared complaints about violence to file with the US Marshals in Montgomery. Even if the officials did nothing in response, we were creating a record. Or so we thought. I could type a little, but I didn't come all this way to be a secretary. I wanted to register new voters.

During the few days I worked in the office at the church, I got my first glimpse of dissension among our leaders. There were whispered conversations and intense talks under the trees in back of the church. It seemed to me that the white "Revs" didn't respect our experienced black leaders as much as we students did. They spoke completely different languages. John Golden critiqued Dan Harrell's sermons, which I thought were brilliant. Dan and Major didn't always seem to agree between themselves, although we didn't hear as much as we did of John Golden's and John Williams's disagreements. The two seminarians wanted to work with white people in town but had different ideas on how to go about it. I knew from orientation that we were not supposed to engage with white people unless they were solid movement people, and there were no overt movement whites in Wilcox County. I couldn't wait to get back out in the field.

In the church office there was thin light from one frosted glass window. We tried without success to keep our things off of Rev. Freeman's desk. Like most ministers, Rev. Freeman served several churches besides his home church and had another job as well. I seldom saw him, and when I did, I confused him with the deacons who really ran the church. The church ladies were the most constant presence; they would pop in at all times of day to see how we were getting along and to make sure we weren't doing anything to cause unnecessary trouble. Maybe they were not happy to have white students bringing increased danger to their church. Most of the local adults seemed too preoccupied to introduce themselves to us, so I didn't learn their names. One of the church ladies always looked critically at Connie and me if the local young men chatted with us for long.

Working on an old Underwood typewriter to make copies on carbon paper was a tedious task even for a great typist, and my typing was marginal at best, slow and inaccurate. If you made a mistake, you had to start over—many reports from that summer were sent error-filled to Atlanta. If you wanted more than one copy, you had to use an ancient hand-cranked mimeograph machine that made poor copies even if you babied it. We used that machine to reproduce boycott and mass meeting flyers. It was tedious, thankless work that I left to others with relief once I stopped coughing.

At the end of a long day, a skinny white official from the attorney general's office in Montgomery pulled into the church parking lot to pick up the reports on the recent arrests that we had telephoned him about the day before. Connie handed him the neat stack of papers that had taken the two of us all day to type. He rifled through them without removing his sunglasses, snorted, then threw them in front of his left tire, slammed himself back into his official car and drove over our reports as he roared out of the dusty church parking lot. I avoided typing after that, and as soon as I was well enough, I begged to be sent back out into the field.

7

Out in the Field

As soon as I was well, Bob Block literally took me by the hand. He explained everything that Major and Dan had told us all over again because now I needed to understand how it really worked in the field. I immediately picked up on the movement terms. "Locals" meant black people and "local leaders" meant black activists, people working in the movement. So did "movement man" and "movement woman." "Folk" meant black residents in any community. "Cracker" and "honky" or simply "*them*" were the terms most commonly used for whites. "Negro" was the respectful term at that time, not "Colored," which was what the separate facility signs throughout the South read. Some students were starting to use "Afro-American" (not African American), but our leaders told us the older folks would be offended, they were Americans not hyphenated with another continent. "Black"—always capitalized—was beginning to be popular with the younger activists.

"Mass meeting" was a rally aimed at getting locals to take direct action: register to vote, attend voter literacy classes, demonstrate, or boycott. Mass meetings usually took place at churches but not during services. They always began and ended with prayer and song, and to my untrained ears, the speeches sounded like sermons, too. "Canvassing" was the work of going door to door visiting unregistered voters and providing them with the information they needed to become registered. This included arranging transportation, sometimes explaining the entire voting process, and a whole lot of persuasion about why someone should take a life-threatening risk for the simple right to mark a ballot that had never yet had a black candidate's name on it. "Reddish" was the local pronunciation of "register" and was commonly used in this sentence "I'm gonna reddish at the courthouse tomorrow or die tryin'." "Carry" was the verb used to describe driving someone someplace, as in "We carried five carloads in from Lower Peachtree yesterday."

"KKK" or "the Klan" meant the Ku Klux Klan, an active group of the secret society organized after the Civil War to reassert white supremacy through terrorism. Everyone knew or thought they knew who was Klan. Klan members felt so confident of their support by law enforcement that they didn't try very hard to be secretive, although they still wore hoods or pulled nylon stockings over their faces when they went out to burn crosses or fire bomb houses. "The Man" meant the bosses, plantation owners, and people with economic power over workers—white people who were part of the establishment.

The local kids we worked with became "our kids." "Field worker" and "freedom fighter"—that was us! Bob and Chuck wore the SNCC uniform: old blue jeans with a bandana in the pocket to wipe the constant sweat, a blue chambray work shirt with a pack of cigarettes in the pocket, and a white T-shirt underneath. As he blew smoke rings, which I thought was incredibly cool, Bob explained why he smoked Lucky Strikes. "I like short unfiltered ones and Camels are too harsh. See this red bull's eye here on the label? I put 'em in this pocket over my heart so when they shoot me, they'll take good aim and I'll die straight away, not be maimed." His gallows humor gave him confidence, but it gave me the creeps. I hated the way Bob and Chuck always talked about getting killed.

Bob usually wore a pair of old sandals that had nearly disintegrated before I arrived. His feet were dyed red or black from the rich soil of the unpaved roads he trod all day, even though he tried to rinse the soil off under his host's outdoor water pump. I had to wear a cotton dress or skirt and blouse, as did all women in the Camden movement. Pants were not yet acceptable outside one's own home. Even women working in the fields wore old cotton housedresses.

The way canvassing worked was once or twice a week Dan and Major would call a meeting late at night or over a sunrise breakfast of hot grits, usually made by me if we were at the Academy. Gripping cups of strong coffee, we'd hunch forward to listen to them tell us who was going where with what team. Then we were loaded into the cars and one of the adults drove us to places like Possum Bend, Boiling Springs, and Coy; these had become "our" communities. If possible, one of the white "Revs" drove white kids separately to reduce the chances that we would be chased off the road, since those incidents were increasing. If Chuck Bonner was in the county, he drove us in one of the SNCC powder blue Valiants that he said could outrun the KKK and had, many a time.

At our next staff meeting, hunched around the tiny table in the stuffy church office, Major boomed at us, "You are responsible for getting folks out to vote and for doin' like we say. If you mess up, you gonna land in jail and get folks hurt. You'll not only mess up the movement, you could get these here folks fired, moved off their place or killed. We're trusting you to act right, act smart like you oughta be—you're college students." It felt like a big responsibility. I wanted to do a good job like I had been trained: to listen to people respectfully but to use my whiteness and the words of King to give them courage, to get them to agree to meet our drivers at designated places on the next registration day.

Major Johns had his hands full with logistics and coordination, so any history lessons we got were on the fly. Once when I asked yet another "why" question in a staff meeting, Major waved his big hand at me and said, "You ain't studyin' history now girl, you're makin' it. Just go out, canvass the people, and tell 'em God is on our side." And so I did.

Once we were dropped off, we didn't have access to cars. At first they paired two SCOPE workers to canvass together with a local youth, but as soon as Dan and Major felt we could handle it, they sent us out in pairs of one white and one local worker so more residents could be reached.

Pine Apple and the Crawfords

The town of Camden didn't really have outskirts to speak of. There were long stretches with very few small homes and even fewer good-sized ones along miles and miles of nearly empty road, winding through the rolling hills and twisting along the Alabama River and its countless creek tributaries. Most of the way out Highway 10 was just sycamores, oaks, pines, grass, and some cotton fields.

For almost two months before I arrived, Bob had been working in opposite sides of southern Wilcox County where he established strong ties with two families: the Bob and Georgia Crawford family in Pine Apple and the Rev. Frank and Etta Pearl Smith family in Lower Peachtree. Both families loved him for his enthusiasm, warmth, and the genuine respect he always showed them. I was beginning to love Bob too, but I tried to push that thought into the back of my mind as much possible. We agreed that the work came first—at least that's what we told each other.

Out in the field we thought we knew where we were, but probably lots of times we were in some other community than what we called it when we reported back to Dan and Major. There were no signs, usually just a church or two—a Baptist and an African Methodist Episcopal (AME)[1] and maybe a small, unpainted, wood-framed store selling sodas, rice, and beans at inflated prices. We didn't have any maps, and post office names didn't always

7. Bob Crawford Sr., Wilcox County freedom fighter, 1960s. (Courtesy of Joy Crawford-Washington.)

match the names the locals called their communities. There must have been some big fancy homes in white sections of these areas, but we never walked through them, and the locals were good at pointing us away from where we might get shot at.

As we set out to canvass together, Bob explained more about how he came to the South. He'd been on a Route 66 road trip with his high school buddy Nat when they saw footage of Bloody Sunday and heard Dr. King's call to come South for the big Selma to Montgomery March. They left Chicago and drove in Nat's car straight to Selma to walk all the way to Montgomery, five days and nights in the rain. After the march Bob stayed around Selma with his new friend, Chuck Bonner, looking for some more civil rights action, but there didn't seem to be much for white kids to do there. "We heard about this student demonstration planned from Camden Academy and Chuck says 'do you want to go?' I came over and never left. Dan Harrell asked me 'Do you want to stick around?' so I did."

Bob fell in love with the beautiful rural region, and the "can do" attitude of local movement folks. After earning his stripes by getting tear gassed and cattle prodded in an early April Camden march, Bob stayed in Wilcox County. He'd been there when King came through and even met him, but he said he wasn't all that impressed. He admired the local leaders more than King and was especially close to the SCLC's Dan Harrell, who would stay in Wilcox the rest of his life. By June, Bob was Dan's right-hand man in grassroots organizing and training the summer volunteers. Bob's main turf was Lower Peachtree and Pine Apple, but he came to see me wherever I was, whenever he could.

Pine Apple was about twenty miles out of town in the southeast part of the county. I spent a few days there with Bob, but each evening I was taken back to the Academy to sleep. We often walked more than ten miles a day. Once in a while we rode on someone's mule, which was painful for short-legged me and only marginally faster than walking. A few folks had plow horses, but usually they were working the cotton or cornfields and not available for riding.

Bob Block was one of the most down-to-earth people you'd ever meet. Two months in Wilcox and he had already gone native. His Jewish heritage blessed him with a dark complexion that deepened over the summer. He was medium short, well muscled, and had a huge grin with deep dimples that captured my heart. He teased me by saying he was glad that he met me or he might have surrendered to some of the offers he was getting from local girls, which would have gotten him into a world of trouble.

When it came to canvassing, Bob was all business. Everyone said he was the hardest worker out there. He'd rise before dawn, put on his blue work shirt and jeans stiff with sweat and dirt from the previous day, chug down a couple of strong cups of coffee with some grits, and off he'd go, with me in tow. He taught me to make a quick connection with whoever answered the door, often a child. "Hey there. We came from California to help you have a better life. Is your mama home?" or "Dr. Martin Luther King sent us, you know him, right? Well, we're here to help you get your just rights, your right to vote."

Then, the secret was to let the child get the adult if there was one or to talk to the oldest child in the house; mostly we'd let them talk. Some young teens had their own stories of going to jail or being tear gassed during their protests. It helped that Bob could say, "Yessir, I was there; they got me right good with that old cattle prod, those crackers."

When we went out canvassing, Bob told me to act like we had all the time in the world while moving the conversation to action with something like, "We're having a mass meeting over to Mt. Olive Wednesday night. Can I put you down as standing up for freedom? Do you need a ride? We can pick you up down on the highway at six thirty if you need rides. How many? All right then."

Then we'd thank them and walk to the next home, many times a mile or more away. We were grateful when there were little clusters of homes, but that also meant that folks could see us coming and decide not to come to the door for fear of being seen talking to us. At the time, I didn't comprehend that folks might be with the movement but have very good reasons not to be seen talking with civil rights workers for fear of losing their jobs, being put off their rented land, or worse. I'm ashamed to admit that in private we called them "Uncle Tom and Aunt Jane."

One day we walked up to a cabin where a girl about ten years old was shaving an old man with a straight razor. "That's an accident waitin' to happen if I ever saw one," Bob whispered.

Since I had to wear glasses from the time I was a child, I reminded him that we almost never saw elders with glasses and said, "They don't get to an eye doctor so it's probably a good thing to have a young person who can see doing the shaving. They don't have electricity, so shaving in the sunlight is the best they can do." He hadn't thought of that. Most kids here didn't get their eyes checked; they just squinted and some did poorly in school for lack of eyeglasses.

Because I grew up rural working class, I was less surprised than some northerners at the poverty and poor health conditions we saw in the black communities, but the extremes still shocked me and hurt my heart. I wrote home asking friends to send medicine and antiseptics. They said they did, but most of those packages never reached me. When we were alone, Bob and I talked about how bad the conditions were and how if folks would just get out the vote and elect some of their own, it would all change. That's what we'd been taught and that's what we believed.

Whether it was because we were in college or because we were white, or a combination of both, we were popular with the local youth and could get them to convince their parents to come to mass meetings, to allow them to distribute flyers for the boycott, and to help watch the church office at night. Whites had always been seen as more powerful even if wrongheaded. Now here we were on their side. Many rural youth told us they had never before spoken with a white teenager as equals. They were thrilled and so were we.

Although I didn't sleep at their home, the Crawfords in the Newberry area of Pine Apple were wonderful hosts to any field workers who stopped by. If I was lucky, after a long day canvassing, my ride wouldn't come until after Mrs. Crawford served dinner. Mrs. Crawford was short like me, but she had a forceful yet loving presence that more than made up for her height. Her warm round face and flashing dark eyes assessed every situation, and there seemed to be nothing that she couldn't deal with, so unlike my often helpless mother. Mrs. Crawford wore her housedress and apron as if it were armor for the day's battle, whether to deal with unruly chickens or sometimes-clueless civil rights workers who visited her home. Everyone called her "Mom Crawford," and she treated us all with the same loving scrutiny. She had an ample stomach for her small legs and ankles, causing her to rock from side to side when she walked. She was always on a mission.

The Crawfords had an old farmhouse with four or five big rooms, a huge kitchen, two fireplaces, and a high-pitched tin roof. They said it had been a plantation home back in the days of enslavement. The kitchen was the center of it all, with Mrs. Crawford generating a whirlwind of cooking, washing, ironing, and dealing with fruits and vegetables all farmed on land Mr. Crawford had proudly purchased from a white widow after years of savings.

There was a huge peach tree in front and many more in the orchard to the side. They had a few cows and the first vegetable garden I saw to rival ours in California. The Crawfords, who were in their mid-fifties, worked hard and lived better than many folks, though they still lived poor by anyone's calculation. Mr. Crawford was powerfully strong from his hard labor job at a sawmill, where he was paid just thirty cents a day, but we suspected that he made his serious money from a weekend bootleg liquor business. When he was home, Mr. Crawford was king of the castle and was respected as such. I didn't see any moonshine, but Bob did. He explained that Mr. Crawford was gone most of the time he wasn't working, stayed over in Monroe County Saturday evening and always had extra money on Sunday. Bob liked the glamour of staying with someone who was defying "the Man," as we called white men in authority.

Mrs. Crawford ran the farm with help from her son, Bob Jr., who was in his late twenties. An only child, Bob Jr. had grown up doing both "boy" chores and "girl" chores, including milking, chopping wood, and heating irons for his mother's ironing business. Now, he visited on weekends to do as much as he could and to see his little girl, Debbie, who lived with her grandparents.

Mrs. Crawford was the glue in that household. She did backbreaking work from sunup to sundown. She cared for her young granddaughter, picked and put up peaches, sold eggs, and took in ironing that she smoothed with an iron heated on the same wood stove she cooked on. And cook she did! Greens with fatback, rice and beans, chicken, grits, of course, and incredibly delicious peach pie that I could not get enough of. She sewed most of her family's clothes, mended them all, pieced the household quilts, and still found time to go to church at Mt. Olive AME near their home, although they were on record as members of Bear Creek Baptist two miles away. While the distinction between AME and Baptist was clear in their minds, twenty miles was too far to travel on a Sunday, a day that could never be a complete day of rest for farm folk, even to attend their own denomination.

After dinner we'd sit and talk on their big, wide, open front porch that ran the width of the house. Mr. Crawford often took time to sit with us and philosophize. He usually held a smoking pipe below his moustache and waved it for emphasis when he pronounced his views, which were as profuse as they were profound. Mrs. Crawford's hands were always busy with shelling peas, shucking corn, or working on a quilt top in the early summer dusk. She smiled when I reached out to grab some corn to shuck or hold the fabric taut for her; it showed I had been raised right. "Um hum, mmm . . . some of those younguns come down here seem like they must have been raised with maids. They've got no sense, but you're all right, young lady, you all right." I glowed in her praise.

We ignored biting mosquitoes in the gathering dusk as Mr. Crawford tipped back his chair. "I agree with Dr. King; we all gots to work together, Black and white. This separate thing ain't working at all. Keeps everyone down. It can't be all one nor t'other, needs to be mixed up. Long as you is good people, it don't matter if you are Black or white. Just treat ever' body like they treat you, that's what I believe."

Bob Block said that later, after someone came to take me back to the Academy to sleep and Mrs. Crawford went in, the men would pass around a pint of moonshine. Before too long, Bob would wash up at the pump and then fall asleep in a small windowless back room where they put him for safety.

Lower Peachtree and the Smiths

Lower Peachtree was a tiny community about forty-five miles from Camden near Rosebud in the southwest corner of Wilcox County, just in from

8. Rev. and Mrs. Frank Smith family (left to right): Gwendolyn Geraldine Smith, Frank Smith Sr., Carolyn Jean Smith, Frank Milton Smith, Etta Pearl Smith, and Jesse James Smith, Wilcox County freedom fighters, Lower Peachtree, Alabama, 1950s. (Courtesy of Carolyn Smith Taylor.)

the Clarke County line. We asked folks what happened to Upper Peachtree. Someone told us a plantation owner changed the name to Clifton back in enslavement days, but I don't know if that was true. The little downtown had several blocks of large homes for white folks and the usual unpainted shanties on the edge of town and back into the woods for black folks. Rev. Frank M. Smith was the opposite of the expansive Mr. Bob Crawford. The tall, slim fifty-five-year-old teacher and minister scarcely spoke to us, although we knew that he encouraged his boys to be active in the movement. Whenever his two daughters came home from college for the weekend, they were all over Bob for stories of Hawaii, where he claimed to be from because he thought it was better than to say he was white and of Jewish heritage. He had spent some summers there with his grandmother so he was able to regale them with credible tales of surfing and volcanoes.

For Rev. Smith, like most black ministers, preaching was a calling, not a job. He pastored a run-down little church next to their home where organizing meetings and mass meetings were held. The wooden sign out front said "Pleasant View Baptist." Rev. Smith had graduated from Selma University and taught at Lower Peach Tree High School, a segregated, underfunded all-black public school. He also participated in civil rights training and organizing meetings in Selma and Birmingham. He and his wife, a lovely, tall light-skinned woman ten years younger than her husband, were solid movement folks, as was their teenage son, Jesse. Unbeknownst to us when we met the family, the Wilcox County School Board was already planning to fire Rev. Smith as punishment for his civil rights activities. He fought his wrongful termination for fifteen years and ultimately won a financial settlement. The school board may have controlled his primary livelihood but not his fiery spirit. On Sunday mornings, Rev. Smith would peer over his glasses, stroke the sparse moustache growing on either side of his thoughtful lips, and deliver sermons with a combination of intelligence and passion that got everyone on their feet.

The Smiths had a nice little white wooden house with electricity inside and pecan trees out in front. Mrs. Smith may have dressed and pressed her hair like the proper schoolteacher and preacher's wife that she was, but she always welcomed us warmly and her pecan pie ranked up there with Mrs. Crawford's. I loved six-year-old Larry who liked to play hide and seek among the trees. Skinny as he was, he could hide pretty well. Their son Frank was away at Morehouse College in Atlanta, and the attractive Smith daughters, twenty-one-year-old Carolyn and twenty-year-old Gwendolyn Geraldine "Geral," came home from Alabama State College every weekend to help out. Rev. Smith seemed very strict with his children. I had no idea the kind of pressure he was under, so I just kept my distance.

When we went out to canvass with Jesse Smith, who with the support of his parents was an active local leader at age sixteen, Bob explained that we should stand back and let Jesse take the lead. We didn't realize at the time how fortunate we were that he tolerated us with our outsider attitudes. Some folks wouldn't open the door when they saw Jesse because his family members were known leaders in the movement. Him coming up the path with white civil rights workers put a scare into many who depended on whites for their livelihood. I was disappointed that not everyone was ready to join the movement, and I didn't really understand the constant harassment they lived with.

I liked working out in the country with Bob. I especially liked that we were so well received and well fed at the Crawfords and Smiths. It also felt safer out there. Most local men had guns, and they weren't afraid to use them. That wasn't what Dr. King preached, but it didn't take very long to understand that there wasn't going to be any other protection than God and guns. I prayed that God alone would keep us safe.

Young Love

At a staff meeting in Camden, we heard that Rev. Blackwell was in a stew over reports from other SCOPE counties about the summer volunteers' loose morals. This was a Christian movement according to him, and we'd better behave ourselves like Christians, regardless of what our parents let us get away with at home. I didn't much like Bob staying with the Smiths' pretty college-aged daughters on weekends. I never met them but heard they were real attractive. He talked them up to make me jealous, although he gave me plenty of reassuring attention that I was still too insecure to fully appreciate. As soon as Major Johns could see Bob and me getting tight, he kept us apart as much as possible.

In high school, I had serious boyfriends; I went steady with one for a year and another for two years. But I had never gone "all the way." Bob told me he had "done it" once with a high school girlfriend after a beer blast, but that after a pregnancy scare he never had sex again. I thought he was experienced. I wasn't sure I was ready even though I was now on the pill.

Bob explained that he avoided forming attachments so that he could concentrate on the work. At the same time, he flirted with me constantly. Then he'd say that having a girlfriend would tie him down, take him away from the "pick up your toothbrush and be in Peachtree in the morning" lifestyle that was such a contrast from his life back home. Early on, I had believed his story about growing up poor in Hawaii. Thinking of my family's little box of a home in Penngrove, I had felt more at ease. Later, when I discovered that he was from the upper middle class, it made me nervous.

We both knew the danger of intimate relationships. One reason soldiers and civil rights workers were told not to fraternize with the opposite sex was that you should not put anyone, even yourself, before the good of the team. In a situation where arrest or death was a possibility, it was better not to be overly concerned about just one person. And, there was the fear that the whites would use their knowledge of a romantic relationship to torture us or, more realistically, to discredit the movement by providing evidence that we were a bunch of amoral, atheistic Communists.

One day Bob and I were standing on the Nettles's porch across from the church when a powerful feeling swept over us. Neither the fear of getting chewed out, his unbrushed teeth and sweaty armpits, nor a hard rain could stand in the way of that first, inevitable kiss. Bob stepped back, looked into my blue eyes with his golden ones and said quietly, "Damn!" That kiss threatened to pull him back to school, family, and his former life. At that moment,

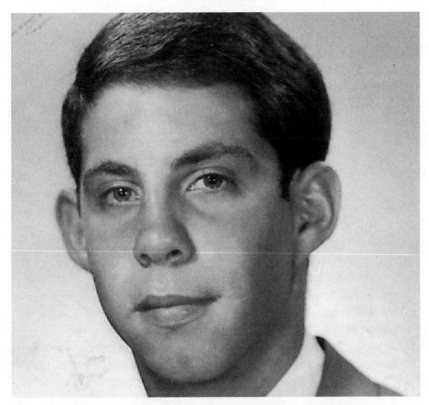

9. Luke (Bob) Block, California, 1964. (Courtesy of R. Luke Block.)

he both loved and hated me for all that our passion might do to his concentration on the freedom fight and his own personal freedom.

I stepped back amazed and excited by the power of the kiss and its promise. Then the old boards gave way and we both fell through. The kiss that tied us to each other began as a porch wrecker. Bob and Charles Nettles repaired it later that afternoon. As soon as Major caught wind of this turn of events, he said I didn't need any more training and hustled me off to the other end of the county to work.

Coy and Ethel Brooks

The first area where I was dropped off alone was Coy. It was scarcely fifteen miles from Camden to a four-way intersection without stop signs where dozens of narrow dirt drives rippled out in all directions for many winding miles. My only instruction from Major was to stay at the house where he dropped me until a local youth came to canvass with me. Our leaders often assigned the local kids far from their homes, so that they would not be recognized by whites who might come after their families.

That first day in Coy, I was completely lost, and not only geographically; I had to adjust to the weather and the way people spoke, both so different from Northern California. It was hot, in the nineties by mid-morning, and the temperature often soared into the humid hundreds before it would begin to rain midafternoon, then cool back to the eighties for a sticky night. I stayed with Mrs. Boykin, whose Alabama accent and expressions befuddled me as much as when my Irish-accented Spanish language teacher would return from her annual summer vacation in Mexico and refuse to speak English to our class. Short, heavy-set Mrs. Boykin may have had a little schooling, but her sentence structure and accent sounded like a foreign language to my ears. It didn't occur to me that I might sound equally unintelligible to her. Despite the fact that much of our communication consisted of "Hmms" and "umms" accompanied by smiles and gestures, we managed all right. With my ear for music, I picked up on rhythms and expressions quickly and by summer's end sounded like a black country girl myself.

Her faded whitewashed cabin had rickety steps that led to a long, wide front porch with loose boards, and then into a kitchen with two small rooms on either side. There was no indoor plumbing, no electricity, and only a wood stove for cooking and heat—standard for black homes in the area. There was a strong smell of kerosene used to light the lanterns and start the wood fire. Her home was much smaller and in worse repair than the Crawfords or Smiths. I don't recall who else lived in that house, but there were no men during the time I was there, although I always shared a bed with a child or young woman.

I was out canvassing from dawn until dusk for a couple of days before they moved me to another area, so I didn't get to know the Boykins. Sometimes Dan Harrell or a local leader would pick me up to go to one of the agricultural co-ops to talk with the workers during their lunch break and then again in the evening for mass meetings at Little Zion Church. I told the workers about food commodities and government loans. Dan had been telling them all along, but he said they paid more attention to someone from up North. I hardly knew what I was talking about, but people were attentive.

My first speech at a mass meeting was a surprise to everyone, including me. I had been faith coordinator for the Pilgrim Fellowship youth group in my rural Congregational church, and for one year I was statewide faith coordinator, so I'd given more sermons than one would expect from a teenager.

It was early in my stay out in Coy, on a Wednesday I believe. I was the only white person in the throng of a hundred or more congregants filled with the Spirit. Dan had already whipped the crowd up into a powerful frenzy of "Amens" and "Halleluiahs." I was awestruck as people shouted, swayed, sweated, and called out during his talk about freedom and the right to vote.

At the end of the meeting Dan suddenly asked me to say a few words. I tried to recall my training in Atlanta, but I gave up and spoke from my heart. "I want you to know that there are thousands of people, white people, who support your right to vote, your right to dignity and a fair opportunity in life. People in California, where I am from, are praying right now for the success of your struggle, our struggle. We believe that only when every person is treated with dignity can we all live in dignity. I am not here to tell you what to do and I know that the people of this community of Coy have already taken a lot of risks in the freedom fight. But if we get more folks registered it will bring pressure on the president to sign the voting rights bill this summer and there will be more protection for you. Thank you for the hospitality and kindness you have shown in welcoming us here. With all of us working together, we *shall* overcome!"

The folks very kindly gave me a rousing round of applause followed by singing the movement anthem, "We Shall Overcome." We formed a circle, our arms crossed one over another as our voices filled the humid sanctuary. I loved the feeling of connection as well as the attention I was getting, although I worried that I shouldn't. I second-guessed myself while plowing ahead, a habit stemming from constant criticism from my parents. Bob seemed so sure of himself, while I was always questioning whether or not I was doing things right, which was exhausting. I wrote most of my worries in my notebook and kept them out of my letters. Some of the other kids, both black and white, seemed to think this project was more fun than I did. It was fun sometimes, but our work seemed pretty serious to me.

My favorite local canvassing partner was sixteen-year-old Robert Powell because he was fearless and had a smile that charmed doors open. I'd stand back and he'd knock. Then he'd introduce me, or sometimes we'd both stand at the door. Robert had good ideas about what would work best with which residents. If they only saw me, sometimes the door wouldn't open or we'd be quickly asked to leave. Often women were working at home farming, doing laundry, ironing, and cooking. Sometimes we got lucky. A woman would open the door with a wide smile and look of near disbelief. "My, my, my, Lawd have mercy—look at this!" A painfully thin lady with her housework rag wrapped around her head waved me in, "You is the first one of them to ever to set foot in this house by invitation. We had the sheriff come out once and break everything up after my son was in the march but that were no invite. You are most welcome here, young lady, most welcome."

As soon as I began canvassing in my assigned areas—Pine Hill, Pebble Hill, Coy, Boiling Springs, Arlington, Catherine, and Alberta—locals told me why they had not yet registered. They repeated stories of lynching in the too-near past, recent beatings, and people being fired from scarce, decent-paying jobs at the okra-canning or box-making factory.

One afternoon, Robert wanted to stop for a soda at Pate's little shack of a country store up near Canton Bend off of Highway 28. We were not supposed to go into any place where whites might see us together, but I went in because I didn't want Robert to think I was afraid. There was a white man in the store. He threw one glance at me before he started for Robert, who took off running. I ran in the opposite direction. I wasn't quite sure how to get back to the church, but growing up in the country did me some good. I walked along the road until I saw trucks where the highway might be, and then proceeded along the shoulder until I spotted Major's old white Chevy cruising along as if he expected to find me there.

Robert and I were lucky that we both got away safely. In nearby Haney-ville, only a few weeks later on August 20, Jonathan Daniels, a white semi-narian, was walking out of a small store with SNCC workers and another white seminary student. Daniels was shot and killed by a racist incensed at seeing the integrated group of civil rights field workers who were buying sodas just after being released from jail.

In spite of the constant threat of violence, Coy became one of my favorite places to work because it was where Ethel Brooks lived. Ethel was only five years older than I was, but I looked up to her as one of the most active, progressive, and exciting adults. Ethel was an attractive, high-energy twenty-four-year-old with medium-dark brown skin, dimples, a huge grin, a wandering eye that gave her a sultry look, and thick unruly hair that she often let go natural, which was every which way. She was a single mom with a seven-year-old son that her mother, Julia, watched while she and her father, Jesse, did community organizing. She had already been in the Camden jail several times and kept in the backseat of her car a pair of old paisley pedal pushers that she called her jail pants.

I wasn't the only person attracted to Ethel's fiery brand of leadership. She had organized dozens of students who participated in the January Children's March and Youth Rally in Selma, where they were arrested, and then she had convinced dozens of high school students to join her on the infamous Bloody Sunday march in Selma. They were proud of their feisty community leader who was neither a preacher's wife nor teacher, but someone they could identify with as an older sister or aunt, a farmer's daughter with some college education and fire in her eyes. Ethel was a natural leader and very outspoken. She once said, "I don't think the mayor [Reg Albritton] has anything to say to Negroes except those that go into his office to get somebody out of jail."[2] That was typical no-nonsense Ethel. Well, I can't say she was completely no-nonsense. In fact she could be outrageous at times. One day as we drove back from her place in the bend area of Coy to Camden, a Lane Butane pickup truck started chasing us. Ethel tried to outrun them, driving faster and faster over the bumpy one lane road. At the crossroads where Harvey's Store was, she pulled onto the sidetrack in back and hid until the pickup passed us. "Narrow escape!" I congratulated her as I exhaled. Then, to my horror, she pulled out behind them and started tailgating them with her window rolled down, yelling and laughing wildly. Another worker and I were in the backseat screaming at her, "Ethel stop! Stop!" We were laughing, but at the same time we were scared half to death. Finally, she backed off. The white men glared back at her with faces that said, "Crazy lady. We'll get you next time," before they roared on. She wasn't always nonviolent, but her reckless courage made me feel braver.

It added fuel to my fire that Bob kept saying he was impressed with me, especially since the other white girls mostly worked at the church office or taught Head Start in Camden, while I was out canvassing. Based on results, my recruiting spiels were improving, too. More folks agreed to be picked up, to be taken to Antioch, and to walk up to register in a group. I expect that a whole lot of local workers had as much to do with the increase in numbers as we did, but Dan gave us credit in private while cautioning us to be humble in public.

Success wasn't always immediately evident. One hot humid afternoon I was teamed up with Robert Powell somewhere far outside of Camden. I knocked on a weathered door at the end of a long weed-filled path. An old, old lady cracked open the door and stood there staring at me with absolutely no expression. While we were coming up the path, I had noticed that her pump was broken. Robert introduced me as "from Atlanta," which in the most recent sense was true and was as far away a place as she might know. Anyway, that didn't cut any grease with her. She didn't know Atlanta; she didn't know the United States or even the State of Alabama. She didn't know of any jurisdiction larger than Wilcox County. Challenged as to why she should put on her Sunday hat and wait by the road for a local leader with an unreliable car to pick her up for a long dusty ride into Camden for what might be a futile attempt to register, I looked around desperately for some personal goal connected to her life. "That pump! That pump could be repaired and then you could get the whole area on water, on a county water line. If you vote, if you vote you'll at least get to tell them what you want, what you deserve." She looked at us pityingly, shook her head, and shut the door. But the next Monday registration day, when Robert and I passed her place on his father's red mule, the lady was sitting out by the mailbox on a wooden bench, with an ancient straw hat jammed on her head, her purse on her knees. She nodded in faint salute as we waved wildly and shouted "Freedom Now! Freedom Now!"

Boiling Springs and the Robinson and Lawson Families

There may have been a spring somewhere in Boiling Springs but I never saw one. This isolated area almost an hour northwest of Camden off of Highway 28 had no town center and scarcely had fifty families. Boiling Springs was where I ended up doing much of my fieldwork. Families here seemed desperately poor. Many worked as sharecroppers, scraping out a living on land that they would never hope to own. The only water came from backyard hand pumps supplied by seasonal wells. Plumbing consisted of a tin sink in the kitchen and an outhouse shared by many family members. Thick trees and brush made the community nearly invisible from the highway. Small cabins were strung out along miles of winding, narrow, rutted, red dirt roads closed in by huge sycamores leaning toward each other and draped with long gray Spanish moss. Paths through forests of pine trees led to small farms of some independent black landowners. It was easy to imagine a Klansman behind every tree, but when I could block those fears, it was a place of incomparable beauty. Some days, the intense red soil and deep green foliage drew me into a kind of reverie.

After the inevitable warm afternoon thundershower soaked my thin cotton dress and Keds, I told Robert that I was going to sit out on a fence rail in a sunny spot for a spell. The hot sun boiled the rain into mist and dried out my dress. Birds were singing, and for a moment, it felt like home. But Robert was impatient to get to the next house and understandably impatient with me. He reminded me of my cousins back home who seldom stopped to look in wonder at the fields and farms they worked so hard. He couldn't wait to get away from Wilcox and I couldn't blame him. There were no opportunities for young men here and only a handful of girls that he wasn't related to.

Robert explained, "Sometimes me and my buddy, L. V. Baldwin—he's away this summer working—sometimes we come up here to Boiling Springs Baptist 'cause L. V.'s daddy is pastor at the church. That way we can visit with the young ladies after service and not get their parents mad. They are very protective of their girls up here. Don't want them running with any fast Camden boys." He flashed his trademark smile. I could easily imagine that the girls would be interested in handsome, smart, and ambitious Robert Powell.

Boiling Springs Baptist was a simple white clapboard building with a steep roof and small steeple, built in the late 1800s. Rev. L. V. Baldwin, an eloquent dynamic preacher in the rural black church tradition, was one of many pastors in the county who "worked the circuit," as they called it, going from place to place as well as working at the sawmill. Rev. Baldwin "whooped" (sang) his sermons, as did most southern black preachers from the time of enslavement to the present. The congregants would shout out, "Tell it!" and "Amen," rising to a fevered pitch. These same phrases were called out during our mass meetings, provided we inspired the crowd. When that happened, I imagined that I was in heaven, a place where people who had been denied were free to take the reins of leadership from the hands of the evil racists.

The Robinsons were my favorite family to stay with in Boiling Springs, not because they had a comfortable home—far from it. They had but three rooms and no front porch, but they were solid movement folks. Besides the now familiar scent of kerosene used in the lanterns, at the Robinsons there was also a strong odor of turpentine that came up from the ancient pine floorboards when they were scrubbed, which was often. The cabin was so weathered, it might have been built during slave times, but Mrs. Robinson kept it spotless. Mrs. Robinson always greeted me with a big hug and then scrutinized me to make sure that my clothes were as clean as those of her well-scrubbed children. She was tall, light, with high cheekbones, a muscular body, and a steady gaze that made it clear that I should not bring shame or unnecessary danger to her family. One morning I found her scrubbing out my filthy clothes in a galvanized steel tub filled with water she had to haul from the pump outside and then heat over her wood-burning stove. I felt it was wrong to let her take care of me, but I loved her for it. She did all her work with complete dignity, not the servility that I thought I saw in some others. I tried to help clean up after breakfast but she shooed me away from anything further. "You get those lazy folks out to vote; that's your job. My gal can help with all this. She's going to have a better life after we get the vote. You go on now, don't worry about us." But I think she worried about me. Sometimes she'd stand out front with a look of concerned concentration until she saw me meet my ride or companion for the day's trek on the highway that ran in front of the house.

Some neighbors, the Lawsons, shared the burden of hosting me by preparing the evening meal. There were a flock of kids who led me back and forth across the field and into the woods between the Robinson and Lawson houses. We'd walk half a mile over to the Lawsons for dinner most evenings, through the dark woods where screech owls sometimes made me jump. As we came back through the tall damp grass swinging a kerosene lamp in the darkness, chiggers bit ferociously. Soon my bare legs were swollen and scarred with bloody scabs.

Both families set out generous platters of high carbohydrate, high fat foods. Grits served with Aunt Jemima maple syrup were the usual breakfast food; the black mammy on the Aunt Jemima label always made me cringe. The Robinsons didn't have chickens or cows so I didn't eat eggs or drink milk there. No one served green salads like the ones we ate every evening in California. Dinner and supper, what we called lunch and dinner at home, might be cornbread, beans, and greens with fatback. The only meat was the fatback in greens. I ate what was put before me. Even though I often had only two meals a day, the high-fat diet started to show up on my belly and thighs. Despite all the walking, my thin cotton dresses felt tight.

There were a lot of us sleeping in the Robinsons' small house. I slept in a big old saggy bed with a tall, serious teenage girl who appeared much older than her thirteen years—Mae was her name as I recall—and with three or four little children tucked in at the end of the bed. I learned early on not to ask details about why children in the same family looked so different from each other and why some had different last names. At that time, many women did not have choices of sexual partners or access to birth control. Many years later I learned that the Robinsons actually had twelve children and that the babies were all theirs. I didn't consider that possibility at the time.

Being in the country and not having much in the way of material goods felt familiar, but in truth, it was another world. I had grown up thinking my family was poor because we had to share rooms and wear hand-me-downs, grow our own food, and only took vacations to camp in the woods. But here was a level of poverty that defied anything I'd ever seen. Most people worked as hard as they could, but the system was set against them ever acquiring anything. Many sharecroppers lived in multigenerational debt. Most worked hard, but some men had given up. They sat on stoops of country stores nursing a soda with some moonshine in it or just stayed at home and drank themselves quietly to death while the women and children pieced together a living.

During the school year many undernourished children walked miles to unheated one-room schools where dedicated teachers tried to uplift their minds and spirits using torn, marked-up, outdated textbooks sent to their segregated schools by the all-white county school board. Teachers had no support from the board of education in fighting against the inevitable drop in attendance when young boys and girls were pulled out to work on seasonal crops; corn and cotton had to be brought in so that their families could survive another winter. Black schools were heated with wood donated by parents. The boys had to pile and carry the wood to the potbelly stoves the teachers tried to keep stoked in the cold Alabama winters. Separate and totally unequal was the rule. The Presbyterian mission schools, especially Camden Academy, fared a little better because of donations from well-meaning northern whites.

In the summer, most children had heavy chores at home, including caring for younger siblings, and far too many were still working the fields despite periodic gestures by state officials to enforce child labor laws. I had to do hard work as a child too, so I didn't think much about this aspect of poverty. I was too young to fully understand how racism ground folks down, and I was too optimistic to imagine that whites would continue to hold economic power and control access to government aid for years to come.

I naively believed that these poor communities would be magically transformed into a series of rural paradises just as soon as black folks had the opportunity to vote. That naive belief got me out of bed in the morning and comforted me as I tried to get situated in the crowded bed at night. Sleep came only from exhaustion; relaxation eluded me. I'd lay in bed staring at the stars through a small hole in the tin roof, grateful that it wasn't raining right then, and wonder: If God could do anything, why would He put these particular folks through such a hard time? I tried to pray for President Johnson to sign the Voting Rights Act, but mostly I couldn't help but be mad at him and Congress for making our job so much harder by dragging their feet all summer. It may have been summertime, but the livin' wasn't easy in Boiling Springs. I lay in bed breathing kerosene and smoke as the wood fire burned down to coals. These were the smells of Alabama poverty to me and the smells of home to my hosts.

Back in Camden, things were getting tense, not only between law enforcement and our project leaders, but also among our leaders, who were engaged in internal disputes. Despite feeling somewhat safer out in the county, I wanted to go into town for a strategy session to see if I could calm things down, to take a real bath, and more than anything, to see Bob.

As soon as Major dropped me at the Academy I took a shower. Indoor plumbing—what a luxury! After my shower, I headed down to the church. By now, I defiantly walked through Camden collecting children who came running to tell me their latest news whether of a new baby sister, someone's brother beaten, or their parents saying trouble was brewing. White people pointedly stared with hatred and sometimes swore at me. I picked up one of the smallest girls and carried her in my arms, feeling her little heart beating and smelling her sweet breath. She reminded me of my little sister Cindy, thousands of miles away. Suddenly a white woman in a Buick swerved and nearly drove onto the sidewalk on Claiborne Street. In her world, black women were supposed to carry white children. Well, I thought, her world is just about to be turned upside down.

8

Things Heat Up

Bob stopped by the Academy to warn me that "the shit is just about to hit the fan." The county voting registrar was still blocking new applicants by being closed for long lunches, asking for documentation not required by federal law, and generally making it difficult to register. During the first week of our project, two local kids were beaten while watching the church office, and five locals and SCOPE workers were arrested and spent a night in jail. Despite these challenges, more than 150 new voters successfully completed the registration process in June alone.

Local leaders of the NAACP and Wilcox County Progressive League met with Rev. Threadgill, Dan, and Major to call for a boycott of stores that refused to hire blacks. Since the county was 78 percent "Negro" and 99 percent of all businesses were white owned, this meant a boycott of nearly *all* business. If we were successful in getting the entire community to participate, it could have a big economic impact. High school kids worked with us to make signs and mimeograph flyers at our church office. We began walking in teams of two or three through the Quarters, knocking on doors and telling everyone not to shop downtown.

The students wanted to expand the boycott with a march to the courthouse. Their spring protest marches had galvanized the community, and they thought this was a good time to attract more attention while white students were here. A couple of northern reporters were hanging around looking for a story, and we hoped they would feature Camden; after all, Selma had captured the national news for months. The press had little interest in the grinding work of voter registration, but they loved confrontations. Some local adults were in favor of a demonstration, but Dan Harrell had orders from Hosea Williams, SCOPE project director, to stay focused on voter education and registration. We would only be allowed to march if conditions were right. Seminarian John Williams argued that we shouldn't demonstrate because he still believed the white folks were going to come around to reason. He accused us of being hotheaded and stirring up the local youth, when in fact it was the experienced young students who argued for marches. Some local adult leaders agreed that it wasn't the right time; it was too dangerous. The racists were beating and arresting people already; it could turn deadly if we provoked them further, and what would it gain? Nothing was going to change until the black majority controlled the politics and policies of the county.

Bob and I sided with the youth, as did Chuck. We held passionate discussions at staff meetings but were overruled. I wanted to be in a march; that's what everyone back home knew about—marches and tear gas—but the no-demonstration contingent won out. There were plenty of hard feelings over that decision, feelings that lasted the rest of the summer and even caused a few workers to leave for counties where they thought they might see more action.

Eric Jones went back to Selma saying they never should have let "honky kids" come down here. "Now it's all about protecting you all. They never gave a shit about our kids, our Afro-American kids." That was the first time I heard someone use that designation, instead of "Negro" or "black." Afro-American sounded powerful and exotic. When I got a chance, I asked Ethel about the term. She said, "That's cool for when you're in Selma, but don't be calling my daddy or mama Afro-anything. They just want to be called Human Being, that's all."

Later that night when we were alone together, Bob told me about an incident out in Pine Apple earlier in the week. "Chuck and Eric took me out to this little nightclub—though you know this county is dry—so it's kind of an illegal place deep in the woods past Crawfords, way out there. I couldn't find it again if my life depended on it. Anyway, we go into this so-called nightclub, the Dew Drop Inn, that's what they called it, just a hole in the wall, really. So we go in and Chuck and Eric get some white lightnin' and I get a beer. After a while two white guys come in and I'm thinkin', 'that's nice, maybe they want to integrate the place'; it was all black except for me. Then all of a sudden Chuck and Eric grab me and say, 'Let's go. Now!' and drag me outta there. Eric yells, 'Those crackers gone for tire irons!' They throw me in the backseat and tear off for Crawfords' place. They tell Mr. Crawford what's goin' on and out come the guns."

"You mean you had a gun?" I asked, incredulous. "We're not about that, Bob." I was shocked.

"Nah, I didn't have one," he replied, "but Mr. Crawford, Chuck, and Eric did. They were each at a window in front of the house. After a while, nothin' happened so I went in the back bedroom and went to sleep."

I didn't think this was funny, but Bob got a real kick out of it. Boys liked danger it seemed. I didn't, but I liked being with him, and when I was with him I went to mush inside. I realized how scared I'd been when I was out in the field and how scared I was still, knowing that the men who harassed us at the church and the men out in Pine Apple who chased Bob would just as soon see all of us dead. Still, it was good to hear that Eric and Chuck had looked out for my sweetheart.

That night, Bob didn't go back to the Crawfords. We talked until we fell asleep in my upstairs room at the Academy. Early in the morning, Charles and Grady Nettles came racing up the stairs and burst into my room to tell Bob that the sheriff's posse broke in and messed up the church again. Our office had been vandalized several times so our leaders thought it best to have someone protect our typewriter and files, and the church itself. The office was where we kept lists of assignments, records of attempts and denials of voter registration and of violent incidents—KKK and police violence— documents we didn't want to fall into the wrong hands. After we began actively supporting the boycott, teams of youth began to spend the night inside the church.

The boycott was an additional hardship on everyone as Sam Ballard's store on Claiborne Street was the only black-owned grocery store in Camden, and it only carried minimal supplies. Folks in the Sawmill Quarter risked harsh treatment at work if they didn't continue to shop at the company "comminsery," as they called it, and most didn't have cars so they had to buy their groceries close to home. But families teamed up; some folks went to Selma to get basics and carried them back to families honoring the boycott, while others relied on stored-up staples and their garden, if they had one. Ladies at the church organized and distributed food donations.

We had been eating sometimes at the one and only "Negro café" as everyone called it, which was one reason I was quickly running out of the money I'd raised. As soon as we joined the boycott, the sheriff told the café owners, Mr. and Mrs. Reynolds, that if they served civil rights workers, he'd shut him down, so Mr. Reynolds told us not to come there anymore. As we stood there looking into the café owner's bloodshot eyes, I guessed that he had done some serious thinking about the consequences, but at the time, I thought he was wrong. I figured, every time someone gives in the racists win. There were three times as many black people as whites; why didn't everyone stand up and stop taking this abuse?[1] Where were all those white liberals the Revs said are lurking around here; where were they now? We were disappointed that some black folks kept shopping, kept on with their lives like always.

With this turn of events, we SCOPE workers had no place to eat when we were in Camden. My mother had stretched a single chicken to serve a family of five, then six, so I knew how to cook on a budget. Now that I was on my own, I focused on having enough food and on sharing it. I counted my remaining traveler's checks and asked some local girls to help me make a run to Ballard's, where I bought stew meat, a big bag of potatoes, a few limp carrots, some moldy onions, bread, peanut butter, and eggs. The young girls helped me put it all in the big old refrigerator in the basement kitchen at the Academy dormitory. We even refrigerated the bread because cockroaches were everywhere due to the dampness, despite my swabbing the floor with diluted Lysol. Cooking and eating together calmed the adults and connected us with the youth. The Academy was their school, so the students felt at home there and would often show up at mealtime to eat, hang out, and talk about the day's adventures.

Bob ate well at the Crawfords and Smiths, while I seldom stayed with families as comfortable as theirs. No one I stayed with had extra food or room. In every home an adult or older child was displaced, usually going to stay with another relative, and I was still sharing a bed. I felt bad about that. We were supposed to be making life easier, not harder for folks. I had raised the $200 that we were told to bring to cover our food, transportation to the orientation, and travel home, as well as any personal needs for the summer. It appeared that I was one of the few who took the requirement seriously or was prepared to share what I'd raised. Decades later, I learned that SCOPE host families were supposed to receive a stipend for housing and feeding us, but due to budget shortfalls they were never paid.

On the few nights when there wasn't a mass meeting or church service, I'd corral some kids to help fry up a bunch of chicken, mash some potatoes, or make a big pot of beef stew. We sat around an old wooden table in the dark, dank, concrete dormitory basement. The kitchen had slits of windows running around the top of the wall where you could see headlights after dark at times when there should not have been any. Members of the posse had started driving around the Academy grounds during the day, and at night would park their cars with headlights shining in to the front of the building. We'd go into the back rooms, sing and pray, leaving someone in front as a lookout in case they decided this was their night to storm the place. This harassment made me nervous, but I talked bravely in front of the local kids because most of them went to school here. In the fall, boarding students would come back to sleep in this dormitory. We wanted the campus to feel safe for them, and for ourselves. Despite long, tiring days, I wrote my supporters and my family regularly for their emotional and financial support. My parents wrote criticizing my fund-raising letters after someone in their church mentioned receiving one.

From a June 1965 letter to my family:

Please send vitamin pills. We are having a boycott on *all* white stores that won't hire Negroes & there isn't a drugstore between here and Montgomery that will serve us.

You don't seem to realize how primitive things are here. It is like another country. I hate to keep asking but there is no place to get things. Also—I do not have enough money to continue living here or to get back home. I don't feel badly about accepting gifts & I wish you wouldn't assume responsibility of refusing them for me. I'm trying to get money for a scholarship fund for civil rights workers, too. If you are embarrassed to have people involved in my financial affairs, please have them write directly to me & then you needn't be concerned about it. It's difficult to tell you the truth about things around here without scaring you unnecessarily. The whites are really trying to scare us off & they are doing everything they can to keep us from registering voters. But, they aren't going to kill us. If we refuse to be scared then they will just have to give in.

Please don't be alarmed at how or what I write. Things are so different here & I'm just trying to tell you.

My least favorite part of our work was staff meetings, except when Chuck was there to add political theory to our discussions of food, shelter, and the increasing violence all around us. Meetings became increasingly tense. Bob and I sided with the locals who wanted more direct action. I don't recall what the other white SCOPE students—Mike, Bill, Connie, and Ann—had to say on the subject. Major and Dan seemed to have some tension between them, as did the white seminarians. During one meeting, Chuck Bonner introduced us to the concept of "criticism-self-criticism" where you could call out others' erroneous, racist thoughts and actions as well as your own, things that could harm collective action. I recall some stinging remarks, but most of them were not aimed at me. I actually enjoyed learning from my new friend, Chuck, who was clearly more sophisticated than I was.

The SNCC workers discussed ideology while we were driving, walking, or talking late at night. I began to understand that democracy didn't necessarily eliminate racism. Before I arrived, Chuck had loaned Bob the same copy of *The Wretched of the Earth* by Fanon that he'd offered me. Bob was still in a stir about it. Fanon's explanation of the Algerian struggle to overthrow French colonialism was a major philosophical guide among progressive civil rights workers. I agreed with the need to eventually get rid of the very concept of "black" and "white" but worried about the idea of throwing off all vestiges of the dominant culture. I liked classical music and running water. For sure I liked being part of the "Beloved Community" and wasn't at all sure about the complete revolution that Eric talked about. Bob and I agreed that this was just the beginning. Who knew where it could lead? As white people, maybe we were going to be excluded, and maybe that was necessary. But right now, we were in the thick of it and we loved it. The people we cared most about—Dan, Major, Chuck, and the local kids—all wanted us there. They didn't seem oppressed, at least not by our little white selves. We were young, and being accepted and feeling like we mattered meant everything to us. This summer was a dream come true for a feeling of belonging, and at the same time it was a nightmare for personal safety. I took comfort in Bob's strong body and his reassurances that we were in the right place at the right time in our lives and at the right time in history. We agreed that there was nowhere we'd rather be; we belonged here as long as they wanted us, and we definitely wanted to stay together.

As our relationship deepened, Bob confessed that his family had always had money. Although his parents were divorced, they both remarried prosperous professionals. He was of Jewish heritage, but his family attended an Episcopal church. His Hawaiian experience was limited to the summer he sailed to Hawaii on the luxury liner the *Luraline* with his grandmother during his parents' divorce. Bob didn't want to be "the Oppressor." He thought maybe he'd stay down here in the struggle and make up for whatever damage his family had done by having more than they deserved.

At first we talked about delaying sex until marriage because that's what I believed in and also because we were afraid, even though I was on birth control pills. Our experienced adult leaders were in a stew over our hot young love, so they tried to keep us apart working in opposite ends of the county. But whenever we were in Camden at the same time, we shared my single bed hugging and kissing, fully clothed in that sultry heat. Every time we rolled over and the springs squeaked, John Williams in the front room below would exclaim, "My God! I can't take it!" We defended ourselves by saying we weren't doing anything, which at the time was true.

Bob made every effort not to let our passion affect his work, or mine. While running off boycott handbills at the church one afternoon, I noticed that Ethel was wearing her paisley jail pants. I asked her what was up. She reminded me that she had a nose for trouble and predicted that we'd all be arrested soon. I laughed.

The next morning I walked Wilson's Quarter with kids handing out boycott flyers, and I talked about the boycott with people who couldn't read. When we ran out of the handbills, I walked back to the church to find the sheriff's posse and Camden police swarming all over the place. Before they saw me, I crossed over the highway to Mr. Nettles's house to see if Bob was there and to ask him what I should do. At first, Bob wasn't there. All of a sudden he came running up in his mud-caked sandals. He breathlessly told me that he had to get to Selma because his sister's class from California was on a field trip to see where the marches had been. I couldn't believe it when my new boyfriend handed me his pack of cigarettes and said, "I gotta get to Selma and you gots to go to jail. That is the only place you'll be safe. It has to be done; it's your time." He pecked me on the cheek and headed into the bushes by the creek.

"How'll you get there? When are you coming back?" I didn't understand why I would be safer in jail and called after him. But he was gone.

When I crossed back over the highway to the church, some of the little kids ran up to me and asked what was happening. I told them they should go home and tell their parents that we were going to jail for freedom, for their future. After I waved good-bye to the children, watching one of my favorites with her little plaits flying as she ran down into the hollow, I climbed into the back of a police car where I had to sit on someone's lap.

Softly I began singing "Ain't Gonna Let Nobody Turn Me 'Round." The other arrested workers started to join in. The officer who was driving turned around and yelled, "Shut the fuck up!" We did. This was nothing like my imagination of being brave and calm, nothing like the photos of marchers lined up with dignity outside the Birmingham, Montgomery, and Selma jails. We were fifty miles from the nearest US Marshals office, and based on the destruction of our reports earlier, we knew we couldn't count on them for help. Our leaders told us that in the past, the federal officers either wouldn't come to Camden or stood by while protesters were brutalized. We were on our own. I began to panic. Another police car with Ethel in the backseat pulled ahead of us. She flashed me her trademark grin as she gestured toward her paisley pants and mouthed, "I told you so." I felt more confident, for about a minute.

9

The Terror Continues

During the short drive to jail, I tried not to think of the constant threat of being taken deep into the piney woods and raped by God-knows-how-many crazed racists. I thought about what Bob said—that it was safer in jail—and hoped that he was right. I desperately wanted to follow what we'd been instructed to do, which was "cooperate, not capitulate." So I shoved those dark thoughts back in my mind and visualized a day when these policemen would be black because we had gotten the locals out to vote. A few days after we got out of jail, I wrote this letter for my roommate in San Francisco to type and mail to my friends and family list.

From a June 1965 letter to supporters:
Dear Family and Friends,
On Monday, June 28, 1965 at 11:00 A.M., I was at the residence of Charles Nettles. I looked out the window and saw a Lane Butane truck [KKK] parked by Antioch Baptist Church. There was a white man by the truck holding a large stick in his hand. There were a large number of Negro children in front of the church, so I ran across the road to see what was happening. Some of the little girls threw their arms around me and I hugged them and told them to go on home.

Then I went on into the church. Most of the SCOPE staff was sitting in the front pews. Mayor Albritton was there with several policemen and posse men with guns. I sat down with the others and they asked me my name, age and whether or not I was a paid staff member. I replied no to the last question.

Then they asked us to get in the police cars. Eighteen arrests were made at this time. When we arrived [at the jail] they asked us to line up. The boys were asked, one by one, to put their hands against the wall while a policeman frisked them for concealed weapons.

While we were standing in line in the dirty, dark, humid Camden jail hallway waiting to be booked, I watched in horror as they slammed eighteen-year-old Don Green into a metal wall after they searched him and pulled out a small pocketknife from his orange sock. Don was booked on a concealed weapons charge while the rest of us were terrified into silence. When they frisked me, taking extra time through the breast and pelvic area, I left my body and felt my mind float above me on the ceiling. I dissociated so thoroughly that I didn't come back to myself until we were all crowded into one holding cell.

For a short time we all stayed in the one cell. There were five white girls (me, Connie Turner, Ann Nesbitt, Judy, and Sherry), one white man (Mike Farley), and fourteen black men.[1] I didn't see the black women, including Ethel. After a while they asked all the "colored" men to step out. They put them in a large cell across the hall from us. Then they took Mike Farley, the one white man, into a cell one away from us girls, on the same side.

I remember being afraid for the black women and girls who had been driven over to the jail, but it turned out that they were released without booking. Some worked in white homes and their employers wanted them at work and away from the bad influence of "outside agitators." When I called out for Ethel that first afternoon, she didn't answer. She was my big sister, the one who always had an answer for every situation, but she wasn't here with us now. They didn't arrest any of our leaders; they wanted us to feel scared and alone.

Although I was only in jail overnight, I didn't have any idea how long I would actually be in or what was going to happen next, so my mind ran wild. Fear of rape by cattle prod gripped my body. The constant noise of slamming cell doors and filthy conditions inside the jail kept us on high alert. Black trustees and white guards leered at us and tried to grab us if we got too close to the bars. We were deprived of privacy and a functioning toilet. My renewed attempts at singing freedom songs were quickly stopped when our jailers told us they would beat the boys if we girls continued to sing. I borrowed someone's lipstick and wrote "Freedom Now" and "One Man, One Vote" on the wall of the cell, but that didn't feel like anything except a message to the next prisoners.

The white guard hung around outside the bars making lewd comments, such as, "Now if I wasn't a law-abidin' God-fearin' man, I'd be takin' that young thing out in the woods . . . and whoooee!" If someone absolutely had to use the toilet, we stood around her to form a human screen.

We sat on the two bunks and talked. A little before 1:30 we heard some commotion in Mike's cell. I heard loud noises like someone was being punched and falling against the cell wall. Mike was yelling. This continued for a short time—maybe three or four minutes. I was sick with fear and revulsion at what I could imagine happened to him. We joined hands and I prayed very hard.

After a long time Mike yelled down to us. He said that the guard had made his white southern cellmate, Crow, beat him. He said he felt like his head was broken and that he needed a doctor badly. We tried to offer encouragement but there wasn't much we could say.

Around 4:30 they (black inmates with jobs in the jail who were called trustees) brought us five plates of beans and cornbread. We ate some of it then most of us passed the remainder of our food to O.T., a psychotic man in the cell next to us. I couldn't eat anything.

We tried to lie on the bunks with two on one and three on the other but it was hot and sticky. The toilet didn't work and urine overflowed onto the floor. The cell was filthy dirty. The water in the sink didn't work so our only access to water was the hot shower. When we finally decided to try to sleep we dragged one mattress onto the floor. Two of us lay on the floor, one on the top bunk, and two on the bottom. They didn't turn out the lights so we had to unscrew the light bulb.

Around 11:00 P.M. Mike yelled to us that he thought Crow was going to beat him again. He asked us to rouse the guard. We thought perhaps there was some way to talk Crow out of it so we hesitated. But as Mike's voice grew more urgent and we heard a few sound slaps, we began pounding on the cell wall with our fists and shoes. Mike yelled, "Guard, guard." It took several minutes before the jailer arrived. We couldn't hear what happened after that—we could only hear loud voices.

I was numb with anxiety and numb with pain from my old back injury. My main concern was for Mike and the people on the outside. Who could know what kind of harassment the local folk were getting, with all their leaders in jail?[2] I finally fell asleep from exhaustion around 3:00 A.M. At 5:00 A.M. I awoke to find a black hand stroking my hair and my face. It was O.T. in the cell next door. I tried to move my head farther away from the bars but there wasn't room enough, so I got up again and paced the floor.

Sherry and Judy, the two white girls who had come over after the Selma march, had been arrested before and had snuck in some money in their bras. The second day, they paid the trustees to bring us hamburgers and sodas, for which I was grateful, having eaten nothing for twenty-four hours. I contemplated the long fasts of Dr. King and Dick Gregory and knew that they were better people than I could ever be. I fought dizziness; this was the last place on earth I'd want to be unconscious.

The second day, they took Connie and me downstairs one at a time. She was gone for a long time and didn't return. My heart was racing when a white jailer came for me with a pistol in his hand and motioned me into the hallway. As we walked downstairs, he said, "I wish I wasn't taking you to the station," and jabbed the gun into my back, right at the bra line. In an unplanned and potentially lethal reaction, I whirled around, smiled, and said, "You remind me of my father." He looked slightly sheepish, lowered the gun to his side, and let me walk ahead.

I was relieved when I entered the fire chief's office and saw the two white "Revs" with the sheriff and several men from the posse. Connie was there too, but I couldn't read anything in her face. John Golden asked if we were being treated all right, and first I, then Connie, replied, "yes." The bloodshot eyes of the men fixed on us as they asked us to sniff a jar of corn liquor—moonshine—that they were passing around. Some of them were visibly drunk and grinned at our discomfort. "No, I am not familiar with that smell," I lied. They laughed. After a while Rev. Golden said not to worry, that they were working on getting some bail funds from SCLC but that it might be another day because money had been sent to Chicago, where Dr. King and Jesse Jackson were leading demonstrations and a large number of people had been arrested.

One guard walked both of us back to our cell; this time the gun stayed in his holster, but we had no idea what was coming next or how long we would remain in jail. I don't know if that was their strategy—to make us sick with worry—but it worked really well on me. My stomach was churning and my dress was soaked with sweat. Late in the afternoon, someone came to the cell door and called Connie's, Ann's, and my name. This time I was truly terrified. I don't know who paid our bail, but we were released onto the street in the late, humid afternoon. Officer L. C. Albritton adjusted his policeman's cap and grinned as he marched us down to the gas station his brother, the mayor, Reg Albritton, owned. "Y'all be right back here if you don't git outta Camden, you hear?" I bristled at being spoken to like a child.

Downhill at the gas station, Mayor Albritton leered at us while he lectured, "What you nice girls wanta come down here and mix up with our nigrahs for? You ain't gonna do them no good. Y'all go back home. We don't need any you agitators. Especially not pretty little things like you." He reached out and planted his hand on my hip and left it there for a minute while I flushed with fury and shame. The imprint felt like a branding iron on my backside even as we ran away from this horrid man and back up toward the Academy.

I started yelling like a madwoman, "Free at last, free at last, thank God Almighty we're free at last!"

One of the local kids sitting on the steps of the dormitory remarked,

"That was nothin'; we was in for three days with no food and they beat us every day." I knew he was right; I was no hero, but I had been to jail, even if it was just for a little while. I felt like I had earned my stripes.

While we were shocked to be released so quickly, we worried about our young men who were still jailed, and about Mike. They kept Sherry and Judy until the next morning, when they released everyone except Don Green. They didn't really want to keep and feed us, just to seriously scare us. And they did. It was evil in there, pure ugly, dirty evil. I burned my blue cotton jail dress in the incinerator behind the kitchen because it felt like I could never get that evil smell out of it. And I only had three dresses altogether.

At the beginning of the project, I had the sense that someone—Dan Harrell, Major Johns, Rev. Threadgill—somebody was taking care of us. Slowly I realized that no one but God was looking out for us, although Dan and Major did their best. I wondered how they could soldier on the way they did. I began to think that going back to San Francisco might be a good thing, but I pushed that thought out of my mind. While there was still work to be done, I needed to keep my complete attention right here. I couldn't be daydreaming about anything, but I sure wanted to see Bob. That night, Bob returned to me. He told me he'd walked along the creek until he was out of town then caught a ride with some locals into Selma. He found his sister's class, gave them a tour of Selma civil rights hot spots and stayed the night with the Webbs in the housing projects. How he got back to Camden I never did learn, but I was never so glad to see anyone in my life. We went upstairs to my room, hugged and talked for hours until we fell asleep, even though Bob had planned to join a group of young men guarding our office at Antioch Baptist Church that night.

Boys Beaten at the Church

Antioch Baptist Church had been vandalized several times already, so everyone thought it best to have someone there at all hours to protect our project equipment and files. The group of teenagers watching the church that night—all of whom were between sixteen and eighteen years old—included Emmanuel Hardley, Robert Powell, Frank Connor, Charles Nettles and his younger brother Grady, Henry Robertson, William Truss,[3] and one other teenager. Don Green would have been with them had he not still been in jail on his concealed weapons charge, and we were still worried for his safety. Bob felt conflicted. He was supposed to stay with the young men, but he needed rest and wanted affection from me. The teens told him they could handle it, after all, his girlfriend had just got out of jail. Bob still kept his jeans on when we slept together. We hadn't even fallen asleep when a car raced up the dirt drive and skidded to a stop in front of the dormitory. Major Johns jumped out without turning off the engine. We ran downstairs to hear Major shout to one of the white Revs to phone Good Samaritan to make sure a doctor could be ready for Emmanuel, who was sitting in the front seat sopping up a bloody nose with his T-shirt, and Frank, who was lying groaning in the backseat with a bleeding head. Another boy was crouched in the backseat holding his head too, but I couldn't make him out in the dark. The racists had broken the church windows again, severed the phone lines, shot up the wood framing of the door, and come at the boys with tire irons. Five of the boys managed to run away, so these three took the brunt of the beating. It was the Klan all right; the boys who fled saw their trucks, and the ones who got caught and beaten saw their faces through their nylon-stocking masks. Major told us the next day that one of the kids pulled a stocking mask off of Frances Gordon, who owned a gas station downtown. Others they could identify were Bob Lane, who owned Lane Brothers Butane Company (Lane Butane), and Bob Spencer, who worked for Lane. The boys were all hurt badly, but Frank Connor was beaten the worst. I ran upstairs to grab my pillow to put under Frank's head. Bob held me back. "No—it's the only one you have for the whole summer and it'll be ruined. He's not likely to make it anyway."

After they drove away, I didn't want Bob to touch me. I was appalled at him seeming so hardened. But after we went upstairs, I saw that he was shaking too. He was sick with guilt for leaving them there alone. "They were after me. It should've been me. Oh my God! God damn!" We held each other and wept at our utter uselessness. There wasn't anything else to say. After Bob fell asleep, I went out on the upper veranda in the warm, now peaceful night. I sat on the swing and looked at the moon and stars through the big pecan tree. I prayed, "Please God, don't let Frank die, most especially don't let him die because of us."

After that, no one stayed all night at the church. We moved most of our strategy sessions to the Academy or met in cars or on someone's back porch. The racists were relentless. We never heard of a single white local trying to stop them, even though the seminarians said there were a lot of good whites in town. I just never saw them. The harassment stepped up. The sheriff told Mr. Sylvester Nettles that he could no longer be responsible for his safety if he didn't get rid of the civil rights workers living at his home. Judy went back to Selma and I never saw her again. Sherry planned to go back to her home near Boston. A reporter from the *Chicago Daily Defender* interviewed Bob, although we didn't see it because we didn't have access to newspapers at the time.[4] The local *Wilcox Progressive Era* newspaper did not mention the attack in the church or any other civil rights activity during our entire stay in the county.

The morning after the attack, Bob and I went with some others to assess the damage to the church. There were bullet holes over the main entrance. Almost immediately, Sheriff Jenkins showed up with a couple of the men in his posse and pointed his shotgun at us. With the sheriff's shotgun at our backs, we filed out into the hot sun and watched helplessly as he padlocked the church door and wrapped a thick chain through the handles. I was relieved when he didn't drag us off to jail again. The sheriff lied to the national press about the church closure, saying that the Antioch Baptist Church deacons asked him to get rid of us. Courageous Rev. Freeman sawed off the padlock and resumed church services three days after we were removed at gunpoint, but we field workers went into the church office only one or two at a time and stopped going to services in order not to cause more problems for the congregation.[5]

Our ongoing boycott of white businesses was what the sheriff had used as the puny excuse to arrest us. The boycott meant no movement or African American money was being spent in Camden. We couldn't estimate the economic impact of the boycott, but it certainly had the impact of infuriating the white business community. "Conspiracy to boycott" was apparently a made-up felony offense in the state of Alabama. Later I learned that we were also charged with "felony trespassing" for staying at the Academy. Although we had the permission of the Presbyterian Church, which owned the property, we did not have permission from the trustees of the Wilcox County Board of Education, who had some kind of authority over the school.

After they closed down the church, members of the posse started to come onto Academy grounds more often. They would drive around gunning their engines during the day, and at night they'd park with their headlights shining in the windows for a long time. We knew they had been drinking and they were armed. Sometimes we just kept doing what we were doing, but if they got too close or fired a shot, we'd go down to the basement kitchen and lie on the cold concrete floor underneath the high windows and wait until they left. It was such a helpless feeling. We couldn't call the police because they were the very people authorizing our terror. Our leaders said we had to get out of the Academy and stay out. This was the only place I stayed that had running water, and the only place Bob and I could be together, so I was particularly upset.

But what made me really crazy was the Klan hurting the local youth, whom we considered our kids. These teens were incredibly brave. They either had parental permission or defied their parents to continue what they had begun that spring, working openly in the movement. Frank Connor was deathly ill in the hospital. He had lost a tremendous amount of blood from his head injuries and remained hospitalized for months. I had no idea what happened to Mike Farley, who was beaten in jail. I hoped that he was able to travel and get home. Don Green was finally released from jail and went right back to work canvassing.

The other survivors of the church beating came home wearing their bandages like the heroes they were. Bob worried that these young men were the ones taking the worst of the brutality and would be left to face it long after we were gone. Dan Harrell told Bob and me that he'd appreciate it if we could stay on after the 1965 Voting Rights Act passed, which he expected soon. We could explain the importance of registration and accompany the new voters to the courthouse, where it was expected that federal observers would protect all of us. It was early July and we still had no word on why Congress hadn't sent this important bill to President Johnson to sign.

10

A Brief Reprieve

As the violence increased, Bob and I spent the night together in my room at the Academy whenever we could, although most nights we were out in the field separately. The Revs took us aside for talks. They warned us: "You are putting us in danger by being a couple. You are breaking the rules. You are setting a bad example for the local kids." We were righteously indignant and explained what had been true up until then—that we were sleeping fully clothed just enjoying the comfort of hugs and kisses after long difficult days apart. When they continued to pressure us, I retorted, "Well, John and Ethel are staying in his room some nights. Is there a double standard?" A red-faced married John Golden replied that it was different, they were grown-ups and they were not doing anything, just talking. But my outburst put an end to the issue.

The night we finally made love for the first time, we didn't discuss it. Thanks to Rev. Al Dale back in San Francisco, I was on the pill, so I wasn't going to get pregnant. Considering we might not make it out alive, I was ready. Bob told me he was experienced, which gave me the confidence to undress completely with him for the first time. Our lovemaking was hurried and sweaty. We tried to be as quiet as possible now that we really were "doing it." Afterward, Bob fell asleep quickly. As I cleaned up in the hall bathroom, I stared into the mirror for a long time to see if I looked any different. If I'd changed, it didn't show. I walked out onto the upper porch in my cotton nightgown, sat on my favorite swing and rocked. While looking out at the full moon, I smiled to myself thinking, "Now I am a woman." My very next thought was: "I am going to be in so much trouble." And then the thought that fixed everything: "We love each other, Bob says we'll get married. It will be all right." Across the way I saw a light on in Rev. Threadgill's window and prayed that he'd never find out that we'd desecrated his campus.

The handful of nights I was able to shower and sleep at the boy's dormitory were entirely due to Rev. Threadgill's intervention with Principal Hobbs and the board of education. While I seldom saw him except during meetings with our adult leaders, his presence on campus and his admonitions to behave were constantly on my mind. Despite how stern he was with us—especially compared to Dan Harrell who tried to cajole his uppity white student charges—I knew that Rev. Threadgill was our protector, that we owed what little respite we did enjoy primarily to him. Whenever I was staying at the boys' dorm, I used to face in the direction of the Threadgills' home when I said my nightly prayers. In the middle of the summer I added a hope that he would forgive me for taking refuge with my new love under those ancient eaves. On the occasions when Rev. Threadgill stopped in at our SCOPE field staff meetings, discussions generally went more smoothly. In a spirit and tone similar to Dr. King's, he reminded us that we should begin meetings with prayer, a practice that had fallen by the wayside after staff sessions had become tense.

Over the Fourth of July weekend, we got some relief. On July 3, Bob and I went in to Selma to party with SNCC kids at the Chicken Shack, the Selma movement hangout. My first impression of the Chicken Shack was that it was like the Roost Club, our high school hangout back in Petaluma. Except in Selma, there were no watchful chaperones to keep you from dancing too close, and the drinks were not limited to sodas. The Chicken Shack was a simple wooden building with a corrugated metal roof that added to the percussion when the summer rain beat down. The concrete floor was beer-stained; the air was filled with sweat, cigarette smoke, and lust. A jukebox with colored neon lights made for most of the light and all of the music. There was some kind of bar that served beer and mixed drinks. I drank rum and coke—sweet and not too strong, but as a nondrinker up until recently, anything was too much for me. We were hot, thirsty, and drank a lot. It felt exciting and risky to be in an integrated club—really a black club with white civil rights workers coming in by invitation only. It was great to be able to dance, let our hair down, and get away from all the Revs.

I loved the music! It was miles away from music popular with white kids in San Francisco, like Sam the Sham and The Pharaohs' "Wooly Bully" or Petula Clark's "Downtown." Even the then-scandalous Paul Revere and the Raiders' version of Richard Berry's "Louic Louie" seemed tame compared to real soul music. We danced to Fontella Bass singing "Don't Mess Up a Good Thing" and the Temptations' "My Girl." Bob and I clung to each other as if our lives depended on it, dripping sweat to Otis Redding's "I've Been Loving You Too Long (to Stop Now)." Now that we were lovers, I melted into him the way I had watched other girls do but had never let myself do before.

Marvin Gaye's "Can I Get a Witness?" got us all into a line dance shouting out "Can I get a witness, witness, witness, witness?" grimacing at the bitter irony of the many civil rights' murder acquittals despite witnesses. Wilson Pickett's "In the Midnight Hour" took us places that the Beatles never could. Soul music became the secular flip side of our civil rights sound track. We mixed in new lyrics with the freedom songs we sang in church, in mass meetings, and in jail. Those songs became engrained in us—body and soul. Driving late at night with Chuck, all of us more than a little drunk, was a stupid move, but we felt invulnerable as we sang our way back to Camden. None of us wanted to miss the Fourth of July picnic out in Coy.

One of the most relaxing days we ever spent was out at Ethel's with her parents, Jesse and Julia, and little Jesse, who was running around with a flock of cousins, dashing in and out of the woods that surrounded their farm. Since the holiday brought out the worst kind of patriotism in the white population, we all got out of town. The Brooks women and some neighbors made a memorable meal that I helped serve: corn on the cob with real butter, pickled pigs feet, fried chicken, black-eyed peas with ham, okra with pot liquor, and pan bread. Boone's Farm strawberry wine was Ethel's favorite. I joined her, my first time drinking in the dry county. The wine tasted liked Kool-Aid with a kick to it. We sat around a table covered with a red-and-white-checked oilcloth, laden with food, under the eaves on the long porch talking about when the revolution comes. That was what SNCC kids said: it's gonna take a revolution. We sipped strawberry wine until the sun went down and the mosquitoes began to drive us in—not that the Brooks had good window screens to keep the bugs out.

As I was helping Ethel dish up pie, made from their own pecans, I went outside to get cream for the strong black coffee. Jesse Sr. had rigged up a refrigerator plugged in on the porch with the wire going straight out to the road. He said that he connected it himself; the power company didn't know he was tapping into their line, which excluded black homeowners. I called to Ethel and asked her if the little glowing insects I saw could be fireflies. She squinted, nodded, and began to sing, "This little light of mine, I'm gonna let it shine." I chimed in; my soprano and her alto harmonized as we carried in plates of pie and cups of coffee, ready to share.

Whenever we'd get discouraged, Ethel would say it was time to do a little singing. She'd begin to clap her hands and hum in her sweet alto voice, "Oh Freedom, oo-oh freedom, oo-oh freedom, oo-oh freedom over me, over me. And before this campaign fail, we all fill up that jail," changing the phrase

10. Ethel Brooks and her father, Jesse Brooks, Wilcox County freedom fighters, Coy, Alabama. (Copyright © 1996 by Bob Fitch.)

from the old spiritual "before I'll be a slave (doncha know) I'll be buried in my grave." Filling up the jails was a form of protest that had been used since the early 1960s Freedom Riders. Ethel had been arrested in Selma and Camden, too. I wished I could be as brave as she seemed; I had hated jail and didn't plan on ever going there again.

After having to house and transport protesters all spring, "our" sheriff, Lummie Jenkins, routinely practiced catch, harass, and release so he could collect bail but not have to take up room needed for his regular prisoners— mostly down-and-out locals who were mentally ill, had drinking problems, or got "uppity" with a white person. More often, the sheriff's posse beat black and white civil rights workers without bothering to jail them. Sheriff Jenkins was infamous for ignoring legal process and encouraging extreme physical violence.

Ethel taught us how to be legally civil but not subservient when we were stopped by the roadside or booked into jail, something with which she had lots of practice. The spring demonstrations, the march from Selma, her SCLC training, and Dr. King's visits convinced her that change was going to come and now was the time for everyone to stand up to the racist system. Ethel was frustrated with those locals who felt they had too much to lose to participate in the movement, and she criticized them publicly, which didn't add to her popularity with some folks.

The next day was a beautiful one made more so when we were told that by swimming together we were integrating the pool at the "Negro playground" for the first time. The Bessie W. Munden Playground was named for an early Camden Academy teacher who collected twenty dollars a year from other teachers until they had enough to build a place for the children to play. I slipped into the cloudy, lukewarm, unfiltered water with leaves and pine needles floating all around. Nearly fifty of us filled up the tiny pool and stirred up the gritty dirt collected on the bottom, but the water was cooler than the ninety-degree air and it was ours for the moment. I thought we were deep in the woods; later I saw that the park was only a little ways off of Highway 221 on the edge of town. As with all-black only areas, the roads were unpaved, and there were no flush toilets or drinking fountains, just a pump for filling the pool. The little kids leaped from the edge into my arms, and then I taught them to float and paddle on their backs. The water seemed too dirty to put your face in, although naturally they did. We splashed, sang, and yelled, feeling far away from the white people gathered at the fairgrounds to shoot off firecrackers. "Crackers with firecrackers, shootin' off their mouths," someone quipped. We were supposed to love everybody like Dr. King said, but it was getting harder every day.

Dan Harrell and Juanita came by for a while. Juanita was so pretty! It was clear that she and Dan were deeply in love as well as committed to the movement. They headed our voter registration project, ran literacy classes, and worked on bringing in federal funding. Dan was in charge of SCOPE in seven counties, yet we saw him several times a week. He wore his slacks and white short-sleeved shirt, dressed to meet SCLC's trademark respectability requirements, even to a picnic.

As he waved his ever-present pipe in the air, Dan told us proudly, "You know this is historic, integrating this pool. Some day because of what you all are doing this summer, all the children of Camden will have nice places to play, to swim, to go to school—black and white together. You enjoy your day; we gotta go to Selma to meet with Rev. Blackwell." That couldn't be good news. Rev. Blackwell was director of the entire SCLC state Voter Education Program (VEP)[1] that oversaw our project, and this was a weekend. Off they drove in their yellow Chevy convertible that some supporter had provided. It gave leaders a certain status with the locals if they had nice cars. It also really infuriated the whites to see black people driving them.

We stayed until dusk eating watermelon, singing, and talking. Charles Nettles started spitting watermelon seeds, mocking the stereotypical voice of an old black man while we all laughed. Near sunset we sang songs like "I

Love Everybody" and "Change Is a Comin'." For a few hours in the woods it felt like maybe we could hurry up change in Camden. Change was being hard-fought, but like the song said, there was no way it wasn't going to come.

While we were having fun over the Fourth of July weekend, more of our local kids got roughed up in the Sawmill and Wilson's Quarters. I didn't hear details, but Dan and Major ordered us to disperse and not be sitting ducks at the Academy. The school board was pressuring Principal Hobbs to get us off campus. I was glad to go back into the field. I was in more than a bit of shock over losing my virginity and starting to drink, not to mention having been in jail. I began wondering what kind of person I was turning into. Would my college roommates recognize me? What about my family? How could I keep all these secrets? Also, it turned out the training was right. It was harder to concentrate on the good of everyone if you were thinking about your lover's safety first.

Sometimes I'd wake from a nightmare where Mike was screaming or imagine that O.T. was pulling my hair through the bars of my cell. If Bob were with me, I'd snuggle into him. The sweet-sour smell of his sweat, Pepsodent toothpaste, and Old Spice deodorant, and his strong arms wrapped around me, made me feel more secure. If I were alone, I'd go sit on the upstairs swing and rock until my heartbeat slowed down, but I never could really relax. The slightest sound and I was in full alert. When I was staying with families out in the county, I often lay awake staring at the ceiling, listening to the sleeping children breathe until a rooster signaled the coming of a new day. When I wrote to my family, I tried to minimize my fears.

Excerpts from a July letter to my family:

It is now July 5th. I had to move out of the Academy—it's too dangerous to be in Camden now. Yesterday was a great day & no arrests were made for a change. I don't know when I'll get to write to you again. Thanks for your letters—they mean so much. We'll be canvassing voters all over the county for the next two weeks so it's on the road for me. We'll just stay at folks' houses when evening falls.

PS It's 6:30 AM—July 5th—and we are ready to go out in the field to canvass for voters. There are more little incidents all the time. One of the strongest local leaders [Don Green] a junior in high school, had some moonshine planted in his car. When he drove out of the Sawmill Quarter, the police were waiting for him. They took him to jail, put him in the bullpen—a cell with no windows or ventilation, harassed him, left him overnight & released him. He's been beaten [and arrested] dozens of times, yet he's a wonderful person [meaning, he wasn't bitter or angry]. Well, our ride is here.

11

Back in the Field

From a July 1965 letter to supporters:

I went to canvass the Arlington area again with a Negro boy [Robert Powell] and girl, and a white male SCOPE worker [Bill]. We were walking along Highway 5 when we noticed a white man in a pickup truck with a shotgun on a rack; he was slowing down. We kept on walking and he turned around and came up behind us. He tried to run over us but we jumped into a ditch. After he tried it a few more times we turned around and headed into a Negro café. We tried to call the Academy but that line was busy. The woman who owned the place was so excited and upset that she made us leave before we could get the call through. We ran and hid in the woods. Our friend had recruited his buddy by this time and was cruising back and forth in front of where we were hiding. The Negro boy went to phone again. Almost everywhere he stopped people were too afraid to even let him in the house; obviously someone has been threatening and harassing the people. He finally got the call through and after about an hour a staff car came for us.

I wasn't particularly scared, just provoked. These kinds of incidents are exactly what scare people out of registering. Today at the courthouse they were far too slow. Now they say they won't give us tomorrow to file so we may have to demonstrate. I hope not. The whites are in a brutal mood. If we do demonstrate the SCOPE people will probably not be allowed to participate.

When Major picked us up, I flung myself into the front seat while Robert and Bill got in back. Running from one grassy damp ditch to another, getting scratched up by brambles, and being terrified that the men would get out and shoot directly at us was pretty upsetting. I really wanted a hug, but Major wasn't the hugging kind, certainly not to white girls. To keep myself from continuing to shake all over, I began singing as we drove back toward Camden: "Swing low, sweet chariot, comin' for to carry me home. Swing low . . ." Major began singing along in his deep booming voice. I changed the lyrics to "Swing low, Dear Major, comin' for to carry me home." That got a bit of a smile out of him. Being in charge of rescuing field workers had to be one of the worst jobs in SCLC, but Major Johns was there for us without fail, and despite his stern ways, I loved him. When I wrote my family that evening, I was still upset but tried to reassure them (and myself) that I could handle the pressure.

From a July 1965 letter to my family:
Dear Family

I had a rather narrow escape today & when I got back to The Academy & got your letters it made me so happy I wanted to cry. I sure think about you all often. I'm so tired of living in constant danger that I can't be afraid anymore. Every nite when I go to bed I just say "Thank God no one got killed today." We *are* getting people registered, tho' the Klan is trying its damndest to see that we don't.

My work right now is mainly going from shack to shack trying to convince people to get off their behinds & get down to register. We usually split up and get local kids to show us around. We never work in white pairs cuz the people are still scared of us.

We get all sorts of reactions and excuses, but we also get the rewards of seeing people stand in line at the courthouse all day & finally walk home with a new kind of pride that says "I'm a registered voter."

By the end of my first month in Wilcox County, bias and barely suppressed terror influenced me; I felt angry with folks who wouldn't register. I wanted to be a heroine. If they wouldn't cooperate and register, I'd be a failure. I tried to invoke the *agape* spirit that King preached, but it wasn't working. I was tired, scared, and in pain.

I flagged down Ethel, who was driving her Dad's truck, and asked her to take me to see Dan and Juanita. I told Dan about the Arlington incident, which he already knew about from Major. I begged him to let me go work with Bob for a day. Dan puffed on his unlit pipe and gave me a "what makes you think you gonna be any safer with him?" look as he surveyed my chigger-bitten legs and nearly decayed tennis shoes. Juanita, smelling of Ivory soap and some kind of hairspray she used to smooth her long brunette hair back into a ponytail, leaned forward and gave me a hug. "It'll be alright darlin'; it'll be all right," she said. She turned to Dan with a sweet smile and said, "You carry her over there or I will."

Bob was surprised but not pleased to see me when we found him in Pine Apple. He looked at my legs and shoes and said, "You're gonna hafta keep up. We don't have all summer, you know." It seemed like every day lasted for an eternity, the way it did when I was a child. But Bob was right, pretty soon the Voting Rights Act would pass and federal examiners would come help these folks register, maybe backed up by federal troops. They wouldn't need us anymore. That day we worked near the Pine Apple sawmill where Bob Crawford worked and almost no one came to the door. The few who opened their doors said they were registered even though we knew from Mr. Crawford that they weren't. There was nothing we could say. When we stopped back at the Crawfords for lunch, John Golden was there. He said Dan had told him to carry Bob back over to Lower Peachtree. Jesse Smith was organizing something at his father's church and they wanted him there. It was getting near the weekend, and I didn't much like the idea of Bob being with those pretty Smith sisters, but Dan was "The Man," for our project.

While John Golden drove me back to the church before taking Bob down to Lower Peachtree, Bob told us what had happened to him the day before. "Dan and I were walking along when this white guy appears out of nowhere. I mean we didn't hear him comin', didn't see a truck, nothing. Just like that, he takes his pistol, raises it right to Harrell's head and presses it against his temple and says, 'You know I would kill you as soon as look at you, doncha?' 'I believe I do,' was all that Dan answered. Man, that Dan, he was so cool. I was just about to beg and cry myself."

Bob said as the seconds ticked into years he saw himself just as dead as Dan right there on that country lane, knowing this guy would never be caught or punished. "And," Bob explained, "this was just an ordinary guy, not one of the sheriff's posse or anything, just an ordinary cracker. Man! They can just do this stuff. Shit!" Bob lit a cigarette and blew smoke out the open car window.

My heart was racing, "How did it end?"

"That cracker just lowered the gun, snorted, spit on the ground and walked away just as fast as he'd appeared," Bob answered.

Then I told Bob what happened to our team out in Arlington and suggested to him, "Your cracker must've been related to my guys. Dan didn't even tell me about what happened with you!" Bob said, "Yeah, I already heard about the Arlington situation. And, for what it's worth, they *are* all related, least when it comes to hating us."

It made me feel good that our elders knew that Bob and I were a couple and that he had some kind of idea what was going on with me even if the information didn't flow both ways. As an eighteen-year-old boy he wasn't the greatest at telling me what I wanted to hear, which was that he'd protect me, no matter what. How could he, when we'd chosen to put ourselves in danger?

There were so many incidents like mine in Arlington and Bob's with Dan that we didn't even report them all. It was the same all over the South for movement folks, in every county, every day for years. Ninety-nine percent of the people attacked were black folks who pressed on in a mostly nonviolent battle for freedom and justice against a continuous onslaught of violence and hatred. Not only were the locals the real leaders of the movement, they also saved our little white behinds time and again. Sometimes we knew what they had done and could thank them; sometimes they just kept it to themselves.

I began to feel confused. The strategy of never staying in one place made it hard to bond with my host families and even harder to get to know the local youth who showed me around. Sometimes the kids didn't show up and I went out completely alone even though I was terrified, imagining a Klansman behind every moss-hung tree.

One day I lost my scarf—just a cheap dime store nylon scarf I used to tie my hair back when it got too stringy from the rain and heat. I burst into tears. All of a sudden, I felt like I had to have nice things, clean things again. I wanted the comfort of a good mattress and hot running water and changes of clothes. Then I felt even worse for being so selfish when local girls like Mae Robinson didn't have half of what I did. I cried for a while, then pushed my hair behind my ears, pushed my growing despair deeper into my gut, and continued on.

George Wallace Comes to Camden

In mid-July, our leaders warned us that George Wallace, the hateful governor of Alabama with his infamous slogan, "Segregation now, segregation tomorrow, and segregation forever," was coming to Camden to rally the already hostile whites. He planned to speak from a platform in front of the courthouse where we sent voters to register. Our leaders told us to get out of town, so most of our workers left for outlying communities, but I was fighting an infection, so I stayed behind at the Academy with one of the white "Revs" and Connie Turner.

Late that night, Connie crept up the stairs and knocked on my door. I barely recognized her. She had put a black rinse in her hair and had "ratted" it into a bouffant style to look more southern, then had gone with *Wash-*

ington Post reporter Paul Good[1] to the George Wallace rally. Good had put her up to a risky adventure. She told me that Good boosted her up into a pecan tree on the square where she saw and heard the whole thing. Connie was breathless with amazement at the hatred Governor Wallace could whip up in the crowd.

She said Wallace had the crowd in a real frenzy. They were screaming, "Kill the Nigger Lovers!" Wallace told the cheering crowd something along the lines of: "Alabama and the rest of the God-fearing South are once again at war with the United States. This time we will succeed because God is on our side. He laid down the law of black and white. It is a crime, a heinous crime to undo God's creation of a superior and an inferior race. Nigrahs never can and never will be equal to white men. We will fight this fraudulent legislation, this so-called voting rights act with every weapon at our disposal. Tonight I tell you my friends that if you defend our freedom and our way of life by driving out these outside agitators, you will be doing the greatest service to this county, the great state of Alabama and to future generations."

I admired Connie's nerve but thought she had made a dangerous move; why risk so much just for the excitement? I was having more than enough excitement myself. Two cars filled with our field workers were shot at as they headed out to Coy to try to avoid the riled-up racists. No one was injured but all were severely shaken, and two car windows were broken. If I hadn't insisted on staying at the Academy, I would have been in one of those cars. Perhaps because the Klan thought we had all left town, no one came up to the Academy campus that night, but I still felt uneasy until Bob slipped into my bed around midnight. "Where were you?" I asked. "Don't ask sweetheart, just be glad I'm here now. Here and alive." He took me in his arms.

Gees Bend and Back to Boiling Springs

When I rolled over and opened my eyes to the already hot sun glowing through the window shade, I saw Bob's penciled scrawl on the edge of a page in my notebook. He must've left while I enjoyed a rare deep sleep. The note looked like it said "Lower Peachtree," with a heart in front of his name, but maybe it was just a circle. I splashed on some Jean Naté and slipped on the new homemade cotton shift my mother had sent and a clean but now gray pair of socks. My old blue tennis shoes were not going to last much longer. Downstairs, John Golden said Dan wanted me out of there for several days and said that was "an order."

I was happy to hear that I was being sent back to Boiling Springs and also to Gees Bend, although I was worried about Bob. He was at the other end of the county, and we had no way to be in touch. What if they really were after him in particular? He was getting carloads from his communities to come in to Camden to register. Frank Connor's bleeding head kept flashing before me. I said a little prayer for Frank, tried to banish that gruesome image, and said another one for Bob, simply, "Please God, let him survive so that we can get married."

As we drove out Highway 28 toward Gees Bend, I tried to sort out my confused feelings. Suddenly John Golden slowed the car to a crawl. A chain gang of black men in black-and-white striped pajamas and sweat-soaked cloth hats were carefully filling potholes with hot asphalt while a white man wearing a badge sat in a truck with a shotgun pointed out the window right at them. Heavy chains around their ankles shackled the men to each other and slowed their movements. One man dared glance up and make eye contact just before I slouched down below the window; I didn't want to be seen. At that moment, I hated being white. "I Love Everybody" seemed like a cruel meaningless slogan. John's jaw tightened as he gripped the wheel and began to hum some hymn under his breath.

Gees Bend is an area about fifty miles from Camden by land in a deep U-shaped bend of the meandering Alabama River. We had to take the long way through Alberta since we'd been told that if we civil rights workers ever tried to take the ferry, we'd be sure to find ourselves on the bottom of the Alabama River.[2] I was curious about Gees Benders; I'd heard a lot about their independence and contributions to the movement. They said it was 100 percent black up there, that they weren't afraid, and that all the preachers were with the movement.

John dropped me at a little community center, buzzing with ladies serving lunch. Off to the side, a couple of ladies were piecing a lopsided quilt with bright strips of cloth. A Mrs. Pettway pushed me to eat a plate of rice, beans, and cornbread although I wasn't hungry yet. Then she introduced me to another Mrs. Pettway, who told me I'd stay at her house and go to church with them in the morning.

When we walked the mile or so down to her place, I was surprised. It was one of those neat little white painted houses with a screened porch and proper roof, more fixed up than anything I'd seen on that side of the county. There was an outhouse and pump in the yard but they had electricity, and this Mrs. Pettway even had a telephone. I wondered if they were well off, but later, when they served beans and cornbread for dinner, I guessed not.

When Mr. Pettway came in from the fields, he told me about the federal government Farm Security Administration (FSA), whose representatives came to Gees Bend back in the late 1930s and found the people nearly starving. The FSA gave them some land, set up a farming cooperative, and constructed these little homes that they called "government built" houses.

Now most everyone had their own little farm, but some were in debt to the government and others refused the loans because they wanted to be independent even if that meant staying desperately poor. They did all right for a while, but when large mechanized agriculture swept the South, once again the black farmers lost out. One reason they organized was to get the federal government to oversee fair elections to the powerful County Agricultural Committee that oversaw farm subsidy allotments. Roman Pettway's general store, where some of the local youths printed the slogan "Freedom Is Near" out front, served as a community gathering place; people came there to find out what was going on. There was a post office and a couple of churches. And sure enough, it was an all-black community. By now, I felt safer when there were no other white people around.

Mrs. Pettway told me that we were going to Pleasant Grove Baptist in the morning. "Isn't that where Rev. Lonnie Brown preaches?" I asked all excited.

"Heavens child how you know about Rev. Brown all the way out from California?" I said Dan and Major told us about the Gees Benders, how they marched to the courthouse before just about anybody. She smiled broadly, "Well that's right, that's just about right."

Pleasant Grove was a pretty little church, better furnished than the simple Boiling Springs churches. These isolated landowners were deeply spiritual in a tradition that mixed the ecstatic with the fundamentalist. Ladies dressed all in white swayed with their eyes closed as Rev. Brown "whooped" his poetic sermon. Some women would rise, shout, and swoon while others would catch them, and fan them with paper fans from a funeral parlor over in Catherine. One woman shouted out in tongues. It was the first church I attended where no one paid me much attention, which was a relief.

Suddenly, everyone was leaving the sanctuary, but it didn't seem like the service was over; it was more like a procession. Outside, three women completely swathed in white were being lifted onto a pickup truck that drove off slowly a little ways down the road. The entire congregation followed and I did too. A path led down to muddy Foster Creek, where I witnessed my first full-immersion baptism. The look of ecstasy on the face of the woman, a mother in her twenties, was as if she had died and gone to heaven. I whispered that to Mrs. Pettway and she whispered back, "Child, she done that. She gone to heaven without dyin', and if she stay right, she dwell in the house of the Lord forever."

We all walked back to the church; the newly baptized women appeared in clean dry clothes looking like brides at a banquet as we ate on tables spread out under the trees. No heat, no mosquitoes, no doubt about the efficacy of baptism could diminish my feeling that the spirit had entered those women, for sure.

My time in Gees Bend, and later in Possum Bend, predated the national acclaim for the quilters, some of whom I got to meet. The bright, irregularly geometric quilts brightened up their homes and kept them warm in winter. These ladies had pride in their work and a few of them brought in a little bit of money through their handicraft. Despite the self-confidence this independent work generated, only a few area residents were registered to vote. The memory of recent violent attacks on those who attempted registration and a lack of clear understanding about why voting was so important kept some away while others waited to see what would happen with the lawsuit the farmers had filed over the poll tax. Our work was to support the efforts of local leaders and talk the people into understanding the potential power of their vote. It was a tough row to hoe since we had no clear information on when the federal government would pass or actually enforce the Voting Rights Act, and as lowly field workers, we were uninformed about current voting rights lawsuits.

Sometimes I gave up and just empathized with folks' desire to "keep things peaceful around here." When I was sitting on a family's porch stringing beans, shucking corn, listening to the frogs and crickets, and trying to chase off the flies and mosquitoes as the women hummed sweet praise songs and talked about the new day "that is a comin'," their viewpoint made sense. As nice as it was for me in Gees Bend, after a few days I was sent back to Boiling Springs.

That Thursday evening, after a revival meeting at Boiling Springs Baptist Church, I was both stunned and thrilled when the pastor called on me to say a few words—"a message" he called it. "I've been walkin' and talkin' with you. I know you have been mistreated, denied basic rights to good education, health care for your children, a life free of fear. My family lives in the country, too, in California, a long ways from here. They aren't rich, but they sent me to a decent public school and now I am getting a good college education paid for by my state's taxpayers. All your children deserve that. Today there are thousands of us all over the South organizing, registering voters so that tomorrow you and your children will have a better life. Please register and if you are registered, get your neighbors to register. We'll have cars here at the church 8:00 A.M. Monday morning. Please help me get folks here. Mrs. Burrell in the back will sign you up. Thank you kindly for your attention and blessings on you all."

After the church service, local movement activist Mr. Burrell drove me back to the Robinsons even though he said they'd gotten threats for keeping me there. Mrs. Robinson seemed glad to see me again, for which I was grateful. The first night I was back in Boiling Springs, Mae seemed kind of distant. She was tall, thin, and strong like her mother. As I lay in bed, I wondered if some kind of pressure was on her because of me staying with them. When you are young, you always think it's all about you. Several children—"the babies"—were stacked along Mae's and my feet with the covers loose at both ends; how I envied their ability to sleep!

The next morning after the menfolk headed out to the fields to work, Mrs. Robinson insisted on making me a bubble bath with her special Avon bubbles. She hauled water from the outdoor pump, boiled it on the stove and poured it into a big galvanized washtub with a capful of the sweet bubble bath. I protested that I needed to get out to canvass. She looked down at my dirty feet and stringy hair and calmly stated, "You best get into this hot water right now or nobody gonna open the door to you today, young lady." So I complied. As much work as she had to do and here she was scrubbing my back. I knew it was wrong, but it felt so good to be taken care of. A few days later I wrote to my family:

Excerpt from a July 1965 letter to my family:

I've spent the last two days working in the Boiling Springs area & have walked about 30 miles. My legs & feet are swollen but I feel good inside. I'm sending kids out with handbills & Sun nite I'll hold a mass meeting. I'll probably just give a short speech and then get one of the local leaders to give the main address. They always listen to me because I am white, but a local person has a more lasting effect.

When I volunteered to come here, I imagined leading voter education classes, giving speeches, and registering hundreds of voters. But mostly I walked and talked and sometimes got a few people to agree to register and to come to mass meetings. Once in a while I got to teach someone to write his or her name, the way Mrs. Septima Clark showed us at orientation. She had said, "Tell them don't worry right now about learning to read and write. When we get the vote, there will be schools for everyone, children and grown-ups. Right now you just need to make the letters of your name." The federal law said you could just make an "X," but that still wasn't accepted in Camden, and besides, most people wanted to proudly write their name on their registration card.

Sometimes the cabins were so far apart that we walked a mile just to get to one, and then were met with disappointment. One lady was out sweeping her dirt yard with a twig broom, a common custom in the region. She opened her door to show me that the floor inside the house was dirt as well. I had never seen that before and blurted out, "I am so sorry you have to live like this!" That was completely outside what we were supposed to say and ended any possibility of building connection with her. I tearfully apologized at the next staff meeting for my unguarded reaction; maybe I should have gotten used to the poverty and suffering, but I never did.

From a July 1965 letter to supporters:

I spent the week before last working in the community of Boiling Springs. To give you an idea of the living conditions, and not to get sympathy, I will tell you of some of my experience. I organized a group of local youth, 13 yrs and up, to go canvassing with me. We split into teams of two to cover a radius of 10 miles. Our objective was to talk with the people, to encourage them to register, and to notify them of the Sunday night mass meeting.

Houses in Boiling Springs are about 2 miles apart on the average. There are no paved roads, no electricity, no running water or telephones. Few people own cars. Women often work 10 hrs. at the rate of $1 a day in the okra canning factory. Probably everyone here is eligible for Economic Opportunity loans but they can't get them since segregationist county officials administer Federal programs.

The second day there I broke holes through both my shoes and had to go barefoot the rest of the time. Sometimes we walked 15 miles a day and one day I had to ride a mule. But, all the other kids [local black kids] were barefoot too. If they are lucky enough to have a pair of shoes they are saved for Sundays.

Near the end of another week out in the county, I could no longer ignore my lack of shoes or the raging pain from my bladder infection. When Ethel saw me hunched over, my swollen, bare feet with split, dirty toenails, bleeding chigger-scabbed legs, and a desperate look in my eyes she said, "All right. That's enough now. You can't register every Negro in Alabama in one summer. I'm taking you in."

Back at the Academy, with great embarrassment, I told John Golden I needed to see the doctor again. He consulted with Major, some phone calls were made, and John drove me back to Selma. When Dr. Maddox saw my scabby infected legs, he gave me a shot of penicillin as well as an oral antibiotic. I stayed a couple of nights with Jan Baker until the medicine took effect. The doctor took my word for it that I had a bladder infection; there was no way he was going to give a pelvic exam to a white girl. I could not believe that I kept messing up like this, getting sick, and being a bother. But Jan and Chuck were glad to see me.

12

The Beginning of Doubts

Jan was staying in a nice little home in Selma. She had her own sunny, lace-curtained room with a big four-poster bed that she shared with me for a couple of nights. The lady of the house was a single woman in her forties who dressed sharp and had freshly processed curls. She treated us like guests at a bed-and-breakfast. She had indoor plumbing and nice lighting fixtures; her home was lovely. So I was more than a little surprised the first evening I was there when, one after another, men who looked like they just got off work from hard labor started walking through the back door into her kitchen. They were smiling and laughing, but it didn't look like a meeting. Each one got a little jar or asked for a bigger jar with a lid that was put in a paper bag and taken to go. Money was put in a drawer under the counter.

Jan warned me not to drink anything offered: "It'll just about kill you," she said, "pure rot gut." I asked why we couldn't just leave. "That wouldn't be polite. We don't want to hurt her business. Half the reason so many come here is to see me and now you." Oh great! Now I am a greeter at a boot-legger's! But I smiled and chatted a bit with the affable workingmen as they chugged or sipped their brew.

Sure enough, one said, "Little lady, let me buy you a drink. For sure I want to buy you a drink for all you done for us, comin' all this way just to hep us out." He paid for a small lidless jar and handed it to me. I pretended to sip as I stood in the kitchen doorway. Jan winked at me and tipped her head toward a big potted plant in the dining room. As soon as I got the chance, in went the moonshine. I silently apologized to the poor plant, better you than me.

The next day, Doctor Maddox gave me another shot of penicillin and told me to keep taking the antibiotics. In the afternoon, Chuck took me to meet his mother and to visit Selma movement leader Mrs. Amelia Boynton. Fifty-four-year-old Mrs. Boynton was busy, and she just nodded at me from a stack of papers on her desk. I said I was honored to meet her and we left. Chuck told me Mrs. Boynton was the brains behind the Selma movement and that's why the police beat her so badly. She and Bernard Lafayette, and later, Worth Long, organized everything before Hosea Williams and Dr. King got involved. But, I asked, "Isn't Dr. King the one who gets everyone motivated?"

"Naw," Chuck said, "we was already completely motivated. I don't know how much more motivation you need than to get beaten every time you leave your neighborhood, every time you try to get one little right that you all in the North take for granted."

Charles drove me by Brown Chapel in the Carver housing projects where the Selma marchers retreated after being beaten and tear gassed on Bloody Sunday. It was quiet at the pretty brick church that day, but two men who looked like members of Deacons for Defense stood at the door. I didn't see their guns, but I felt their presence. They just nodded at Chuck.

Our next stop was the Selma SNCC office upstairs at 41 Franklin Street. It was a mess compared to the parsonage-like orderliness of the SCLC office downstairs. There were black liberation books stacked on a homemade bookshelf and papers strewn everywhere. Stokely Carmichael, who would become the next chairman of SNCC, was sitting in a large office chair looking like he was ready to have his photo taken. Although my two closest coworkers were impressed with Carmichael's rapid rise in the movement, I was more interested in meeting SNCC's national chairman, John Lewis, and was disappointed to learn that he was in Atlanta. Posters of Malcolm X and Che Guevara hung on the wall. Chuck asked if I wanted to meet anyone at SCLC, which had the ground-floor office. I peeked in the door but declined, "They think I am some kind of problem because I've been to the hospital. I don't want them to know I'm not out in the field," I said. I was glad when we left soon after we arrived.

My impression of most of the SNCC field workers I met was that they were hipper and more sophisticated than I was, although that would not have taken much. Neither SCLC nor SNCC was responsible for my sometimes condescending, uninformed, or patronizing attitude. I was a product of my age, my ethnicity and cultural biases, as well as this new learning about how to think and talk about race. Bob and I thought we knew more than the other white kids working in Wilcox, but we greatly respected our SCLC leaders, Dan Harrell and Major Johns. From my perspective, everyone in the movement was either revolutionary or evolutionary. We were all heading in the same direction. Things were moving fast—strategies, attitudes, and policies changed overnight. We were young, impressionable kids who wanted to belong. We wanted to be part of the change without fully comprehending the depth of historical divisions in the Deep South. Chuck Bonner, his friends Amos Snell and Cleo Hobbs, and most of the other SNCC workers we met were generally appreciative of our efforts and just as generous with their criticism. They felt it was their job to educate us in the ways of black liberation, and I agreed they were right about that. They also liked to party.

That afternoon, Bob joined us; I was thrilled to see him after more than a week apart. The first thing we did was to shop for new sandals since we both had been barefoot for some time. We hated going into Teppers Department store, which wouldn't employ black people, but there was no alternative. The clerks couldn't wait to get us out of there since our infected bare feet and accents made it clear we were some of those "outside agitators." They took our money anyway.

There were large black neighborhoods in Selma where we could walk around in integrated groups without getting arrested, which felt surreal after Camden. Black folks here assumed that white kids mingling with their youth were civil rights workers. We felt safe from Sheriff Jim Clark and his posse since we were not conducting protests or boycotts this summer.

Chuck took us to meet his mother, Bernice, at their house on Small Street. She chatted with us while she ironed clothes on the screened porch. Chuck's mother was so young she could have passed for his sister. As we walked down the wooden steps, Chuck said proudly, "She was only sixteen when she had me, but she and my grandmother, they took real good care of me. They're scared for me, but they back me. Family support is so critical to the movement. I feel sorry for them that do not have it." I grimaced at Bob since we both had families with mixed feelings, but Chuck meant people like him, who were in and out of jail for years, beaten, and thrown out of school. His strong young mother tried not to worry over her highly visible activist son, but it must have been hard for her. Chuck had been beaten by Sheriff Clark during an early student march and had been arrested many times.

Although Bob and I were glad to be together for a little while, we couldn't completely unwind, partially because we were shell-shocked from being under constant attack in Wilcox, but also because some SNCC workers were letting us know directly and indirectly that we weren't welcome anymore. A few would sit and talk with us, then get up suddenly and say, "You gots to leave now. No whites." We began to get the message that it was getting time—if not past time—for us to go. We downplayed what we had done and tried not to say anything offensive, but sometimes our just being there and the fact that we could go back home whenever we wanted offended people. Those were not the majority of field workers, but we were young and felt the rejection strongly. That rejection was part of our decision to leave a few weeks later. Consciousness of white privilege would come to us later in life, but at the time all we felt was hurt.

The guys had been sipping Southern Comfort all afternoon, and I was getting more uncomfortable by the minute as we made the rounds of churches where people had been beaten and the homes of marchers still recovering from wounds, all buddies of Chuck's it seemed. That night we went to the Chicken Shack again. I imagined all the black girls glaring at me and Jan even though I wore my SNCC medallion and Chuck always acted proud to be with us. After a few minutes, I gave in to my nerves and started drinking too, even though it wasn't a good mix with the antibiotics. Suddenly there was a rock 'n' roll song I had never heard before. It was so explicit that it made me blush, but it had a great beat and words. Everyone began to sing as we all danced. The Rolling Stones' "I Can't Get No Satisfaction" told it like it was—what we were going through—"We tried and we tried, but we cannot be satisfied, not until everyone is free" we ad-libbed. It felt like we were in the Beloved Community again. Someone kept refilling my drink.

Later that night, I felt myself leaning against the scratchy stucco wall of the Torch Motel with Bob trying to hold me up; I kept slipping down the wall, asking, "Why can't we go into our room? I want to lie down." It was raining hard as we stood in the small shelter of the dripping eaves. Sounds of radio music and sex flooded out open windows. Eventually the door to our room opened and a young couple stepped out. She straightened her dress as he grinned proudly. He flashed a smile and said, "We didn't go under the sheets. They still good." I picked up a barrette from beside the bed, but they were gone. Next thing I knew I was passing in and out from too much to drink but still trying to make love with my boyfriend who was only slightly less drunk than me. It wasn't pretty.

The next day we had breakfast with Chuck and Jan somewhere nearby. I could barely choke down eggs and biscuits with lots of strong black coffee. We all had bad, bad hangovers. Over coffee with a still muddled brain, I tried to explain that my understanding of nonviolence is that it is like a martial art: "You take the negative energy, the hate rushing toward you, and turn it back on the perpetrator in the form of love. That should melt down his defenses or at least make him stop and think. If you hate or hit back, you become no better than the oppressor."

Then Chuck explained that SNCC still used the word *nonviolent* in their name, but after all the attacks this year, nonviolence was just a strategy, not a guiding philosophy. "We use it when it's convenient, when it will get press, prevent murder, or recruit more folks," he said. "When necessary, we use any weapon: rocks, knives, even guns, especially in situations where you are outnumbered and could be outrun. There's no political advantage from getting beat or shot if no one is there to cover it."

Bob said he absolutely agreed with that, which made my stomach queasy, and not only from last night's liquor. "But, I don't mind getting beat or even dying for the movement, but I sure as hell don't want to die if these guys don't even want me here," Bob added.

"Well, I want you here, for sure," Chuck said. "Y'all been damn straight with us. But it is gettin' time to go. Fact is, me and Jan are thinkin' of heading out there to San Francisco with you all, in a few weeks." Chuck went on to explain that getting an education is a form of activism too.

Jan questioned whether "black power will come through achieving affluence and influence in the tradition of the often-maligned Booker T. Washington, founder of Tuskegee Institute, or through violent revolution?" We groaned in self-mockery at our intellectual talk and the giddy guilt that we could, all four of us, drive away from Selma, alive. That they were coming to California was great news! Bob said that Chuck could stay at his mom's place until they got settled, so I said Jan could stay at the house my three roommates and I were renting, although she'd have to sleep on the couch. For the first time, we talked about going home and going back to school like it was a reality, as if those places we called home and school would be waiting for us, unchanged. Bob and I could slip back into our young lives, and Chuck and Jan could begin a new one together in San Francisco.

The Accident

After breakfast, Chuck drove us back to Camden in one of the powder-blue SNCC Valiants equipped with a switch under the dashboard that allowed the driver to turn off the taillights when it was being followed. We drove Highway 41 to Camden in pouring rain. Amos Snell was in the front with Chuck. Bob and I were in the back. I was carsick, and then . . .

This is what I remembered and told everyone for forty years: It was raining, the road was slippery, and Chuck started speeding because we were being chased by a pickup with a shotgun rack on the back. The rack was empty, which meant the gun was inside the cab with the two men. As we rounded the big Selma curve, I heard a shot, and then we flew through the air, across the highway, in what felt like slow motion. I clung to Bob in the backseat figuring "This is it!" More shots. Then by some miracle the car settled down in a meadow with pine trees all around. I felt a burning pain in my low back. I wanted to get out of the car but the door was jammed. The next thing I recalled was standing in the rain. Bob had his arm around me, trying to get me to talk, but I couldn't. Everything looked green, like I had on green sunglasses. I couldn't hear anything but the pounding of my heart.

After a long time, I could hear a bird sing, smell the pines, feel the warm rain, and hear Chuck's voice as he commanded us to crouch next to the car until he flagged down someone to finish carrying us back to Camden. He and Amos would hitchhike back to Selma and get someone to help them tow out the SNCC car. It was a while before anyone passed by and even longer until someone stopped.

Their car was already full with kids and groceries, but charming Chuck talked them into taking us, saying they would be helping the freedom fight. We crouched on the floorboards in the backseat, with a blanket over us, and the kids put their legs on top of us. I peeked out once to get some air and saw the dark grim faces of the driver and his wife. We rode like that back to Camden, where they dropped us at the foot of the Academy hill and then took off as fast as they could. I could barely walk up the driveway and suspected that I had broken my tailbone; the pain was horrendous.

I didn't write home about the accident. I didn't want my family or anyone to know about it because we shouldn't have been out partying the night before. I blamed myself for being sick earlier in the week, which caused us to be in an integrated car for no good political purpose. I felt guilty about having sex. I was down on myself for not staying in good health, and finally, mostly, I was really, really scared for the first time. When I felt myself flying through the air, I expected to be dead when I landed. All the shocks of the summer combined into a deep, deep terror that I couldn't shake.

After the accident, I wrote fewer and shorter letters home and seriously doubted that we should stay after the SCOPE project ended in August. It didn't seem like we could do much good anymore. Wilcox County was under siege. There were no more safe places to meet and even fewer places where we could sleep. Bob kept saying, "Those SNCC guy's don't want us here. Not Chuck, not Stokely—they've always been fine with me. But, others . . . Just a few months ago they were calling me Brother, feeling all the love from the March. Now, I don't know what . . ." We had a theoretical understanding of racism and felt we had experienced it to some degree, but we craved the approval of our black peers, which was, understandably, hard to come by. We buried our feelings deep inside and seldom spoke of them, even between ourselves.

13

This May Be the Last Time

After the car accident, I continued to see everything through a green filter and my head was buzzing, but I didn't tell the adults. There was no way I was going back to Selma or seeing any more doctors. In severe back pain, I started popping Tylenol from a big bottle my mother had sent in her last care package. Meanwhile, the school board was pressuring Rev. Threadgill and Principal Hobbs to get us out of there by saying that we were trespassing and that they would get the sheriff to remove us. I was shaken to my core since the car accident and was reluctant to go back out into the field. For the first time I was really, really afraid that I might die. Despite my fears, I kept doing what we were trained to do, but my spirits were low. I asked for a daylong assignment, so they gave me a doozy.

Millers Ferry

Millers Ferry, on the edge of the Alabama River just outside Camden, was one of the most dreaded assignments for canvassing in the county. The Millers, and later the Hendersons, were among the last families who kept slaves after the Civil War ended. Somewhere on their property were "the slaughter fields," a place where less than a hundred years ago captured runaway slaves were tortured and murdered in front of the others. Locals said these "lessons" continued into current times in this company-owned mill town. Even with the nearby Prairie Mission School run by the same northern Presbyterian group that owned Camden Academy, fear of violence was extreme and constant, reinforced by grueling hard work, lack of real wages, and abject poverty.

Millers Ferry still operated as a virtual slave plantation in every way except the name. The company owned all the property and deducted rent for the unheated, ramshackle cabins from the workers' wages. What little workers were paid was not in real dollars, but with tin tokens that could only be used at the company store. They were always paid less than it took to feed their families and cover rent, so they were always in debt to the lumber company that owned the entire plantation. Residents there were among the most discouraged and hardest to reach.

Major drove Robert Powell and me over the wooden bridge to the landing. While beads of sweat popped out on his forehead, Major told us that he was going to wait on the other side of the highway and if anything went wrong, to come back there. I wondered why we were going in if this was such a dangerous place, but I didn't question him. My heart pounded in my ears as we entered the landing. There were strong black men tying rafts of pine logs together to pole down river to the lumber mill. In the distance, the sight of the plantation overseer blowing smoke out his truck window sent shivers through me even though it must've been ninety degrees in the early morning.

As we walked along dusty paths between unpainted, gray wood shacks, doors closed and flour sack curtains were pulled shut. Few would answer our knocks. Some cabins did not have proper doors, just a burlap sack curtain hung over the entry. The few folks who were willing to speak ushered us quickly indoors. One woman proudly invited us in. Her shack was swept clean, and she had sewn decorative cloth borders around her bleached flour sack dishtowels. A colorful pieced quilt covered the sagging bed she shared with her husband and three children. She said she had attempted to register several times but the registrar was always closed when she got there. Her quilt and her pride were the only beautiful things I saw in Millers Ferry.

Less than an hour after we began walking through Millers Plantation, we heard the sound of a pickup truck. Sure enough, it was the overseer; he was wearing sunglasses, his straw hat was pulled down low. "Y'all best get outta here right now before the boss man comes. We don't need no trouble around here. Understand?" We understood. Robert walked away slowly, his head held high. It was all I could do to force my shaky legs to walk instead of race across the bridge where we found Major's car in the shade of a tree, the engine already running. My heart didn't stop pounding until we were back at the church.

Bad News: The *Washington Post*

Near the end of July, it seemed like our project leaders' battles had gone from bad to worse. The two white Revs were on the outs. Major and Dan were barely civil with each other, and Ethel expressed open disgust with everyone except her parents, John Golden, and us kids. We didn't see Rev. Threadgill anymore, but I imagined that he couldn't wait for us to leave so he could discover what he would have to deal with after our two-and-a-half-month invasion of the Academy. Courageous Antioch Baptist leaders kept their beloved church open despite the sheriff saying it would stay padlocked until we stopped organizing.[1]

Before we moved out, I was summoned to the Academy telephone to take a call from Randolph T. Blackwell, who directed Alabama SCOPE work in his capacity as SCLC program director. In a resonant voice barely constraining fury, Blackwell demanded to know how I expected them to let me stay when I kept breaking the rules. He recounted my expensive medical bills that cost precious dollars that were needed for bail and other expenses. Then, like a bolt of lightning from a dry sky, he read—nearly shouted—a paragraph from an article published in the *Washington Post* on July 12: "Nineteen year old Joyce Brians from San Francisco State College sleeps at night in Negro homes. By day, she goes out canvassing alone on rural red clay roads with local Negro boys who point out homes of potential voters."

He droned on, but I couldn't hear anything else he said, knowing that the wording about being alone with "Negro boys" and "sleeping in Negro homes" was the type of sensationalism about "race mixing" that SCLC hoped to avoid. I begged to stay, and I pleaded that I didn't know the reporter wrote down anything I had said. I protested that I was tricked into speaking with Good, although I didn't give any details about how I was tricked. I told him I loved my assignment, would never cause any problems again, and begged to be allowed to stay on until the end of the project. After a while he relented, but he told me that if he heard one more word—even one more word about me for anything at all—I could just pack my bags.

Paul Good, a *Washington Post* reporter, had been hanging around Camden interviewing people off and on over the past few weeks. We were firmly instructed not to speak with him. Connie had already gone into Selma with him a couple of times and went with him to the Governor Wallace rally. She said she trusted him, but Connie was marching to a different drummer.

How this article came about was that Paul Good stopped by the Academy when only Connie and I were there and asked if we wanted to walk up to Hangman's Hill above the dormitory to see where the KKK had burned a cross during the spring demonstrations. I remember thinking it must have scared the students and teachers half to death and how brave they were to keep on protesting.

When we got to the spot where I saw the burned cross with a big circle of dark soot all around, I collapsed on a log. How could people use a symbol of Christian love and sacrifice as a symbol of hate and fear? I was shaking. Good pulled out a six pack and said, "Have a beer; it will calm you down." I had never taken a sip of alcohol on Academy grounds, picturing Rev. Threadgill and hearing his stern warnings, and, God knew, I had broken enough rules already.

Good began to ask questions, lots of questions. At first, I told him flat out that we were not allowed to speak with reporters, and that all questions should be addressed to the SCOPE project leaders. He said not to worry, that I wouldn't be quoted, and that this was just "deep background." My doubts were clouded by the shock of seeing that burned cross—the hated symbol of the KKK I had come to fight—the beer, and, most of all, the need to talk to someone outside the movement. Maybe he could understand what I couldn't make sense of myself.

A few days after Blackwell's call, John Golden told me that a certified letter was waiting for me at the post office. I dreaded going there because the all-white clerks stared at my coworkers and me in open hatred, fumbled for our mail, and often made us return two or three times by claiming that we had no mail. Only half of the letters and packages people sent reached me. While I clutched my driver's license identification in my sweaty hand, John drove slowly around the block so I could jump in the car as soon as I finished my business inside.

When I opened the letter, I found my parents' check for more money than they had ever given me in my life: $200 to fly home immediately. Also enclosed was the *Washington Post* article, which had been reprinted in the *San Francisco Chronicle*. The sentence about walking roads alone and sleeping in Negro homes underlined twice. Even though I was in pain and on the edge of a nervous breakdown, I returned to the Academy and wrote a short note saying that I could not leave now and would not leave without my friends. I enclosed the torn-up check and put it in the outgoing mail pile at the entrance to the dormitory. I didn't want to abandon my commitment to the project, and I didn't want to be separated from Bob.

Years later when I found both the *San Francisco Chronicle* and the *Washington Post* articles, I was even more grateful to Blackwell for letting me stay when I read the rest of my statement: "'My happiest days are working out there,' she says, 'But there is a lot of frustration with SCOPE. They spend too much time talking about organizing and there isn't enough action. I mean, the people here want to demonstration [*sic*] against police brutality but SCOPE leaders hold them back.'"[2]

This painful media lesson stayed with me the rest of my life. Every activist's life is lived on the record. If you don't want it published, don't say it. Not that I have lived up to that ideal personally, but from then on when I was involved in political or social justice action, I tried to stick to sound bites that could be on the front page of any paper or make no comment.

Stay or Go?

As I headed out to Boiling Springs for what could be my last time, the old Negro spiritual "This May Be the Last Time" kept playing in my mind: "May be the last time we stay together. May be the last time we fellowship together. May be the last time, I don't know."

Excerpts from a letter to friends and supporters, July 1965:
   I got up at 5:30 a.m. Tuesday and headed out for Boiling Springs. We had to get the folks to register these next five days because we won't be given any more days until August. I walked over 10 miles of cow pasture with a local Negro (James Robinson) and spoke with people about voter registration. That evening we had a student mass meeting and organized the kids to canvass the area the next day. We were quite successful in Boiling Springs and sent 5 carloads of folks to Camden the next day.

I canvassed like always, but I began telling people I'd worked with that we might be leaving soon. The Voting Rights Act that should bring northern federal examiners had finally made it through Congress, and President Johnson was supposed to sign it any day. Since harassment of locals was nonstop, a lot of folks thought it was better to wait it out. After the Voting Rights Act, there would be registration every day and no literacy tests. Due to this expectation, it became harder and harder to register folks before the law went into effect.

We had made an impact. Under a constant barrage of hostility and harassment, we had registered over five hundred people, just like thousands of other local, SCOPE, and SNCC teams in dozens of counties that last Freedom Summer. It was hard to argue with the logic of waiting to be protected while registering, so we focused on education, worked with local leaders to prepare folks for what the forms would look like, and taught handwriting to those who wanted to learn to sign their own names even though now their "X" would be accepted. Sometimes I just sat and talked with folks and told them how proud I was of them and how sorry I was to leave.

As we moved closer to August 6, the date that the 1965 VRA was supposed to pass into law, we were instructed to sign up voters who were ready, willing, and able to register the first day. Our leaders trained people who might be willing to file lawsuits and people willing to document the illegal tactics of the voting registrar by testing the system on registration days. Pushing back, the white establishment believed that its job was to destroy the movement and to terrorize black folks so that they would not vote even when they had additional legal tools to back their rights.

Dan Harrell took Bob aside and asked him to stay on staff. Then he asked me if I'd stay. We had told everyone that we were engaged and that we were a team. If Bob stayed, I would. I hadn't seriously considered that possibility until now. I wasn't sure it was a good idea because we had no money and no place to live, no place to be together. Besides, I was scared and in pain, but still, I was torn. I liked belonging, and I liked making a difference. But, I wondered, were we really helping anymore? Would it do any good to stay? I missed my friends in San Francisco and my little sisters back home. I wanted to finish my education, get married to Bob, maybe have children, and for sure I wanted to live the rest of my life with indoor plumbing. Bob and I agonized over whether we should stay after the SCOPE project ended. I was against it, but wanted to be together so I left the decision up to him.

On the Run—Possum Bend

How Major, Dan, and local leaders like Rev. Threadgill and Jesse Brooks stayed on top of what was going to happen, I did not know. Only now can I appreciate what a pain it was for them to have to worry about us while trying to get their own work done and keep themselves alive. We owe our lives to them.

During our last few weeks in Wilcox, more than once we were woken up and taken to another place because word got out that they were after us. One rare night Bob and I were at the Academy together when someone pounded on my bedroom door and yelled for us to run downstairs into the car where Major was waiting with the engine running. We did as we were told without question or toothbrushes. Major was more tense than usual as he drove us to a place way out in Possum Bend. We didn't know the sleepy, scared men who got out of two beds and let Bob and me take their places in hot, wet sheets. We told Major that we didn't want to be apart, so for the appearance of decency, we made up an improbable story that we were cousins from California who had promised our parents we wouldn't be separated. Major said he'd pick us up at a certain place on the road in the morning, and that we should canvass anyone we saw between now and then. "Tell them we got the vote; now you gots to register," Major reminded us.

In the morning, we found a pot with the dregs of lukewarm coffee. I looked on the shelves in the kitchen but they were bare. "These people are starving!" I moaned. "It's a damn crime, that's what it is, a crime I tell you." Bob paced the floor with half a cup of the old coffee. I bemoaned the fact that almost no federal aid programs like food commodities reached the people because white state officials prevented them from applying or they were too scared or too proud to apply, or they had applied and been told they didn't qualify.

"Just like everything down here. Man, wait 'til they start to vote; those crackers gonna regret their miserly ways," Bob replied.

Before we set out, I cleaned up what little there was in the kitchen and made up the beds although the linens were in dire need of a wash. We passed a few folks on the way and chatted them up. Several had gone in to Camden for the marches or at least seen the demonstrators. As we walked along the edge of the road to our planned meeting spot, I told Bob, "I already enrolled in school. I have roommates counting on me back in San Francisco. You could get reenrolled at the College of San Mateo, couldn't you? Don't you think we can do more to change things if we get degrees and jobs?" I asked.

"Actually, I would be enrolling for the first time," Bob responded, "Nat and I just took off after high school graduation and traveled for almost a year until I landed here. Just let me think, okay?" Then he added, "Don't pressure me. Aw, don't get all teary on me, please. We'll stay together, whatever happens; we're in this together, all right?"

I never let on to my parents that we were even considering staying on, and I ended my last personal letter to them with, "I never could have been the kind of person who could do this kind of thing if it wasn't for all of you."

College plans, friends and family, pain, and fatigue were enough reasons for me to be ready to leave as planned. But for Bob, the deal breaker came as a sudden shock. He showed up unexpectedly one afternoon and said he'd just talked to his friend Jerry Roche who was driving back from National Guard training and could meet us in Alexandria, Louisiana, and drive us home in his '56 Mercury. We could stop at some places along the way, like New Orleans and the Grand Canyon. I asked Bob, "Why the sudden change of heart?"

He tried not to tear up as he paced around telling me what happened. "Damn! I feel like I am the hardest working person out here, at least the hardest working white guy," he said. "You know I hit the ground running every morning and never stop 'til dark. You know 'cuz you were with me some days and lots of times I didn't get to see you for a week. Well, this week I was back in Pine Apple. I walked all day for two days getting the biggest crowd ever to their Sunday night mass meeting. I wasn't going to speak or anything, just organizing. Major Johns talked real plain about the need to keep going, keep the pressure up.

"Somewhere near the end of the meeting, Eric Jones—you know from SNCC?—I never saw it coming. We had just heard all this love and stuff from Major Johns. Then Eric steps up to the altar and starts with something like 'White folks are the cause of all our problems. We gotta get out from under the foot of honkys. We gotta get these whiteys outta here now or we're never gonna be real men.'

"He didn't say civil rights workers specific, but I knew he meant me. You know I've been around Stokely and he never said anything to my face. All of a sudden I realized it was like we read in that *Wretched of the Earth* book; there's no place for us here. It's time to pack."

I argued that this was just one guy, who was likely jealous that Bob got so much praise from the adults and attention from the girls. But I didn't protest too much because I was ready to leave. We told Major and Dan, who said that it most likely was a good decision for us, although they were sorry to see a good worker like Bob go. Dan and Juanita stopped by with hugs, promises to come see us, and to make sure we knew that we were welcome back anytime. John Golden planned to go home to visit his wife, although he would return to work briefly in the fall.

Somewhere along the line the other white students had already left, but we were so absorbed in our own drama that we hadn't really noticed. Bob called Chuck, who said we should go ahead; he needed a few more weeks before moving to take care of some things in Selma, but that he would come get us from Camden.

After much deliberation, our actual departure took place quickly. I wrote a note to my host families, the Robinsons and Lawsons in Boiling Springs. When John Golden drove us out to Coy to say good-bye to Ethel and her parents, I felt like we were leaving them too soon, although Jesse Brooks was upbeat as usual about the future of black voters in the county. He said that he planned to run for tax assessor, a position held for years by a notoriously corrupt white man.

When Chuck came in the now-repaired Valiant to take us back to Selma so we could catch a bus to Louisiana, I was in a kind of haze and Bob seemed depressed. Chuck kept up a lively conversation, recounting all our adventures and misadventures, laughing and waving his hands like he always did.

In the backseat, I stared out the window at the tree-lined highway and red earth embankment, wondering if I would ever see this place or these people again. I hoped and prayed that we had done more good than harm for the freedom fighters of Wilcox County.

In Selma, Chuck and Jan told us they definitely would be coming out to the West Coast in a few weeks, and we were glad about that. It would feel strange to lose every connection with the movement all at once. We shared a final meal of fried catfish sandwiches and Pepsi at Walker's Café on Washington Street, the same café where Rev. Reeb had eaten his last meal before being murdered. We didn't dwell on that fact. "I tell you one thing I won't miss," I said spitting out the bones, "back home we clean our fish before we cook them."

We were too low on cash to stay at the Torch Motel so Chuck took us to the cheapest, most run-down motel in Selma, the Thunderbird. He took Bob's cash and paid for the room so they wouldn't see that we were white; he even registered us under a fake name. We hugged, Chuck said they'd be seeing us in California in a few weeks, and then we watched him drive away. The room was tiny, dingy, and smelled of stale cigarettes and dubious linens. The bedspread was already wrinkled and there was a machine to put quarters in to make the bed vibrate for twenty minutes. Unfamiliar grating music came through a metal box that didn't have any dials or way to turn it off. Bob tried to unplug it, but finally he tied one of the pillows over the speaker with his belt to muffle the sound.

I just stood there in shock. "My God, this is just like Dante's Inferno! This is pure Hell!"

"Why do you always have to be so dramatic?" Bob complained.

"I am not being dramatic. I am being literary!" I replied.

He wanted to make love, but I was too grossed out. He fell asleep. I tossed and turned and tried not to listen to groans from adjacent rooms. I must have fallen asleep at some point. Next thing I knew someone from the motel was knocking on the door saying, "Get up. Get out now. You gots to go, right now!"

Bob said he guessed this was the kind of place usually rented by the hour and our hours must be up. Our Trailways bus for Alexandria wasn't leaving until 3:00 P.M. What were we supposed to do until then? First we had some breakfast at Walkers Café. This was our first time being just two white people in the café together, and the service didn't seem as friendly as when we'd been with Chuck and other black kids.

Bob cleared his throat and said, "I have some business I have to take care of. You can't come with me." He looked away as he told me he had to say good-bye to a young lady he'd met during the march, someone he liked a lot but she was too young, only sixteen. He had stayed with her family, the Webbs, and had been warned to stay away from the young girl. He thought he might have hurt her feelings, and he wanted to tell her what a privilege it had been to meet her. He also wanted to say good-bye to the rest of the Webb family, including Sheyann, who at age eight had been one of the youngest of the many young children active in Selma demonstrations.

I didn't know anyone in Selma except Chuck and Jan, and we had already said good-bye. As a white girl alone, I wasn't sure if it was safe for me to walk around inside the projects, and I sure as hell wasn't going to "pretend to be white" and walk around downtown. So I sat in the café sipping coffee and furiously smoking cigarettes, writing in the last pages of my notebook for as long as I could. More than an hour later, Bob returned with red eyes, and we walked in silence over to the bus station.

As we waited at the station, I held out as long as I could and then had to decide between using the filthy "Colored Only" or the clean "Whites Only" restroom. Bob said, "You have to go back to bein' white, at some point. We don't have anyone to bail us out anymore. You can do it. Besides, Joyce—look in the mirror when you get in there—you really are white, you know." The truth hurt. After ten weeks in the movement, I felt my heart and soul were black, even if my skin was still pale.

I compiled the notes for my last letter, used my last stamp, and sent them to Jeanne Searight with a personal thank you to her for typing and maintaining this record of my unbelievable summer. I told her that I looked forward to being her roommate and to telling everyone at the Ecumenical House what we'd seen and done. The following letter was written several days before we left, but is the last one I have.

Excerpt from a July 1965 letter:
Dear Friends and Family,

Things are more peaceful now in Wilcox County . . . at least on the surface. A recent meeting of the local Klan drew a crowd of 2,000 according to Camden's Mayor Albritton, but there haven't been any more incidents that we are aware of. Since there are only two more days of registration this summer the white folks are not too worried anymore. We haven't come anywhere near our hopes of registering thousands of Negroes. About 500 have been actually registered in Wilcox this summer. The SCOPE people (both White and Negro) have been hampered by local people and by administrative conflicts. But more than anything they were hampered by you. By all of you who didn't put pressure on Congress to pass the Voting Right Bill; by everyone who didn't write his Congressman, by everyone who didn't voice his opinion of this bill. If we had the bill to work under this summer we could have registered 100 persons a day, five days a week, all summer long. I'm sadly disappointed in the American people for letting such a vital piece of legislation sit around in Congress at such an important time.

Now, not all the Negroes are with the Movement . . . obviously or we would have cleaned up this mess years ago. There are those who for a pack of cigarettes will give Mr. Charlie a list of everyone in the Movement so he can fire them, and whip them, and try to hold them back.

But I don't think Mr. Charlie—symbol of the white man—is going to keep folks down. I don't think Uncle Tom—symbol of the humble, scared Negro—is going to help them down. The people who are fighting for their freedom value it above their lives. And I'll bet you the devotion you'll find here to freedom far exceeds any you'll find among our troops in Viet Nam. We are a nonviolent army, marching steadily towards one goal—freedom NOW!

Within a week or so, I'll be heading back to California, probably taking some time to tour part of the good old U.S.A. It's been a strange, exciting, terrible and wonderful summer for me. I hope I can accurately relate more of our experiences when I see you all again.

Once again, I want to express my deep gratitude for your letters, concern, and contributions. . . . See you in California!"

The bus pulled up. We boarded along with the other white passengers and sat in the middle seats. Then the black passengers boarded and still went to the back even though that issue had been legally resolved years ago as a result of the work of the Freedom Riders. Bob and I looked at each other; without a word we got up and went to sit in the first seat in front of the self-designated black section.

"What're they gonna do, kick us off the bus? Shoot us?" Bob grinned and put his hand on my knee. "Say good-bye to Selma, sweetheart; it's all over now."

Tears welled up as I looked through the grimy window, wishing there was a brass band, waving hands, any sign that we'd been part of some kind of progress. There were only old newspapers blowing around the dusty parking lot.

II
Looking Back, Moving Forward: Stories of the Freedom Fighters

14

The Intervening Years

If you just put your hand in mine,
We're gonna leave all our troubles behind.
Keep on walkin', don't look back. (Don't look back.)
(The past is behind you, let nothing remind you.)

"Don't Look Back," Smokey Robinson and Ronald White

Bob and I were miserable on the long bus ride from Selma to Louisiana, where we met up with Bob's buddy Jerry Roche. We held our breath when we had to change buses inside the state of Mississippi, and we spoke as little as possible to anyone else and to each other only in whispers. After a restless night in a cheap hotel in Alexandria, we convinced Jerry to take a long side trip to a weathered cabin in the middle of cornfields outside New Orleans where Benet Luchion, the SCLC staff member who had saved me from attack at the Atlanta SCOPE orientation, had family. Benet wanted us to tell his folks that he was still working with SCLC and in daily danger but still alive. Sadly, no one was home. We penciled a note and hung it on a nail on the unpainted door: "Benet sends love. He is safe in Atlanta, Friends of Freedom."

In New Orleans we tried to party, but the poverty, segregation, and excessive alcohol consumption depressed me. Conflict over leaving instead of staying to help Dan Harrell with community organizing consumed Bob. It was far from the guys' trip that Jerry and Bob had originally planned. Adding to my physical discomfort was the pain of leaving our Wilcox County friends behind, knowing we hadn't accomplished all that we set out to do. I wondered whether things would really change now that the 1965 Voting Rights Act finally passed, and I worried that the movement might not be successful without outside civil rights workers.

When we returned to San Francisco, Bob and I announced our engagement. His family objected on the grounds of our youth and my rural background. When we went up to the country to see my folks, my mother searched my suitcase, found my birth control pills, and told my father. He shouted that Bob had turned me into a whore and told both of us to get out of his house. For several years afterward, my parents prevented me from spending time alone with my younger sisters.

Apparently there had been dissension about my civil rights work even in my mother's liberal family. While I was still in Alabama, there had been some furor at a family reunion when she read my letter about my arrest to our relatives. According to my cousin Sheri, the letter created so much dissension that the reunion ended early. Two uncles thought what I was doing was terrible and that blacks and whites had their respective positions and should keep them. My aunts, especially Ruth and Dorothea, were proud of what I was doing. Sheri said that my mother seemed proud, but that my father seemed ambivalent.

Decades later, my cousin Bob Brookover told me that while I was in the South, his mother hitchhiked to Oakland to attend a Black Panther meeting. Soon after, he came home to San Francisco to find a small gathering of her Women's International League for Peace and Freedom (WILPF) friends and men with big Afros discussing how whites could support the Panthers. One of the men was Huey Newton, who along with others cofounded the Black Panther Party for Self Defense in Oakland in 1966. Learning this story so many years after the fact brought back sadness that my parents' rejection resulted in me not seeking out my amazing aunt Ruth and sharing our stories of that summer. Before she died at age ninety-seven in 2012, Cousin Bob told her how much she influenced me.

When we first returned, my Bob enrolled at the College of San Mateo, and I continued at San Francisco State; we lived separately. We spent weekends together when we could and were forced to be intimate in secret since even in the mid-1960s my roommates did not approve of premarital sex. After our extraordinary experiences in Wilcox County we tried to find a new normal. But we couldn't adjust. I suffered from the inability to concentrate on my studies, nightmares, and low back pain caused by the car accident. It was so painful to sit that I stood during my classes.

When I stopped by the SNCC office on campus, they told me that Friends of SNCC was defunct and that even though I was a member in Alabama, northern SNCC was now for blacks only. I gave talks at a few churches and at the Ecumenical House, some solo and some with Bob. We attempted to explain to our mostly youth audiences why the Voting Rights Act was important but that its passage didn't mean that black people were going to gain equality and access to power overnight. We raised a little money and sent it to SCLC. My letter to the Robinsons and Lawsons in Boiling Springs was returned marked undeliverable. Although I wrote promising to return to Wilcox the following summer, Bob believed that the time for whites in the movement was over, and I reluctantly agreed. It would be more than four decades before I returned to search for these brave families. Bob was sickened

by the fact that Jerry, who drove us cross-country, had to report for National
Guard duty following the Watts uprising in Southern California. We understood the outrage that was tearing that nearly all-black community apart
and believed that the National Guard and police were just making it worse.

In San Francisco, my activist friends focused either on black power or ending the war in Vietnam. It was painful to observe the growing split between
white people in the peace movement and people of color who served dispro-
portionately in the military. There didn't seem to be anyone who wanted to
hear about voter registration or ongoing racism in the South. My college
roommates talked about boyfriends, food, and their courses. They didn't
ask about my summer, even though they had read the letters I wrote. After a few months, I stopped talking about my time in Wilcox County too.

Chuck Bonner and Jan Baker arrived in California a few weeks after Bob
and I returned. I had hoped their arrival meant we four could find some
kind of West Coast movement to get involved with together but that didn't
happen. Despite never having lived in San Francisco before, Chuck and Jan
set up a household in the Haight-Ashbury district, found jobs, enrolled in
school, made friends, and immersed themselves in the flowering hippie culture while quickly establishing ties with Black Panther organizers in Oakland. Their apartment became a crash pad for young civil rights workers
leaving Selma. Their postmovement adjustment appeared to be far smoother
than ours. As an interracial couple, it seemed to me they were living the
dream, but Bob and I were having a hard time with our relationship and
with me being in constant pain.

Despite the excellent physical therapy provided on campus, surgery was
recommended to remove my broken coccyx, which I had done over the winter break. My parents were so upset that I was no longer a virgin that they
didn't even come visit me in the hospital. I didn't have health insurance, so
Bob paid for part of the bill with some of his college money and Mt. Zion
Hospital wrote off the rest in exchange for my letting an entire class of medical students watch the surgery from a glassed-in gallery over the operating
room. They thought I was some kind of hero because I had been injured in
the Civil Rights Movement. I felt like I was getting credit I didn't deserve,
but I needed the subsidy so I guiltily encouraged their assumptions. The operation did not go well. Postsurgical complications and cortisone injection
treatments led to my near incapacitation. The medical doctors abandoned
me to a psychiatrist. I began to fall apart; nothing seemed to help my pain.

The following year, when I was between roommates and apartments for
a few weeks, I slept on the window seat at Chuck and Jan's Parnassus Street
apartment. While I was there, one of their Selma visitors stole my silver

SNCC medallion that meant so much to me. It seemed like every piece of evidence that I had been a civil rights worker was disappearing. Among ourselves we didn't talk about the Selma or Wilcox movements. Chuck and Jan were moving forward, creating a new life for themselves. Bob and I stayed stuck in our summer experience for a while longer, not talking about it, but not moving forward either.

The pressure on Bob from his family to break free of me, finish college, and pursue a profession was intense. I clung to him like the drowning woman I felt myself becoming. Decades later, doctors confirmed that the large doses of steroids injected into my spine could have contributed to anxiety and depression from which I suffered. We were both shell-shocked but didn't have a word for the strange sense of dislocation we both felt. Nothing seemed as real as our summer in the South.

The emotional gap that opened up on our long car trip home widened until neither of us could see our way across the divide. Bob could have had free rent in his mother and stepfather's luxurious Atherton home, but he wanted to identify as one of the people, so he moved into a funky apartment with some guys in San Mateo who had a band called the Wildflowers. Soon he dropped out of school and began working in an antipoverty program in Oakland with John Golden, who had returned from Wilcox shortly after we had.

Meanwhile, my parents refused to help me and I didn't want to depend on Bob, so I tried to find a part-time job. Bob's stepmother, Marge, was vice president of Bank of America in San Francisco; she told me she would pull my application through if I applied for a job there. I was shocked when she informed me that I could not be hired due to my criminal record: I had convictions for felony conspiracy to boycott and felony trespassing in Alabama. No formal charges were filed or hearing dates set that I knew of when I was in Camden, but when I returned to California, more than one employer told me that I was blacklisted. Macy's, a large department store, told me that I had a record of felony trespass, presumably for staying at Camden Academy.

I struggled to create a new life without school, family support, or a job. The strong Christian faith that propelled me into the movement had been shaken. I began to question everything and everyone, and most dangerously, myself. Without some degree of self-confidence, it was nearly impossible to make good decisions. To his everlasting credit, Bob hung in with me for a year and a half until I foolishly broke up with him by striking up a brief new relationship with someone older, someone I thought was more sophisticated. Bob was a constant reminder of the mental turmoil I wanted to escape.

Even after Bob and I split, Chuck and Jan continued to be my friends, but I was disturbed that they seemed to believe that revolution was going to bring change more rapidly than peaceful protest. At the same time, doubts gnawed at me too. Even after the 1965 Voting Rights Act passed, economic and historic disparities prevented the fulfillment of true equality. We continued to hear of kids jailed, beaten, and tear gassed during protests not only in the South but also in cities across the country. Over the next decade, state troopers shot and killed both black and white students on college campuses at Jackson State, Kent State, and elsewhere.

Even though I seldom attended class, I reenrolled in college in the fall semester of 1966 in order to secure a part-time job at an inner city Boys Club on Page Street as a recreation director. The Boys Club members were 85 percent African American while we staff were 99 percent white. I led art projects and cooking experiments for the five- to seven-year-old boys, calmed them when a raccoon got in their tent on a campout, and tried to protect them from the bigger boys at the club. I threw myself into work beyond my job description by reading to them, comforting them when they had difficulties at home, and talking with their parents about their special interests.

A couple of incidents at the Boys Club hit me with particular force. A young boy whose family I had visited drowned in the crowded indoor pool. His family relied on the club to watch over their boys while they worked multiple jobs. The lame excuse of the swim coach who served as lifeguard was: "He was the same color as the pool drain so we didn't see him right away." I was furious, but the director shrugged his shoulders in acceptance. I left early in shocked silence. None of the staff was invited to the funeral, and no one spoke about it after the first day. Soon after that tragic event, while I was walking home after work around sunset, I inadvertently walked in between two groups of teens with knives drawn, ready to fight. As the two groups moved closer in the dim light, one young man called out, "That's Joyce from the Club," and they moved apart to let me pass.

These events were common for the times, and it slowly sunk in that I had blinders on when I left San Francisco thinking that racial inequity was a southern problem; it was everywhere, every day. I began to recognize institutionalized racism, sexism, and homophobia in government and businesses. Systemic bias wasn't limited to the Deep South; it was only more obvious there. I wasn't aware of a movement in San Francisco that made sense to me. There didn't seem to be any way to wrap my arms around subtle California bias, so I just wrapped them around individual kids.

The Boys Club position was government subsidized, paid minimum wage, and required that I be enrolled in college. When my new boyfriend and I split up and I needed to pay rent again, I dropped out of school and took a full-time job, for which I was grossly underqualified but well paid, as secretary at a unionized machine shop on Fulton Street.

In my search for not only a new lifestyle but also an entirely new life, I bleached my hair blond and began to wear the minidresses and boots with net stockings that were in style at the time. I pulled my hair up in a French twist for work and let it down on weekends. I wrote poetry for hours in the I Thou Coffee House on Haight Street and danced with hippies in Golden Gate Park.

As I disconnected from activism in San Francisco, the struggle for black self-determination continued unabated throughout the South. The influx of new voters did little to stem the tide of racist violence. The murder of civil rights workers after we left deeply affected some of the people I had been closest to. On August 20, Rev. Jonathan Daniels, a fifty-four-year-old white Episcopal seminary student from Massachusetts was shot and killed by Tom Coleman, a white deputy sheriff in Haneyville, Alabama, just forty-nine miles from Camden. Daniels had participated in civil rights demonstrations in April 1965 in downtown Camden, where he and his family were tear gassed.[1] Shortly before his murder, he had been released from custody in the city jail along with others in Lowndes County. On the day of his death, he was simply walking out of a store with another white priest and SNCC members Jimmy Rogers, Ruby Sales, Joyce Stokes, and Gloria House, who had just been released from jail also. Despite witnesses, the murderer was acquitted.[2]

A few months later, on January 4, 1966, in Tuskegee, located 116 miles from Camden, Tuskegee Institute student and civil rights activist Samuel "Sammy" Younge Jr., a military veteran, was shot for trying to use a whites-only bathroom behind a gas station. Dan and Juanita Harrell were former Tuskegee Institute students and Dan had spent summers with his grandparents in nearby Union City, so Younge's death must have been particularly disturbing to the activist couple. A subsequent not-guilty verdict delivered by an all-white jury resulted in a student demonstration in the streets of Tuskegee.

Only three weeks after Younge's murder, on January 23, 1966, the Camden community was shaken to its roots by a slaying in the grassy parking lot at Antioch Baptist Church. After a funeral and before a mass meeting planned by Dan Harrell and Rev. Frank Smith, with the Wilcox County SCLC, a white farmer deliberately bumped into thirty-two-year-old David Colston's car.[3] When Colston got out to complain, Jim Reaves shot him in the head in front of his family and dozens of community members coming out of the church. A rapidly organized protest march the next day was met with silence from the police who, perhaps for once, feared the crowd. Dr. King, whose life was constantly threatened, came quickly and quietly to comfort the family and Camden community members and to encourage them to remain nonviolent as the struggle continued.[4] Despite numerous witnesses, Reaves was not charged.

It would be decades before I learned of the deaths of these and other civil rights martyrs who were mourned by my former comrades, but I shared the shock and grief of the entire world when Martin Luther King Jr. was assassinated in Memphis on April 4, 1968. By this time I had lost touch with Chuck and Jan. Feeling isolated from the thousands of mourners elsewhere in the city, I wore a black armband to work, but my boss at the machine shop told me to take it off. Over lunch I had a long talk with the mailman about how upset we both were that we had to work that tragic day. While hundreds of thousands of people mourned Dr. King's passing peacefully, pockets of riots made worse by overreaction from police broke out in major cities within days, including Baltimore; Washington, DC; Memphis; and even my own San Francisco—the capital of peace and love. Young, nervous, mostly white National Guardsmen enforced curfew in the Haight-Ashbury, where I lived. I feared the armed men, but I didn't identify with the mostly white protestors either.

Less than two months later, on June 6, former attorney general and presidential candidate Robert F. Kennedy, who many credit for arm twisting southern officials into complying with some federal antidiscrimination laws, was murdered in Los Angeles. We activists thought that both Bobby Kennedy and his brother, John, who was murdered while president in 1963, had dragged their feet on civil rights policy. But in the black community, they became heroes. When I returned decades later, I learned that most African American households in Wilcox County had a poster tacked on their walls with photos of King and the two Kennedy brothers. Faces of the three murdered men and the words "Freedom Fighters" were featured on the back of paper fans used in the hot, humid churches. Beyond the tragedy of the curtailed lives of these young leaders was the sense that if people as privileged as the Kennedys and as famous as Dr. King were not safe from political assassination, how could a sharecropper in rural Alabama expect safety at the voting booth?

In spite of the unrelenting violence, the fight for fair elections, school equality, decent jobs, farm loans, and economic security continued in Wilcox County. Long after the passage of the 1965 Voting Rights Act, activists continued to be fired from jobs and put off of tenant farms for registering to vote and for organizing others to register. Activist teachers were fired, losing some of the most respected and best paying positions available to them at that time. Until 1973, Wilcox County defied federal mandates to integrate public schools through a series of countersuits, fully backed by the state of Alabama.[5] When all appeals were finally exhausted, rather than integrating the schools by assigning white teachers or students to the African American schools, or allowing black students to attend white schools, the county board of education closed and then literally destroyed most of the historically black schools in the county. Even with a clear majority of new voters registered by spring of 1966, it wasn't until 1978 that the first black officials were elected to county offices. Intimidation, death threats, attacks, and murders didn't end with acts of Congress. Against constant harassment and white economic advantage, the courageous freedom fighters of Wilcox County pursued the nonviolent battle on every front—political, legal, educational, and economic.

The effort that had begun in the late 1950s to bring information, organizing tools, fresh bodies, and strategies to the long-standing, ever-growing Wilcox County freedom fight continued through the mid-1970s. Along with field workers recruited by SNCC, SCLC, and CORE, national organizations including the NAACP and the American Civil Liberties Union (ACLU) filed complaints with the federal Department of Justice on behalf of the beleaguered citizens. Counsel for these national organizations worked closely with federal authorities. Local residents initiated complaints of attacks and threats by calling the Department of Justice in Montgomery directly. They knew there was no point in complaining to the all-white local authorities.

In spite of the risk of harm—even death—that civil rights organizers faced, small "Freedom Schools" sprang up all over the South, many organized by SNCC. In Wilcox County, locals who had been trained by SCLC Citizenship Education Project (CEP) staff established most of these schools. The CEP continued to increase literacy and political education among black Alabamians. In the spring of 1966, SCLC's Septima Clark, Dorothy Cotton, and Anelle Ponder came to Millers Ferry, Mission Prairie, and Anniemanie schools in Wilcox County to teach civil rights history, literacy, and voter education through the CEP. Among others, teacher Albert Gordon and community activists Rosetta Anderson and Virginia Boykin Burrell received training from SCLC and led literacy classes around the county.[6]

"Big Lester" Hankerson and James Orange, two of SCLC's most effective grassroots organizers from the Alabama SCOPE staff, were among several civil rights leaders who visited Camden to teach nonviolent resistance strategies and to lend support to ongoing demonstrations. Additional civil rights workers, both SNCC and SCLC, came to work in Wilcox over the next few years, although SNCC concentrated their efforts in adjacent Lowndes County and in Mississippi. White Volunteers in Service to America (VISTA) workers came to teach school and stayed longer, some of them left lasting memories with the families whose children they taught and embraced. Some families believed that self-determination was essential and were concerned about northerners influencing their children by their urban talk and dress. After decades of independence (and neglect) by national organizations and the federal government, little Wilcox County became a centrifuge of well-intentioned, impassioned young people with different agendas, philosophies, and life experiences.[7]

Until the spring of 1965, the federal government had no record of any registered black voters in Wilcox County, despite a more than 70 percent majority and repeated legal appeals by voter applicants. In the spring of 1965, prior to the SCOPE project, twenty-nine men from Gees Bend who marched on the courthouse succeeded in completing registration applications, and by May the FBI reported a total of thirty-seven "Negro" voters. During our project we reported registration of five hundred new voters to the SCLC office in Atlanta. By October of 1965, Hosea Williams credited SCOPE with registration of 1,237 out of an SCLC total of 3,627 in Wilcox County. SCLC's work in Alabama netted a total of 49,372 new voters between April and October of 1965. Some of these registrants may have subsequently been purged from the voter rolls, a tactic used throughout Alabama to prevent new registrants from voting.[8]

Despite continued obstructionist tactics, on May 3, 1966, the new registrants were able to vote for the first time in a primary election with state and local candidates on the ballot. Newly created districts laid the groundwork for the eventual ability to carry primarily African American communities in areas such as Gees Bend and Coy. Candidates ran together on the People's Choice Platform and campaigned vigorously. Walter J. Calhoun ran for county sheriff against Lummie Jenkins, James Robinson ran for county tax assessor, James Perryman for commissioner in District 3, and Donnie V. Irby for commissioner in District 1. Lonnie L. Brown, the intrepid Gees Bend preacher and insurance agent, ran for state senator. For the first time, federal observers protected and assisted black voters at the polls, along with local leaders and civil rights field workers. Despite the high turnout of new voters, all of the first candidates were defeated.

By October 31, 1967, there were 3,780 registered "non-white" (the term used in the federal report) voters in Wilcox County[9] and a total of 155,695 new black voters registered in the state of Alabama, indicating that the majority who intended to register did so as quickly as possible after passage of the 1965 VRA.[10] An unintended side effect of getting out the African American vote was increased white voter participation. US Department of Justice statistics record 2,974 white registered voters in Wilcox County in 1960 and 3,679 in 1967.[11] Although black voters outnumbered whites and civil rights organizers continued to work the county, ongoing threats and bribes from white land and business owners, who still controlled employment and housing opportunities, meant they also controlled the outcome of elections. In a county historically plagued by official corruption, no one believed that fair elections would come to the region anytime soon.

For many years, despite diligent efforts and superior numbers of black voters, the traditional good old boys of white Wilcox County continued to be elected to county office. A notable exception is credited to SNCC, which organized a targeted campaign to get locals elected to the important county agricultural committees responsible for applying for and distributing federal farm subsidies. Although denied seats on the powerful Wilcox County Agricultural Stabilization Conservation Service Committee, in 1967 ten black farmers were elected to the Community Committee, which served as an advisory group. For the first time these farmers had an official voice.[12]

As the fight for fair elections continued, reprisals against activist educators and the destruction of historically black schools in Wilcox County led to years of student protests and limited educational opportunity. With the full support of Governor George Wallace and the Alabama state legislature, the Wilcox County Board of Education continued its battle against school integration long after all legal appeals against the federal ruling requiring equal and integrated education had been exhausted. A federal court order sought by the Department of Justice in November of 1965 and issued in August 1966 mandated the integration of Wilcox County schools. But court orders did not change the minds of the all-white school board or the minority white community they represented; they only stepped up their strong-arm tactics.

Among the early wave of teachers fired shortly after the passage of the 1965 VRA were respected civil rights leaders Rev. Frank Smith, Rev. Thomas Threadgill, and his wife, Mildred Threadgill. Movement teachers continued to be harassed and were blacklisted from other employment. The official pretext for the firings was that the county office of education was not receiving enough daily attendance funds from the state to justify the number of teachers, since most of the students were out demonstrating. That all the teachers fired were active in the movement or married to activists clearly was not a coincidence. As late as 1975, wrongful discharge suits were brought to federal courts by teachers who were fired for participating in school de-segregation protests in Wilcox County.[13]

Students from Camden Academy continued to demonstrate from 1965 until the school was closed in 1973. Many students missed the majority of their classes as they continued to protest the segregated school system, pick-eted stores that wouldn't hire their parents, and drew attention to illegal practices that prevented qualified black candidates from winning elections. Local police confronted student activists with guns and tear gas, and even young teens were sentenced to thirty days at the county prison farm. There were only a few years, from 1968 to 1971, when a handful of black students enrolled in existing white schools in an attempt to integrate. These brave students were mistreated, especially at Wilcox High School.

The final assault on the students and teachers came when the federal court order to integrate was finally enforced in 1973. In retaliation, the county board of education closed all of the black mission schools, took the proper-ties by inverse condemnation, declared them integrated public schools, and then closed them. They then built fewer, consolidated public schools they had no intention of integrating. Camden Academy, the pride of the black community, was destroyed—the buildings actually torn down.[14]

Historically important Snow Hill Institute, founded in 1893 to provide education and vocational training to former slaves, had become a public school in 1924 and was also forced to close under orders to desegregate. The board of education could have repaired and integrated Snow Hill but chose instead to build a new elementary-middle school in Pine Apple and consolidate the entire county into one high school, Central High. The new schools ostensibly were built to consolidate the existing segregated schools, but whites refused to attend the new schools, so all public schools became entirely African American, which they are to this day.[15]

On another battlefront, the Harrells continued to bring federal programs to Wilcox County. They had opened one of the very first Head Start pro-grams in the United States during the summer of 1965. This and other proj-ects helped fulfill SCLC's mission to "organize communities around issues of political disfranchisement, educational deprivation and poverty."[16]

By January 1966, SCLC stopped paying all SCOPE Alabama staff, but Dan and Juanita Harrell stayed on in Coy where Dan guest preached and worked full time on his passion: African American economic community development. When activists lost jobs and were forced off of their rented or sharecropped land, Dan Harrell, Albert Gordon, Thomas L. Threadgill, and Rosetta Anderson of the Wilcox SCLC applied for and were granted funding by the new Office of Economic Opportunity to establish an antipoverty program intended to create jobs and co-ops for the displaced workers. Before the funds were received, Governor Wallace pelted the media and Washington with allegations that Wilcox was a hotbed of "Black Power" separatist activists who excluded white residents from their boards and funding applications. His outrageous tactics succeeded in delaying grant funding for months and the denial of a much-needed "self-help" housing grant to build housing and provide home loans for the newly homeless activists.[17] The irony of Governor Wallace accusing Wilcox County SCLC of being black separatists and extremists at the very time when the tactical and philosophical split between SCLC nonviolent activists and SNCC "by any means necessary" proponents was growing to the breaking point, was likely lost on the federal government. In reality, SCLC worked with federal agencies such as the Office of Economic Opportunity and continued to recruit integrated teams of civil rights workers based on a belief that true equality would best be achieved through integration with dominant culture institutions. As SNCC moved even more strongly in the direction of self-determination and self-defense, nonviolence and integration remained bedrock principles of SCLC.

After several years of application and effort, Wilcox County SCLC received federal antipoverty grants that provided housing for many displaced activists and employment for the Harrells, Threadgills, Smiths, and others.[18] Despite relentless obstruction by state and county officials, Dan Harrell managed to receive a grant from the Community Action division of the US Department of Agriculture to start a cooperative for one hundred cucumber, pea, and okra farmers who had been displaced from their tenant farms due to their registering to vote. The income from the co-op was supposed to provide capital for a cooperative housing project for those who had been evicted. Dan envisioned a farmers' credit union and also helped get some funding for cucumber pickle processing sheds in Gees Bend to complement the work of a small okra processing cooperative already in operation near Coy. Despite his unflagging commitment to documenting the poverty and discrimination the farmers faced, a change in officials at the Office of Economic Opportunity saw the collapse of Dan's fully expanded plan.[19]

Although the freedom fighters in Wilcox continued to face what often seemed like insurmountable obstacles after passage of the 1965 Voting Rights Act, they shifted their strategies whenever necessary to meet the resistance they faced throughout the 1960s and into the next decade. Voter registration efforts finally paid off in the 1978 elections. By 1979 Wilcox County elected its first three black officials—sheriff Prince Arnold, tax collector Jesse Brooks, and county commissioner Eddie Beverly. Additional black officials were elected in subsequent years, and eventually, the majority of officials in Wilcox County were of African American heritage.[20]

Far from news of Wilcox County, I struggled to relocate my place in the world and outside of my family. In 1969, I married poet David Gitin, whose father's family descended from a long line of Jewish rabbis. In my search for a new identity, a new life, and renewed faith, I began studying Judaism. At the same time, I changed my first name to Maria, the female lead in the play *West Side Story*. I felt kinship with the passion and idealism of the young romantic Puerto Rican woman. David's parents welcomed me into their family although they were horrified by my non-Jewish name choice and our hippie marriage in Golden Gate Park, to which I arrived barefoot with daisies in my hair. We worked in the post office and for Greyhound bus lines, wrote poetry, and constructed our own reality. David was a bohemian and an intellectual who had never been politically active. We didn't talk much about my time in the South.

I was a twenty-two-year-old newlywed when I began studying for conversion to Judaism with David's uncle, progressive Reform rabbi Joseph Gitin of San Jose. My impetus for conversion was partially fueled by disappointment with the church and its failure to continue to fight for civil rights, but my main motivation was to please my husband's parents. My own parents distanced themselves from me when I returned from the South changed beyond their ability to comprehend, and we never regained familial closeness. I wanted to belong, and I needed a spiritual center. I embraced the beautiful traditions of Friday night Shabbat dinner, the prayers, music, and High Holidays. Uncle Joe presented Reform Judaism as more progressive than the Congregational church of my childhood, with better food and music. In Judaism, there is no concept of individual salvation—it is all about community—and in Reform Judaism, that community especially includes the dispossessed and disadvantaged. It felt right, and I have kept the faith to this day.

In January 1972, David resumed graduate studies at the liberal University of Wisconsin. Soon after we arrived in Madison, an FBI agent contacted me. Two years earlier antiwar students had bombed the university's research building, killing a researcher and wounding three others. In a flat voice over the phone, the FBI agent said, "We know that you are here. We know you changed your name. This call is for your own security. We advise you to stay away from campus radicals." I hung up in shock and forced myself not to think about still being followed as if I were a terrorist instead of a student and poet. Our older poet friends, George and Mary Oppen, had fled to Mexico for twenty years after being stalked by the FBI for their membership in the

Communist Party. Memories of the HUAC films I had seen at San Francisco State still frightened me. While in the South, I learned that speaking out against the prevailing system could land anyone in jail. David thought it was best to take the threat seriously and to avoid even signing petitions that could be considered too liberal. At that time, oblivious to the women's movement, I took my cues from my husband and followed his suggestion.

It may have been coincidence, but around the same time, Gerald Marwell, one of the University of Wisconsin researchers conducting a longitudinal study of SCOPE volunteers, contacted me. The threatening tone of the FBI agent who had called kept me from responding to Marwell's follow-up study that was filled with questions about ideology and Communism.[21] Because I was paranoid about the FBI following me and because David shied away from politics, my Wisconsin political activities were limited to a few anti–Vietnam War marches and working on George McGovern's failed 1972 presidential campaign. It felt like too many people I didn't know knew where I was, even with my new name. After Richard Nixon won reelection, I was so discouraged about American politics that I didn't vote again until Jimmy Carter ran for president in 1976.

During the 1970s I focused on writing two books of poetry and a cookbook. As I explored my buried feelings in my journal, I wrote myself out of what had become a deeply troubled marriage and back into college. Fifteen years after I began at San Francisco State, I finally earned a bachelor's degree from Antioch University's West Coast studies program in the spring of 1979. In my early thirties I became what was then called a "reentry woman" just in time to embrace feminism.

I discovered an empowered community of women at the Monterey YWCA when my Antioch advisor, Kate Miller, helped me secure a government-subsidized position directing their domestic violence program. Within ten months, I became the executive director and led the founding of the first full-service residential shelter for battered women and their children in Monterey County, California. During my years with the YWCA, I used my SCLC community organizing training often. The national YWCA's "One Imperative" was "To eliminate racism wherever it exists and by any means necessary."[22] This was the very quote from Malcolm X that I had questioned. Now I embraced it as an empowerment tool rather than a call for bloodshed. We hired black, Asian, Latina, and lesbian staff. Now single, once again I felt part of a beloved community and experienced the joy of belonging to a powerful, life-changing movement.

After leaving the YWCA to become a development consultant to nonprofit organizations, one of the greatest joys of my professional life was co-leading diversity training with Charles R. Stephens of Atlanta. I first met Charles at the Center on Philanthropy in Indiana in 1995, where we shared frustration with how diversity was being addressed in our field. We quickly sketched out our Embracing Diversity training on napkins in the cafeteria. Charles shared his stories of the walkouts and sit-ins at Morehouse College in the 1950s. His actions prevented him from getting a job with the Atlanta police department but led to him being recruited by the Butler Street YMCA, a position that launched his rise to national leadership in the fund development profession. We copresented at national conferences and led diversity training across the United States for many years before his passing.

In 2004, I moved to Watsonville, Santa Cruz, California, where I became deeply involved in the predominantly Latino community and with many leaders who had been trained by César Chávez and Dolores Huerta during the United Farm Workers movement.[23] Once again I felt at home in a community where being white was not the norm. Young leaders taught me how to be a better ally as we canvassed precincts, marched in proimmigration protests, and registered new voters. I cofounded the revitalized Pajaro Valley César Chávez Democratic Club with Luis Alejo and served as an adult advisor to GirlzSpace, a program for Latina teens who had been denied opportunities. Within a few years, I met and married Samuel Torres Jr. His Puerto Rican family laughed at the romantic reason I had changed my name to Maria so long ago, but they enthusiastically embraced me as we began a new phase of life together, that of reflective and inquisitive elders.

15

Joyful Reunions

The light that shines is the light of love; lights the darkness from above.
It shines on me and it shines on you, and shows what the power of love
*   can do.*
I'm gonna shine my light both far and near, I'm gonna shine my light both
*   bright and clear.*
Where there's a dark corner in the land, I'm gonna let my little light shine.
*   "This Little Light of Mine," classic civil rights song adapted from gospel hymn*

Over the years, every once in a while, I would meet someone who had been
in the Selma to Montgomery March or worked in the 1964 Mississippi Freedom Summer. I would hear about a civil rights book or a film, but the stories often focused only on violence and had white heroes. Although I was an
active diversity trainer, working on and writing about prejudice on a nearly
daily basis, I didn't read the books or see the films about the movement because I wasn't yet ready to revisit my own memories.

By the summer of 1992, I had moved to Santa Cruz County, where composer and public radio producer Charles Amirkhanian gave me a photo es-
say, *Down Home*, by Bob Adelman. This was the first, and at the time the
only, documentation of *my* Wilcox County. Many of the faces and places
were familiar to me. I pored over the photos for hours, thrilled to find Rev.
Threadgill and Antioch Baptist Church, but I searched in vain for my friends
Ethel Brooks, Dan Harrell, Major Johns, and the Crawfords, Smiths, and
Robinsons.

Around the same time I received Adelman's book, I spotted the name
Benet Luchion in our local paper. There could only be one such man—my
SCOPE orientation savior. He was listed in the phone book, so we recon-
nected easily. Friends warned me that Benet was an eccentric character with
a wheatgrass farm commune in rural Bonny Doon. They said he danced at
every street fair and community event in his distinctive wool suit with a pan-
African sash and was active in environmental justice work.

When I picked up Benet at the bus station—he didn't own a car or any
pollution-producing vehicle—he warmly encouraged the exploration of my
civil rights summer and filled me in on his own history. He was born in 1929
in Gueydan, Louisiana, at the home of his grandmother, and was raised in
the cornfields out in the country on land belonging to his ancestors, ances-

11. Dr. Benet Luchion, SCLC staff member and civil rights activist, Santa Cruz, California, 1996. (Courtesy of the author.)

tors he could trace back to Reconstruction times. Benet explained that he had left his studies at a Trappist monastery in Louisiana to join the movement, then joined SCLC to direct a successful voter registration campaign in Alabama, and was asked to stay on as staff. This was the very place where we had left a note for his parents in 1965.

Benet Luchion served as field staff for SCLC from 1963 to 1967. Now he was a retired science professor, devoting his political energies to eliminating toxic waste and assuring a clean, healthful, worldwide food supply. He was thriving, it appeared, on wheatgrass and purified water. He organized First Sunday potlucks at the Louden Nelson Community Center in Santa Cruz, where African Americans and their allies shared food, fellowship, and support.

Luchion didn't remember the time he saved me from being attacked by nonmovement men in Atlanta but noted that "there were many such incidents." He explained that one reason why my summer had been overlooked in the history books was that Rev. Hosea Williams had become discredited within SCLC for cost overruns and conflicts with other leaders. Also, events such as the Los Angeles and Chicago protests eclipsed our voter registration effort even though SCOPE registered voters in more than sixty counties that summer. The media was more interested in bus burnings, tear gas, and murder than people still fighting for voting rights in the South.

"Before we met at the Atlanta SCOPE orientation, I headed the SCLC voting rights project in Gadsden, Alabama. After that, I worked out of the Atlanta office. They gave me some official title like field director, but who I really was, was leader of human security," Benet reminded me. I asked him about the times I was shaken awake in the middle of the night and moved from one house to another without any explanation. He explained that he and others were on top of the Klan even in my faraway county. The Atlanta office would get word when an attack was imminent and then get a message to our leaders, Dan or Major, who would move us out of there and warn the local inhabitants so they could either leave or get out their guns.

"In SCLC we had to know where every one of our people was all of the time and how secure their situation was," he said. "I knew the name of every Klan member in the South, where they lived and what their modus operandi was—did they work in groups, alone, prefer firebombing or carjacking? I stayed on top of the security situation and went to or dispatched someone to any place where we knew people were not secure. Many times we saved Hosea Williams, Dr. King, and James Foreman, as well as local leaders and field workers like you. If I had to get in my car and drive across Alabama to do that, then I did it: whatever it took to keep our people safe. We had a tight telephone network and handwritten lists. The lists had to be constantly updated because folks were always on the move."

Eventually, Benet Luchion moved to Camden, Mississippi, where he now raises organic vegetables and cattle and rides his horses. When I last asked him what he was up to, he was in his late seventies. He replied, "The same thing I have always been doing, human security. The human security movement is about the security of the people. That's what my whole life is about, what I did back then, what I do now. Everybody talks about freedom and revolution, but until the people are in a safe place with decent food, water, and freedom from constant fear of attack—the rest doesn't matter. Back then, I was like a Mac truck driving that philosophy through the movement. Before any other strategy you need to ask: Are people hungry? Injured? Do they have trauma? I went to the Beijing Women's Conference in 1994 and created a lobby on this issue to get this on the agenda of the United Nations. It took until 2000 but now there is an International Human Security Commission. The basis of democracy is the security of the *polis*, the people."[1] When Benet told me his parents were burned out and lost their farm that had been in the family for generations because of his work in the movement, I was heartsick, but he was resilient. Reuniting with Benet increased my feeling that I needed to document the Freedom Summer of 1965. So many who worked so hard were still unknown, their stories untold. With Benet's help, I made a list of people to contact, but I still wasn't ready to take on a serious search for my old friends and leaders.

Then, in the summer of 2005, former SCOPE worker Willy Siegel Leventhal contacted me about a SCOPE reunion in Atlanta. He explained that SCOPE had been either maligned or ignored by historians because of personal issues between leaders of the project. Authors writing about the Civil Rights Movement, like Taylor Branch and David Garrow, relied on those who criticized the SCOPE project to the detriment of Hosea Williams and our work. With the encouragement of Hosea Williams, Leventhal amassed a collection of SCOPE-related documents and compiled them in his book, *The SCOPE of Freedom*.[2] Although I was unable to attend the 2005 SCOPE reunion at Oglethorpe University, Leventhal told me afterward that SNCC chairman and SCLC board member Congressman John Lewis told the gathering that SCOPE volunteers were no different from the 1964 Mississippi Freedom Summer workers, that we were all in it together, and that we took the same risks. "The SCOPE volunteers stood shoulder to shoulder with us in our struggle for civil and voting rights," Lewis said.[3] This was the first time that I had heard any civil rights leader publically acknowledge our contribution.

Leventhal also told me about Bruce Hartford's Bay Area Civil Rights Veterans organization with a national website.[4] I drove to San Francisco where I spent some emotional hours in Hartford's book-filled condominium. As I spoke with this warm bear of a man, forty years of suppressed feeling spilled into tears. Bruce understood completely. He said many other vets had visited, sharing similar experiences. Other parents had disowned their children, and many vets went years without talking about their time in the movement; everything I was feeling was perfectly natural.

Suddenly, I was consumed with a need to find out what happened to the people of Wilcox County. Where were they? How were they? Who had the children of Camden become? What about my old coworkers, Bob and Chuck? I easily located Chuck Bonner at the Bonner and Bonner Law Offices in Sausalito, California. Chuck—now called Charles—returned my call within an hour, his familiar Selma drawl and deep laugh bridged the four decades since we had last seen each other. We made plans to meet in San Francisco after I led a training session for a health center in Chinatown.

Handsome, tall, smooth-talking Charles hadn't changed a bit. He crossed the hotel lobby with arms outstretched to scoop me up in a big hug, and greeted me with, "How come you and I never got it on?" I reminded Charles that I was Bob Block's girlfriend before he even met me. Charles asked if

I knew where Bob was, and I told him that I was pretty sure he was still in Pettigrew, Arkansas. The last time I had heard from Bob was in the late 1970s, and he'd changed his name to Luke. Charles picked up his cell phone and located Bob in a few minutes. We only spoke briefly, but from then on, it was as if none of us had ever stopped talking.

Charles said that he was always grateful to Bob and me because we were the ones who gave him the impetus to come to California, although it had been his plan to leave Alabama after being expelled from Selma University. "One time when we were arrested, Cleophus Hobbs and I met some guys from San Francisco State. That's when I first got it in my mind to come out here someday. When I met you guys, that sealed the deal," he said. Charles recalled the life-changing moment when he and the other forty students stood up and walked out of chapel. "The day of the walk-out, our footsteps echoed on the wooden floor. I'll always remember the smell of that ancient wooden building. It was the smell of history, and our footsteps were the sound of history in the making."[5]

Chuck had assumed his full name, Charles A. Bonner. After we lost track of each other, Charles graduated from law school and became a successful civil rights attorney in the San Francisco Bay Area. He has four adult children; his son Cabral is his partner in their law firm. Charles serves on many state and national boards and commissions, continuing his work toward peace and justice with a focus on ending international child sex slavery.[6] He has lived in East Africa, and has traveled to Thailand, Tibet, China, and throughout Europe, including a pilgrimage to the Polish death camps. I was impressed with my old SNCC buddy, but not surprised.

In December 2005, Charles arranged a SNCC reunion with Bettie Mae Fikes, Bruce Hartford, Jimmy Rogers, Jean Wiley, Luke, and me at Charles's Clear Lake weekend home in Northern California. Most exciting for me was finally reuniting with Bob, now Luke, the person I had to see to even begin writing the stories that I had waited all these years to tell.

As Bob, he had been my best friend, my first lover, and the one person who saw me more clearly than I saw myself those many years ago. As Luke, I was shocked at how dramatically different he looked: gone were the thick curly hair, clean-cut face, and sparkling golden brown eyes. He was nearly bald with thin gray hair and a bushy beard and mustache that hid his deep dimples and great smile. His eyes lacked luster. At first, he seemed worn down by life.

Luke described life on his sheep farm in Pettigrew, Arkansas—a far cry from the life of a doctor or lawyer that his parents had hoped for him. Luke

12. SNCC reunion: Luke (Bob) Block, Maria Gitin (Joyce Brians), and Charles A. "Chuck" Bonner, November 2005. (Courtesy of the author.)

freely confessed that the anticipation of seeing us again and diving back into the past made him a nervous wreck. But over the weekend as the stories began pouring out, his same crackly voice, easy laugh, and his emphatic "That is just plain wrong!" reminded me of the handsome passionate young man who shared the most important summer of my life. His eyes began to sparkle, and I knew there was still a great smile under that bushy beard. The physical attraction was gone, but the connection we formed that long-ago summer was restored. Over the weekend, Luke agreed that we needed to check up on folks in Wilcox. He said getting away would be tough, but if I could, he would.

Just as we had decades ago, Luke and I clung to each other's every word over the weekend and didn't pay nearly enough attention to the other wonderful veterans who were with us. I was in awe of Jean Wiley, a student-teacher-activist and SNCC staff member in Maryland and Alabama from 1960 to 1967. She was in the movement before any of us, integrating department stores in Baltimore and then teaching at Tuskegee where her home became a safe house for activists heading for Mississippi. Sammy Younge Jr., who was murdered for his civil rights work, had been one of her students, and you could see it still hurt her to talk about him.

We spoke of how it felt to be stalked by the FBI for years and the incredible duplicity of the federal government, as evidenced by President Johnson shaking hands with Martin Luther King on television while at the same time authorizing wiretapping of King's telephone. Bruce Hartford, who had been SCOPE director for Crenshaw County, Alabama, told us that from the time we entered the South, law enforcement officials, as well as the local white supremacists, had a list of all of our names. Bruce recalled, "The day I arrived the chief of police of Luverne, the county seat, pulls up with a box of 5 x 7 cards on the seat beside him and holds one up with my name, details about me and asks: 'Is this you?' He just wanted me to know they had my number."[7]

Others reported the same thing in their counties. We learned later that FBI director J. Edgar Hoover had ordered FBI officers to "scour SCOPE workers for subversive backgrounds" as part of his obsession with proving that Martin Luther King was a Communist and that SCLC was a Communist front.[8] So my paranoia about being followed when I was a student in Wisconsin was not paranoia after all; the government really did waste resources tracking student civil rights workers.

Bruce told us that many, if not most, of the people who contacted him through the Bay Area Civil Rights Veterans group went through long periods, even decades, of not talking about their experiences, or making any effort to connect with the people and places that had been so important to them. Many of us suppressed even thinking about our time in the movement. Luke said, "That was me, that's for sure. I never said word one about it for years. I have hardly told my wife and kids anything at all."

Charles said that he had searched and found Dallas County sheriff Jim Clark in a rest home and got him to sign a 1964 photo of Charles and his high school classmates in a demonstration in Selma, just before the sheriff began to beat them. Charles reminisced, "When Clark beat me the first time, I was still in high school. Our teachers finally decided to get involved in the movement in 1964. We planned to pack the jails with students should Clark carry out his threat to arrest the teachers. We all went out together in the first demonstration at the county courthouse on Alabama Ave. Clark ordered us to disperse. I started to sing, 'Ain't gonna let Jim Clark turn me round.' He and his men beat us with billy clubs and cattle prods. He beat us off the street; beat us into the courtroom. There waiting, sitting on high, was Judge Reynolds, only his beet-red neck protruding from his black robe.

13. Charles A. Bonner and Hudson High classmates demonstrate in front of Dallas County sheriff Jim Clark (in white hat with back to camera) during a student demonstration just before Clark beat and jailed them, Selma, Alabama, January 1964. (Courtesy of Charles A. Bonner.)

Peering down over his wire rim glasses, he thundered, 'Don't you "missus" no nigger woman in my courtroom' to a cowering student who referred to his mother as 'Mrs.' Judge Reynolds, the probate and juvenile judge, promptly sentenced us all to thirty days in jail. First we were sent to Camp Selma, a wooden, white, barrack-type building a few miles northwest of downtown Selma. After sentencing, we were sent to Camp Camden in Wilcox to serve our thirty days. We didn't bail out, and when we got out, we went right back to demonstrating. That's why I had no tolerance for the timid students and teachers at Selma U when I got there. I had been taking my lumps for years already."

I told the group about searching for old Wilcox County jail records. I wasn't the only one who had never sent for my federal arrest records, not wanting to stir up my name in the FBI files. Even without receiving formal charges or notices of hearings, I had been told that I was unemployable due to felony convictions for conspiracy to boycott and felony trespass. The complicity of the government and businesses in persecuting civil rights workers cannot be overestimated. Other veterans reported that they had hearing dates, faced charges, and some had bail paid for them; some went to jail for weeks. Bruce Hartford suggested that maybe SCLC pled no contest and paid our bail, which was why we girls were released after thirty hours.

After a long, emotional day of swapping stories, as I fell asleep upstairs, it occurred to me that I hadn't wanted to think or talk about all of this for so many years not only because of personal trauma that summer, but because I felt so helpless and insignificant. Even though I have worked on antiracism and political equality most of my life, I am still white. I have unearned privilege and it still hurts to face the conditions that the majority of people of color live under in this country. The reason most whites don't fight racism is that we don't want to accept our privilege. The task of redistributing access to wealth, property, and top quality education is too discouraging for most of us.

The next afternoon, Jimmy Rogers and I were standing on Charles's sunny deck overlooking the calm waters of Clear Lake. I knew that Jimmy had worked with SNCC on voter registration and had been walking next to Rev. Daniels when they shot him in Haneyville just one county over from Wilcox on August 20, 1965. Jimmy said he was so close to Daniels when Daniels was shot that blood splattered all over his sweatshirt.

I asked Jimmy if he ever expected to live this long. He stared out over the water and said, "After serving five years in the Air Force, being in jail with other SNCC demonstrators the night Viola Luizzo was killed . . . all that . . . I had plenty chances to be killed. But when that man had his gun pointed straight at us . . . I believed I was dead. Sometimes I still can't believe I am alive. But I guess there's a reason for that. Now, I do what I can to keep people going in the right direction. I worked as a probation officer over in Oakland for thirty-one years; I just retired last year. I'm part of a group that tries to get prisoners a fair shake, try to get them into drug rehab programs. Just because you are in the prison system shouldn't mean you lose all your rights."

Jimmy reminded me that the Selma SCLC and SNCC offices on Franklin Street were right across the street from the Dallas County Jail, where Sheriff Jim Clark loved to lock up civil rights workers. "That way you didn't have far to go if you got arrested and when we you got out, you could go right back to work," he said. He chuckled at the memory.

I reflected, "That was a lot of nerve to put movement offices right there in front of the sheriff. I hardly remember anything about the office except meeting Stokely. I didn't have any idea then how important he would become to SNCC and the black liberation movement."[9]

As Jimmy and I stood there together, Odetta's song, "Mississippi God Damn," came into my mind and then the words of Rev. Andrew Young: "Go love the hell out of Alabama!" I asked Jimmy, "By God, we tried, didn't we? Segregated Alabama felt like it was Hell itself, but somehow, I just could not bring myself to love the men pointing guns at me and my comrades all those years ago. I wonder if I ever could?"

As we continued our healing conversations over the reunion weekend, I realized that feeling ashamed of leaving because of my back pain, and Bob feeling chased away by Eric Jones, were real but useless feelings. The truth was that I signed up for a ten-week student summer project that was always planned to end. SCLC wanted us to go back, tell our stories, organize and influence others on campus to get involved and to fund-raise during the school year, and then return as volunteers each spring-summer. That was the plan.

SCLC leaders like Hosea Williams lived inside the struggle all their lives, as did many SNCC leaders. They thought that experiencing a taste of southern racism would be good for us mostly white students and for their cause— we could get more people in the North to support the southern struggle. No one explained to us that the experience might shake us to the core and make us question absolutely everything: question whether there was anything that could make a difference in the face of centuries of engrained racism as well as question every aspect of white, male-dominated US culture.

The main reason Luke and I hadn't talked much about our experiences or what we had witnessed was because we knew how insignificant we were. Many of us said nothing for decades. Some never did talk about it. A few hardy white people like Bruce Hartford continued the freedom fight complete with return trips to jail and ongoing threats to their lives and with far less media attention than civil rights workers received during the Freedom Summers of 1964 and during the spring of 1965 Selma campaign. Although some SNCC leaders believed that the black community would be more empowered by all-black leadership and that white students were detracting from their efforts, Charles made it clear again that he had always considered Luke and me members of SNCC even if we were also working with SCLC. Regardless of the divisions between the organizations, identifying with Martin Luther King Jr. was such a winning strategy that Bruce Hartford later told me, "Stokely had the sense to use King's influence. When he first started organizing in Lowndes County, folk would ask him if he was one of Dr. King's men and Stokely would answer, 'Yes, Ma'am, I am.' He told King about that, and King just laughed in approval."[10]

Many student activists found expression through the black power, free speech, peace, environment, women's, and other empowerment movements. Some kept faith with the dream through literacy, antipoverty, and prison reform work. Others became highly educated, founded social change organizations, or taught school. Some stayed drunk or stoned for a few years, and some broke down completely and recovered, while others never could put their lives back together. Far too many died from injuries and broken hearts.

In 1965, Luke had returned to a confused but supportive family, no money worries, and plenty of friends, but he hadn't been able to adjust either. He tried college, but it didn't make any sense to him after seeing action in the movement. I teased him about his early lies to me: that he was Hawaiian and that he was just middle class. From my perspective, his family was rich! But after the South, Luke lived nothing like his parents. King had spoken at the SCOPE orientation about "creative maladjustment" as an appropriate response to racism. Since he hadn't stayed in the South, Luke tried to find another way to continue the freedom fight.

"I tried to do what Eric Jones told me, work with white people on racism and poverty. I worked for a year with John Golden in Oakland with the American Friends Service Committee. Then my first wife, Karla, and I took jobs as field organizers for the Southern Conference Educational Fund (SCEF), a small organization whose idea was to get white southern support for the Civil Rights Movement. We worked with Ann and Carl Braden in their Appalachian poverty project in Louisville, Kentucky, for about six months. The Bradens were great, but working with poor white folks? It was like beating your head on a rock; I felt utterly defeated. Eventually, I moved on to environmental activism and continue in that at some level today.

"As far as school goes, I dropped out just one semester short of graduation. I wish I would've finished as it would have made my mother so happy, but for myself it hasn't made much difference. I love my country life, my friends, my family." Luke told me proudly about his artist wife, Willow, their two daughters and a son, and their grandkids—three generations all living together on the family farm in houses they built themselves. They raise prize sheep and have chickens that lay the best eggs. They built their own kiln to fire Willow's ceramics, which are sought after at arts and crafts fairs.

With my eyes closed, Luke easily seemed like the boy I knew as Bob. He hadn't mellowed with age, was still intense, still teared up easily, and spoke with the same self-deprecating humor and extravagant respect for the people he cares for. He kept saying I hadn't changed a bit, and in some ways, I guess that was true.

What surprised me most was that Luke had blocked out so much of his own experience. Only with prompting from Charles did he recall the Dew Drop Inn incident or other times he was in danger. Charles tried to remind him that the first night they were in Camden, the two of them were taken into custody by a sheriff's deputy and driven deep into the woods to be arraigned by the sitting judge. Then they spent two days in jail in separate cells before being released to rejoin the other demonstrators.

"What? I can't believe this! You told me you were never arrested; how could you forget that? They were beating all of the white men in jail. What happened?" I practically yelled at Luke; I was so upset that I hadn't known this essential piece of his history during the time we were involved.

"I guess I just blocked it out," he replied. "Frankly, Charles, I still don't remember a bit of this, although I trust your memory, I certainly don't question that you have it right, but I can't picture a bit of it," Luke grimaced as he strained to reach back to what had to have been some of the most terrifying hours in his life.

When we were alone, I tried to get Luke to talk about it more, but he said there was nothing, not a shred of memory, so I changed the topic and asked, "Were you really sexually experienced?"

"Nah," he laughed, "I just thought it sounded better than if I was a virgin too. No, it was definitely my first time, that's for sure. Could you tell?"

I asked Luke what he remembered about me. I knew I made a lot of mistakes that summer and had complained too much. I apologized for the awful way I broke up with him. "Well, that kind of hurt at first, but I was young. I got over it pretty quick." he laughed.

"When I first saw you, I thought you were incredibly vibrant and alive and open. I thought you were really, really beautiful. You seemed really educated; you told me a lot that helped make sense of what we were doing, like the history of racism. I was getting that from Chuck and Dan too, but you were so articulate about it. I never knew civil rights from an outsider's view because I just jumped right in after the Selma to Montgomery March and learned on the job.

"For me it was love at first sight," he continued. "As time went on, I also saw your dark side, when you were in so much pain from that back injury. But you were such a trouper you were always doin' what needed to be done and doing it well. That summer and beyond, it was always fun being together. All I have is good memories." We spoke briefly about what it would have been like had we stayed together and gotten married, and we agreed that we were both too intense to have lasted much longer than we did. Besides, he was absolutely set on having children and that was not part of my life plan.

When I asked Luke what he thought the lasting impacts of our time in Wilcox were for his life, he considered carefully before he replied. "There were two main things. One, I got in touch with a huge reservoir of anger, which I fight 'til this day. Also, I got in touch with my guilt for having such a privileged upbringing. From this came my belief in the righteousness of poverty. I pretty much kicked that one, but it took decades. Two, the Craw-fords were my model for family and integrity, and surviving on a farm for that matter. I have spent the rest of my life tryin' to live up to their stan-dards. I loved that sign they had on the wall, Do unto Others as You Would Have Them Do unto You. They lived that and I have tried my best to follow that motto. To tell you the truth, knowing them affected me more than the politics of the whole thing."

I asked him about trauma, about how he survived incidents like that man with the gun pointed at Dan while he stood there helplessly. He shrugged it off and said, "You were considerably more sensitive than I was. I probably had some post-traumatic stress, but I just stuffed it and went on. But for sure, the most lasting effect of being in Wilcox was that I 'went country.' Once I lived there in rural Wilcox, especially out at Crawfords, there was never any question of going back to my parents' life. That's why I changed my name to Luke. Everyone was named Bob. My middle name is Louis so Luke seemed to fit. I must've changed it the same year you changed yours to Maria, even though we were no longer in touch."

When I reminded Charles and Luke about our car accident on the road between Selma and Camden, I told them that the accident was one of my strongest memories from the whole summer. They looked at each other, and then told me that I had the story wrong. They didn't recall any shots, only that Chuck was speeding and the car spun out of control. We rolled over a steep incline, but not a cliff like I remembered. It was true that some white men in a truck pulled over and maybe swore at us down there, but they didn't remember any gunshots. And the car miraculously didn't roll over, just went crazy sideways until it settled upright. The worst injury was that Bob slammed Chuck's finger in the door, and it wasn't even broken. But they did remember me screaming and screaming for the longest time. The accident must have thrown me into survival mode and altered my sense of reality. My coccyx had been broken and I was in shock. Luke said he didn't realize until we were traveling back to California, and I kept asking to lie down on the backseat, how much pain I must have been in.

The summer of 1965 was a deep and permanent shock to my system. It was in Alabama that I realized that anyone who crossed the boundaries of acceptable behavior anywhere could easily find themselves in jail or worse. Public safety was only available for those who conformed to the authorities' view of what was permitted.

During our reunion, and later when I attended other Bay Area Civil Rights Veterans gatherings, I realized that many of us did have some degree of post-traumatic stress disorder (PTSD) from the traumas we experienced. Many veterans report flashbacks and nightmares forty or more years later. It had been years since I had been troubled like that, but as I began recreating memories with Luke and others, I started to have nightmares nearly every night. It was only after my first return visit to Wilcox County in 2008 that they subsided.

Over our reunion weekend we listened to each other's stories, we laughed, we danced, and I'm not ashamed to say that we cried. Saturday night we hung out at Mt. Konocti Blues Club, which Charles owned at the time. When Charles introduced us to the audience, it felt corny, but I wept as they applauded us. Forty years after the fact, it was the first time in my life that anyone had acknowledged me as part of the Civil Rights Movement. I wondered if anyone else in this crowded room had any idea what a miracle it was that any of us aging civil rights veterans were even alive.

As if he read my mind, Charles shouted across the table, "We are so lucky that we all survived! One day we'll go—all three of us—to the Selma Jubilee and walk over the Edmund Pettus Bridge together. That's a plan!"

16

Tragic Losses, New Friendships

There's a movement on the road in Alabama,
There's a movement on the road in Alabama,
Black man, white man, Christian, Jew,
We've got to keep marching through.

"Murder on the Road in Alabama," Len H. Chandler Jr., 1965

After our 2005 reunion, I couldn't stop thinking about the people we had known in Wilcox County. I wondered whether Dan and Juanita Harrell, Major Johns, and Ethel Brooks ever got to rest and be respected for their work, whether they finally elected a law abiding sheriff, and whether the schools were integrated. I searched for the few references to the county that I could find and devoured the words.

When they looked back did folks in Wilcox view white civil rights workers as a help or hindrance to their struggle? Did we cause more harm than good? I wondered if the Freedom Summer of 1965 that had sprung back to life for me mattered to anyone else. I felt a surge of affection for places like Camden Academy, Antioch Baptist Church, Boiling Springs Baptist, Little Zion in Coy, and Pleasant Grove in Gees Bend. I wanted to rediscover what it was in the determined, courageous, and loving spirit of the black activists of Wilcox County that enabled them to endure and made it impossible for me to ever really forget them.

I began to outline this project with my author-activist-professor friend Bettina Aptheker, who had become the life partner of my Antioch College advisor, Kate Miller. After months of writing, research, and telephone interviews, my author friend Jim Houston advised, "You need to go back there, see the people, walk the roads; it will come back to you." And so I did. Before, after, and during my 2008 and 2010 visits to Wilcox County, I listened to stories from dozens of people who participated in or whose family participated in the Freedom Summer of 1965, and I eventually spoke with or received written information from more than seventy people; forty of them contributed their own personal stories. Over time, these stories began to take shape like a Gees Bend quilt, with bright, seemingly unmatched fragments stitched together by the common thread of having lived through the tumultuous civil rights struggle. Honoring the oral history tradition, these stories are clustered around primary people and places important to the Wilcox County freedom fight rather than recounted in a linear fashion. Although I was a participant-witness and am not a scholar, I share historian Elsa Barkley Brown's belief that like jazz "history is also everybody talking at once, multiple rhythms being played simultaneously. The events and people we write about did not occur in isolation but in dialogue with a myriad of other people and events. In fact, at any given moment, millions of people are all talking at once. As historians we try to isolate one conversation and to explore it, but the trick is then how to put that conversation in a context which makes evident its dialogue with so many others."[1] Through hundreds of hours of interviews, casual conversations, and searching through old news archives, I gathered many variations of the same events. Some of the people I spoke with explained to me that there were really two phases to the Wilcox County freedom fight: the 1960s voter registration movement and the school equality movement that continued into the 1970s. Because they overlapped, for many of the younger participants who engaged in years of nearly daily protest they blurred together as one long battle.

In preparation for our first trip, and in order to make the most of the limited time Luke could spare away from his farm, I mapped out our visit months in advance. I sought contacts for as many people as I could in hopes of finding our families, our friends from long ago. I began with a long-delayed call to Rev. John Golden, the last person to wave good-bye to us from the Camden Academy steps, and one of the few white coworkers I located.

When I telephoned John, the "good Rev" as we had called him, he remembered me right away. Naturally he remembered Luke more clearly since they worked together in California for a year in 1966. "My first memory of Bob Block is he was riding a mule. He had shorts on and I thought he had black shoes, but it was just his mud-caked bare feet, just dragging along the ground. He was quite a guy!"[2]

John told me that the reason he had been in Camden that summer was that the Presbyterian Church, which sponsored Camden Academy, asked white seminary students from the North to help with reconciliation between blacks and whites. "Rev. Thomas Threadgill convinced us that there were some good white people," John said. He had come out after the Selma marches and began working with Rev. Threadgill's group. After they disbanded, he stayed on and worked with the voting rights activities in Camden, but he didn't consider himself part of our SCOPE project even though he is listed as a field worker in the SCLC SCOPE files.[3] "There was this group of only six or seven white women taking great risks. One woman went home after a meeting and her husband cocked his pistol at her and said, 'You have a choice. You either stop going to those fucking meetings or you are dead, bitch.' The group stopped meeting shortly after that."[4]

I told John that this was the first I had ever heard of any Camden whites supporting the movement. When I had a chance to ask Rev. Threadgill's daughter, Sheryl Threadgill, about a white women's group she said, "It could be possible. I believe my father would have done just about anything for the movement, but I never heard anything about that."

John told me that he tried to return to seminary but he couldn't adjust. "I was there in Camden for that ten weeks that you were, then came back to Berkeley/Oakland briefly and then returned to Wilcox right after Jonathan Daniels was killed. That really affected me. I stayed with the Charleys out in Coy working on the Agricultural Stabilization and Conservation Service Committee. We were trying to get some black folks elected.

"Just before this local agricultural committee was going to vote, a guy from some branch of state government came to monitor the elections. There was a rumor it was going to be rigged. We got some of our people elected but they were white; some blacks voted for the same whites to continue to serve. Voting then could be with an 'X' or a signature. The rules they set up for this committee were that you had to draw a line through whom you didn't want. Many blacks said they could not draw a line through a white man's name."[5]

My main reason for calling John was to ask about Ethel Brooks. I was stunned when he told me that Ethel was dead. I asked if she was murdered, and he said that at first everyone suspected foul play, but the autopsy determined that she died in a solo car accident. Tears for my long-lost friend drowned out my further questions.

To find out more about Ethel, John suggested I call her cousin, Miss Willie Kate Charley, the daughter of Joel and Leona Charley, Ethel's aunt and uncle, who John had stayed with in the fall of 1965. At age seventy-four, the retired schoolteacher was still living in Coy and still sharp as a tack. Miss Charley, who everyone simply called "Kate," not only helped me learn more about Ethel and the Harrells, but also became one of my best sources for who was still around from those days.

When I reached Kate Charley, she was as friendly as could be. I told her how sad I was that my friend Ethel had died so young and asked her to tell me more about what had happened. "Ethel worked a night shift in a convenience store in Camden," she said. "Her son was always in a lot of trouble. He called and asked her to pick him up after she had been working all night. It was about 7:30 in the morning. She ran into the Canton Bend bridge and was killed instantly. I don't know if she got ill or fell asleep or what. Maybe

14. Ethel Brooks, Wilcox County freedom fighter, 1960s. (Courtesy of W. Kate Charley.)

she had a heart attack."[6] Kate said that the autopsy didn't find a bullet in her body, although they looked for one, and there was no further investigation. I had counted on seeing my dear friend again and could not accept her death.

Kate didn't know where Ethel's son, Jesse Jr., was, and Ethel's parents were dead, so Kate suggested that I talk to Mrs. Rosetta Angion, a Coy resident who raised sixteen children by herself and still found time to be a movement activist. Seventy-seven-year-old Rosetta Angion was glad to tell me what she recalled.

"Ethel? She was a young Harriett Tubman. If she came by and told a few of us 'I want you all to go walk across that river; I know you can do it,' we'd go do it. Whatever she told us to do, we did it. It all worked out because she had been trained, she had been to Atlanta for the trainin'. She carried my children over to the Selma march, the one they call Bloody Sunday. She went up to the Academy and got them all to walk out and go over there. They looked up to her."[7]

Mrs. Angion's eldest surviving daughter, Mary Alice Robinson, still lives near her mother. She told me, "I got involved through Ethel Brooks; she'd come around and talk to us and get us to the meetings at Antioch Baptist Church and on the marches from the church to the courthouse. Ethel carried a lot of us over for the first Selma march. On Bloody Sunday—March 7, 1965—we came down from Brown Chapel AME church and we walked across the bridge. My sister Edna and lots of us from Coy walked together. When they turned the dogs on us and tear gassed us, I rolled down the hill into the bushes. I got some briars in my hand and they stayed there for a long time. I left them there as a reminder of what they done to us. We went back to the church, and I didn't go back to the bridge for the Selma to Montgomery March three weeks later. Ethel Brooks, Dan and Juanita Harrell—they really got people out to vote in the Coy area. Before that, black people had no power at all."[8]

In addition to Ethel, I learned more sad and shocking news about some of our friends we had hoped to visit. From Kate I learned that a local black man had murdered Dan Harrell! From Major Johns's sister, Mary Johns, Luke heard that Major died young of an aneurism. All three beloved leaders were only in their forties. Each time we learned of a new loss, Luke would say, "I just can't believe it; I always thought we'd see them again!" The deaths of our primary leaders refueled my commitment to tell their stories and to learn all I could from those who were still alive.

My reasons to return to Wilcox were to revisit the people and places that made such an impression on me and to gather more information. Luke wanted to go mainly for healing, to discover what it was about this time in his life that still choked him up to talk about it. Little did I know what a rich tapestry of connections we were about to weave.

When Luke met me at baggage claim in Memphis, Tennessee, on Wednesday, October 8, 2008, it was the second time I had seen him since we parted ways in 1967. "This is so amazing. I can't believe we pulled this off!" Luke grinned ear to ear as he scooped me up in a greeting hug. Amazement was coupled with the feeling that this reunion was inevitable, completely natural. Even though we were both happily married to others, we knew there couldn't be any other companion on this first journey back to our civil rights home in Wilcox County, Alabama. This was our private pilgrimage, much like two army buddies returning to the scene of their last battle. Next time we'd bring our spouses, but this first venture couldn't be with anyone else. As Luke drove our rental car toward Alabama, we shared our fears, hopes, and nervous laughter while the Dixie Chicks sang "Taking the Long Way Home."

Return to Coy 2008—In Memory of
Ethel Brooks and Dan and Juanita Harrell

Following her telephone directions to Coy, Luke and I found Kate Charley on her family's home place on Songbird Lane, which she named herself when black people finally got to name their own roads. She explained that it was the custom in black families to leave the piece of land with the house to the youngest child who was expected to care for the parents until they died, which Kate had done. Kate had been away teaching in Tuscaloosa in 1965, but her parents were active in the movement and kept civil rights workers in their off-the-road "safe house" for many years. Kate recalled, "You didn't stay here. My parents only kept men and all the men were named John. My dad's inside joke was that everyone in the movement sounded like they were hiding out, on the run. It seemed like they were all named John. John Riley, John Golden, Major Johns—they all stayed with my folks."[9]

We chatted for a while about some of the changes that resulted from the black majority securing the vote. In 1965 there were no paved roads in African American communities in Wilcox County. Most black residents did not have access to running water or a sewer system, and few homes had electricity or telephones. Kate Charley told us, "Earlier we had an outdoor hydrant and plumbed water to a washing machine and sink in the kitchen, but it wasn't until the 1980s we had running water and flush toilets in the house. The whites in Coy had electricity as early as the 1930s. The utility company would run miles of wire right past our little houses to the white owned ones, deep through the woods, just skipped us."[10]

Before we headed out to follow Kate's little blue Dodge truck racing around the back roads of Coy, she handed us one of her famous coconut pies—shredded coconut bound together with plenty of sugar and Karo syrup. We could barely keep up to her speed as Kate led us onto a side road off County Road 13 that we could never have found on our own. Set deep in the woods was the Brooks's hand-hewn plain board home, now sadly run down and apparently abandoned.

The big front porch where we had all sat enjoying fried chicken and drinking strawberry wine was rotted through in most places. The Brooks's had one of the nicest homes in Coy and now it was completely abandoned. The only sign of meals past was a stack of empty Nehi soda bottles. We began to pick our way through the open breezeway, which was filled with trash and ruined furniture, but the floorboards didn't look sturdy enough to continue into the house, and Kate warned us to look out for snakes. I pictured Ethel in her youth that summer, how proud and excited she was about the progress being made. I remembered the time we sang "This Little Light of Mine" while the fireflies flickered all around us.

Today, the orioles and little yellow finches chirped as we picked our way under the huge sycamores and oaks, with wild mulberry and the ever-present kudzu growing all around. We looked for the old pecan tree, but we couldn't find it. The house and outbuildings were returning to earth. We tried to find the sweet water well, but the area was too overgrown. Kate recalled that Ethel was the only one who ever fell into the well. She was just a little girl sent to fetch a great big bucket of water, which tipped her over, so somebody had to come pull her out. It was just like Ethel to attempt something beyond her reach.

Our next stop was Mt. Zion Baptist church, "Little Zion Number One," they call it. Kate had a key to the church and opened the side door. The building has been lovingly updated and maintained. A lot of work and fundraising went into the renovations and new stained-glass windows. I stood at the lectern, looked out at the empty pews, and marveled that I had the audacity to speak to the people of Coy that long-ago summer night. After admiring the new kitchen, lounge, and social hall, we went out a side door to the unfenced treeless graveyard.

Two rough-hewn engraved marble stones sat atop a cement slab. There was an empty upturned flowerpot from some long-past floral offering leaning against the larger stone, which has engraved on it, "The Book of Life." Engraved on the book cover was "Ethel Lenora Brooks—We love you. Dad. Mom. Son," with a small angel carved beside the text. The smaller stone reads, "In God's care." Ethel's headstone was adjoined with her mother Julia's. Ethel died before both of her parents at age forty-four in 1985, just twenty years after we knew her. I half expected her to pop up and say, "Just kidding, I'm still here." I never knew anyone more alive than Ethel Brooks. The memories I had of the vibrant, dedicated activist whose energy and passion seemed inexhaustible were still strong.

We knew before we returned to Coy that both Dan and Juanita Harrell were dead, but initially it was difficult to find anyone other than Kate who would speak about them. The Harrells were among the most important leaders in the county and I was determined to find out what others recalled of them. They treated Luke just like a son. He told me that to this day, he considers Dan the bravest man he ever met. Everyone agreed Juanita was as smart as she was beautiful. They both had been to college at Tuskegee Institute but were able to communicate with country folk and young kids as easily as with northern college students. They did so much for the movement over such a long period of time; it was hard to believe that there wasn't a monument to them anywhere in the county.

The first time I spoke with Kate Charley she recounted their sad story: "Dan was one of the stalwarts who got things moving and organized. Juanita died young; it was very sad; they had a young son. Then Dan died in a terrible tragedy. There was a little black nightclub. Dan was in there trying to get people to come to a meeting or some activity for the movement, and he got shot. It was out near the four-way stop on the way to lower Coy if you turned left to get onto Highway 41. They said it was a personal dispute, but I don't believe that. We heard that there were some whites who got blacks to do their dirty business for them, maybe buy them a case of beer."[11]

The Harrells lived in Coy until their untimely deaths. Dan was only forty-six; Juanita had been even younger.[12] More than one resident lamented that the community felt a real loss made worse by their leaving no trace, not even a gravestone. Cleo Brooks, Dan's younger cousin, told me, "Dan accomplished a lot more than he gets credit for. He was able to build a lot of homes through the Federal Housing Authority. He even had a title, Director of the Southwest Alabama Self Help Housing Project, something like that. We formed the Coy Land Movement and bought forty acres that is still held in the name of SCLC. I live in one of those houses, and there are other tracts all over the Coy area. In 1965, President Lyndon Johnson gave an award to us for building housing for blacks in our community. Coy really was the epicenter of the Wilcox County Civil Rights Movement. We had more people on the bridge on Bloody Sunday than any other community and that's a fact. Most people don't know that."[13]

I asked Cleo Brooks about Dan's murder. "They said Dan had a gun on him. The guy that did it called him out and shot him. They put a gun in Dan's hand so it looked like self-defense. The four to five witnesses were all family members of the attacker, and they testified that it was self-defense. The few other witnesses didn't want to get into it, so they didn't speak up. Everyone in Coy knows it was murder, but nobody said anything. I wasn't here, we lived out in Oakland, California, then. That is just what they say."[14]

Dan's younger brothers, Leonard and Tommy Hal, as well as Dan's son, Eddie, all told me the same thing—that Jim Salsberry had been after Dan for a long time. Dan tried to get Salsberry to stop stalking him. He never initiated a preventive attack, far from it. Leonard reported, "Before the murder, the same man came at Dan with a gun pointed at him. In self-defense, Dan shot Salsberry in the leg; then immediately took him to get medical treatment."[15] Tommy Hal, ten years younger than Dan, was with Dan when he gave Jim Salsberry that warning shot. "He could have killed him right then. Instead, he just wounded him and took him to the hospital. Dan was an expert marksman and knew martial arts, but he was very compassionate. As long as I recall, he never seemed discouraged. I worked there with him building homes for low-income people in 1972. My brother Dan was a person who never saw obstacles, only opportunities. He didn't get excited, kept a level head, and knew how to make things happen."[16]

According to their son, Eddie Harrell, Juanita caught valley fever while on a trip to California to visit relatives before he was born; she died when he was scarcely a year old. After Dan's murder, Eddie's uncle Lewis and aunt Faye brought him to California and raised him as their own son. He was twelve years old and vividly recalls the events leading up to his father's death. The killer had chased young Eddie a week earlier. He had to hide in some brambles for hours to escape being attacked. "The night it happened, I heard three shots. I ran out back, behind our house. My dad was laying there on the ground. I remember Jim was wearing a white shirt with vertical blue stripes. That pattern and those colors are imprinted on my mind along with what Jim said: 'Call the law, because I just killed a good man.'"[17]

A *Wilcox Progressive Era* newspaper photo with an article dated January 10, 1979, shows Dan lying face up with just a sheet thrown over him, not even covering his feet. He was shot three days earlier, on a Sunday. Two guns were found at the scene, but only the murder weapon was confirmed as having been fired, with two shots to Dan's chest. Jim Salsberry, the assailant, claimed that Dan fired at him first and that he shot him out of fear for his life.[18] Locals told me that after an investigation and brief trial, all charges were dropped. Everyone I spoke with believed that the Klan had paid Salsberry to shoot Dan and that Dan had never fired a shot.

Former Wilcox County sheriff, Prince Arnold, told me that he had only gotten to know Dan near the end of Dan's life but learned a great deal from him about working with the community. Arnold was elected sheriff in November 1978, the same election in which Dan was defeated for county commission. The paper reported that the investigation concluded that the shooting was self-defense. When I showed Sheriff Arnold the newspaper article, he made a copy but didn't comment on the incident. He just shook his head and said, "The man was brilliant. I had total respect for him. People here don't appreciate all that he did for us."[19]

Luke and I certainly appreciated what Dan did for the movement and wanted to visit to the Harrells last home. Kate Charley warned us that although Dan had owned three acres with a small house, and a store with a washette that some referred to as a "nightclub" called Harrell's Place, there wasn't anything left—just an empty lot. We followed her penciled map to a curve on County Road 12. We stared out across the dry weedy field. There wasn't a trace of a home or a store; there was no sign at all of the dynamic Harrells. Standing there with Luke, I recalled the day Dan drove us out there and spread his arms wide, telling us about the cooperatives and houses he would build. He envisioned black economic independence in the tradition of Tuskegee and Snow Hill Institutes, but with employment rather than education at the heart of the program since he expected that integrated public schools would prepare students to thrive in a new economy that they would help create. It must have broken Dan's heart to lose his beloved Juanita and then lose a county commissioner election in the community to which he dedicated his life. Was it a coincidence that his murder was immediately after the election of the first black county officials?

In 1965 Dan Harrell and other local leaders were already trying to bring in federal aid, food commodities, home loans, and funds from the new War on Poverty program. Part of our SCOPE project work was to simplify and explain to residents that if they got the vote, they could elect officials who would secure the federal funds they deserved. Even with that incentive, it was hard to convince some folks to take the risk, so for many more years the majority of new black voters continued to elect white officials over black candidates. Elections continued to be rigged; bribes and threats common to the rural region continued for years, some say even into the present.

Cleo Brooks also credits Dan Harrell with the earliest documented effort to integrate public schools, in the spring of 1965. Harrell escorted Cleo, Oscar Huff, and Georgia Blackmon to superintendent of schools Guy S. Kelly's office to apply for the approval required to transfer to white schools. The district denied the fifth graders their transfers. According to Brooks, "Dan didn't want to endanger us by forcing integration with federal marshals like had been done in other areas, but he began the process and kept appeals going, all the way up to the state level."[20]

By the mid-1960s there were federal community action agencies developed under the Office of Economic Opportunity aimed to bypass segregationist southern states, but it was nearly impossible for the programs to get any traction until local whites were finally voted out of office a decade later. According to people I spoke with, the "powers that be," as they still call them, would rather see black people starve to death than give them anything that might weaken white economic dominance. In 1966, after local leaders finally got some direct federal aid and built a commodity building, the very day it was filled with food and supplies for all the people who had been fired or put off their land for voter registration activity, the local racists in Camden burned the building to the ground.[21]

It's no wonder people got discouraged; it is more of a miracle that they persevered. The Harrells took on a system that was institutionally wired to fail minorities, even in areas where they were the majority. The institution of racism as well as individual racists blocked their every effort, but they never stopped trying. With more adequate support and without people gunning for him, I believe that Dan Harrell could have gone much further toward establishing a thriving black economy in Wilcox County. Dan and Juanita Harrell were civil rights heroes and should be remembered as such.[22]

I asked Kate Charley about the Robinsons, Pettways, and Boykins, the families with whom I had stayed, and the Lawsons, where I ate supper sometimes. She said there are lots of families with those names, but that Boiling Springs had pretty much dried up and people moved away. She said she didn't know the Robinsons; they might have been put off their place for housing me. Some folks who kept civil rights workers were even burned out. My heart sank as I prayed no harm had come to them or anyone else because of me. Then Kate told me more about her own folks' involvement.

"My parents and Ethel's were active in the Coy freedom movement along with teachers Mr. Albert and Mrs. Theola Gordon, Mr. John and Mrs. Daisy Cook, and the Jacksons. They all lived more or less near to us," she said. "When the men were out organizing, registering voters, the wives talked until the men came back from Monroe County or wherever they were working. It helped the wives with their stress to stay on the phone, which was easy since we had party lines back then, everyone talking with each other. The women could not get comfortable until the men were back. It was tense, I tell you!

"Then one would say, 'I see a headlight coming. Looks like they got back all right this time,' and then they could breathe a little easier. Of course the phones were tapped—they probably still are. The KKK and the segregationists are lower key now. If they want something done, they get a black man to do it, give him money or drink or buy him a car. They get them to go agitate against the ones who are trying to accomplish something, like our little school, the Camden Christian Academy we are trying to get going. The Klan? I am sorry to say they are still here, but they keep a low profile."[23]

I thanked Kate for being so honest, so blunt, about how she saw and continues to see the situation in Wilcox. She said, "I do what I can, help teachers and students, attend prayer meetings, visit folks, travel, try to keep myself out of devilment. When it comes to tellin' the truth, I'm not afraid. I've been doing it all my life and they haven't got me yet."[24]

Return to Gees Bend, October 2008

Primarily because of its quilters, Gees Bend, the small isolated community I vividly recalled—the full immersion baptism in Foster Creek, the beautiful voices of the Pleasant View Church ladies—has become the most famous of all of Wilcox County's tiny communities.

I had noticed those asymmetrical patterned quilts in Gees Bend and Possum Bend while I was there, but their commercial promotion began only after we left in 1965. Some of the quilters, now in their seventies and eighties, have been on tour to art museums and universities with their quilts. Wherever they go, they sing their praise songs, songs that some folks call "Negro" spirituals. While they speak in simple terms and a unique dialect, the quilters are not as naive as they have been portrayed. When we met some of them, they laughed about how they were romanticized in the media for doing what they have always done.

Although it says "Boykin" on the official road map, no one who lives in the Gees Bend area uses that name, except at the post office. Instead, they call the area after Joseph Gee, one of the region's earliest cotton plantation enslavers. After abolishment of slavery, Gees Benders survived by sharecropping for decades as they strove for economic independence. Community members survived the devastating loss of their tenant farmer jobs and homes during the Great Depression of the 1930s. Despite subsequent federal assistance in purchasing land and building homes, winning the vote, and a strong commitment to community life, as of the 2010 census 49.2 percent of Boykin (Gees Bend) residents lived in poverty.[25]

The quilters' fame brings most of the Gees Bend visitors, but when telling their history, residents are proudest of the group of Gees Bend men who, after a year of planning and organizing, marched to the courthouse to politely demand to be registered to vote in 1963. Although it took all day, ten men were allowed to fill out registration forms, which were quickly deemed unacceptable.[26] Undaunted, the Benders pressed on through legal filings until they won in 1966.[27]

The feisty independent Benders were punished harshly for their early activism. In 1962, even before their heroic trek to the courthouse, the ferry that was the lifeline between Gees Bend and Camden was shut down abruptly as Benders began to organize for their voting rights. The closure of the ferry changed a twenty-minute river crossing into an hour and a half drive each way by the narrow old roads. Many who marched or registered to vote in rural Alabama lost their jobs and some even lost their homes. When the ferry that connected Gees Bend to Camden and the outside world was closed, Sheriff Lummie Jenkins was infamously quoted: "We didn't take away the ferry because they were black; we closed it because they *forgot* they were black."[28]

Benders were early founders of the Wilcox County Civic and Progressive League and worked with both SCLC and SNCC field staff. Dr. King made several visits to encourage the community, and they were proud that the mule-drawn wagon that carried him to his funeral was made in Gees

Bend, symbolizing the undying connection between their struggle and his leadership.

Others have written about conflicts surrounding the original Freedom Quilting Bee and the subsequent Quilters Collective that we were about to visit,[29] but when Luke and I returned to Gees Bend, Luke was interested in the quilts and I was interested in asking about "my" families. Although Gees Bend residents are understandably proud of ferry service being restored in 2006 after more than four decades of punishing absence, we had always driven the long way around through Prairie and Catherine, and so we did again. Luke thought it was important to come in slowly. "I feel like I should make this trip on my knees, like a pilgrimage." I ragged him by saying, "As slow as you drive, we may as well be crawling in on our knees." We laughed and sang along with Sheryl Crow's "Every Day Is a Winding Road" as we drove deeper into our past.

Mary Ann Pettway, the Quilting Collective manager,[30] had told me when I called a few days earlier: "Just phone when you get here or if you're running late, we'll wait for you." As we rounded the bend, the Boykin Nutrition Center came into view. Back in 1965 it was a community meeting hall; it still has the same old tin roof and peeling paint and a faded sign that says "Gees Bend Quilters." There were a couple of out-of-state cars parked out front in the wide dirt driveway.

My heart pounded as we walked up the old steps. Luke was right—I felt as if I were entering a sanctuary. I almost expected to hear ladies singing praise songs. And I did! Gospel hymns on a radio blended with soft voices inside the humble building. The majority of the oldest and best quilts are now owned by collectors and museums, or safely preserved by out-of-state family members of the quilters, not hanging on the walls of this low-security building. But I was there to speak with people; the quilts were a side benefit.

We entered through the empty lunchroom and walked through an open doorway into a long narrow room where dozens of brightly colored quilts were stacked. A heavyset woman with a red headscarf was hand stitching and seemed to be the only quilter in evidence. When she glanced up, I introduced Luke and myself. She told us to make ourselves at home, pull quilts out, and spread them out to view. I said that we were there to meet Mrs. Mary Ann Pettway, and she replied flatly, "She's at home bakin' a cake."

Although we had no plans, nor money to buy quilts, we looked, admired, and "oohed" and "ahhed" over the contemporary designs. There were a few historic quilts hanging on the wall, but most in the stacks were five or fewer years old. The prices of $5,000 and up surprised me, even though I had been

15. Gees Bend quilters with author (left to right): Nancy Ross Pettway, Mary Lee Bendolph, Maria Gitin, and Annie Ross Kennedy, Gees Bend, Alabama, 2008. (Courtesy of the author.)

forewarned. Just then, a thin middle-aged white man from the Midwest selected a quilt and a $7,000 transaction took place. A little while later, two more white men with southern accents who clearly had come to shop, not browse, entered. Why doesn't it ever stop surprising me how money is inequitably distributed in this country? But I didn't covet a quilt. I longed for conversation.

Luke was getting antsy so I picked up a small quilted wall hanging from the $75 pile and told him this would be the one to get his wife if he was planning on it. It was the nicest in that price range, very beautifully done. He set it aside and bought it for her later. For myself, I selected a little sample with just four lines of uneven purple, yellow, red, and gold strips inside a white border. The piece was only $10 but made me feel happy. On the back in a shaky hand was the name "Allie Pettway" with no date, but it was clearly recent.

Luke and I argued about leaving. I had faith that Mrs. Pettway was going to come and that she was making this cake for us. Mrs. Bennett nodded and said, "Yessum, that's right. She'll be here after a while."

Shortly, three energetic older ladies arrived: Mary Lee Bendolph and sisters Annie Ross Kennedy and Nancy Ross Pettway. We spent some time talking over their change of fortune since the movement. The ladies didn't recognize my descriptions of the Pettway, Robinson, and Boykin families I stayed with in 1965. They laughingly reminded me that "near everyone out here is named Pettway and there is plenty of Robinsons and Boykins too."

"You came all this way to ask about people you remember when you was down here?" They were accustomed to people coming to ask about the quilts, but this was something different. I had woefully inadequate information from which to try to reconstruct my past.

In fall 1965, I was distraught when my letter to the Robinsons and Lawsons of Boiling Springs was returned. I had heard that some folks' homes had been burned for housing civil rights workers. I wondered if the Robinsons' address really was wrong or if the white mailman wouldn't deliver it. I had always called them Mr. and Mrs. to show respect and didn't recall their first names. One of the ladies said, "Most of Boiling Springs is torn down; there's nothin' really up there now."

We talked about some of John Reese's photos on the wall, including one of Monroe Pettway and Rev. Lonnie Brown, two of the strongest movement men in Gees Bend. They are regarded as heroes in Gees Bend for leading the first organized effort of African Americans to register in Camden in 1963. The courage of these men who actually entered the courthouse at that time has become legend. Annie Kennedy bemoaned that they loaned a photo of the first Gees Benders registering in Camden to some researcher who never returned it.

As our conversation turned to old photos, I went out to the car and brought in the only two books I have ever encountered that focus on Wilcox County, *Down Home* and *In the Shadow of Selma*. As we combed through the first book together, our conversation sprang to life. All of us sitting there were part of a living history. We knew these people, these places, and they knew far more. They could name nearly every person in every Adelman photo. They pointed out Mary McCarthy, the white VISTA worker who they credited for founding their quilting "cooperative," which is what they called the Collective. Soon, Mary Ann Pettway arrived with her Bundt cake, which we enjoyed along with our conversation.

No one said anything when we came to Sheriff Lummie Jenkins. I guess over the years they all have said what there is to say about him. When we got to the photo of a black man staring out of the Wilcox County jail, I told them, "I was in that jail, that evil old jail."

"Oh you were arrested too; oh good for you! All right then!" one of them said. "No self respectin' civil rights worker could stand up if you hadn't been arrested."

One woman recounted, "I never did get jailed, but two of my neighbors did and they were hurt bad. I had to take them to the doctor. That's history, I tell you!"

Annie Ross Kennedy found a photo of her husband in the book *In the Shadow of Selma* and shook her head. "That's him, my husband, Houston Kennedy, and that's our mule. This picture been all over in museums, books and they always just put 'man with a mule' or 'Gees Bend farmer,' with no name at all."

I offered, "Well, we can fix that right now, at least in this copy. Please sign his and your name right here," as I handed her the paperback opened to the photo of her husband. With great care she wrote in beautiful cursive script, "Houston Kennedy" and signed it, "Annie R. Kennedy, wife."

Luke was just learning about these books. He exclaimed, "You're famous!"

Which prompted Mary Lee Bendolph to say, "Well, like I say when somebody says to me 'You're famous, you must be rich,' I say 'being on *Oprah* don't make you rich.'"

Luke asked, "Were you on *Oprah*?"

One of the women answered, "No, they just had our picture on."

The ladies asked about our experience as civil rights workers. Luke told them about being stung by an electric cattle prod in an early April 1965 march from Camden Academy and about working with Dan Harrell. I told them about arriving in Camden in the middle of the night to find out that Sheriff Jenkins had warned the people planning to house us that he'd kill their whole family if they let us stay there so we had to sleep on the floor of Antioch Baptist Church. They nodded in agreement; that's how things were back then.

We were not getting any closer to finding my families and the ladies had other things to do, so I said that it was a blessing just to be there, and Luke said it was an honor to meet them. I tried Mrs. Monroe Pettway's number again and this time she answered. I told her I was sorry to hear that her husband had died a few months back and what a brave man he was. She said, "Yes he was, yes he was. Thank you for remembering him."

I asked her if I might have stayed with them, and she said, "Heavens no, that was too dangerous." I didn't let her hear me laugh. Monroe and Jessie Pettway lived their whole lives in total commitment to the most dangerous enterprise a black activist could undertake, insistence on their equal rights. Too dangerous to house white civil rights workers? Indeed!

The ladies said they were sorry they couldn't help me find my families.

Then someone wondered aloud if my Pettway family could have been Allie Pettway who lives at the end of the road. It was her little quilt piece that I had just bought from the sample pile. They gave us directions and telephoned Mrs. Allie Pettway to let her know we were coming.

"When I tell people I am writing about my time in the movement, everybody says 'oh you need to talk with so and so,' naming famous officials," I told them. "I say, 'No, these folks out in Gees Bend and the other little towns, they may not be famous but they are the brave ones. They had no FBI or anyone.'"

"Yes! Yes!" the ladies exclaimed in agreement. Their chorus of church-lady approvals wasn't for us as individuals but for the joy of talking about the movement days and remembering the danger and their hard-won victories.

We walked back into the quilt showroom to thank Mary Ann Pettway again for the cake and Mrs. Bennett for being there. After another round of thanks and hugs, we got back in the car and headed down the road to visit Mrs. Allie Pettway.

After a few muddy sidetracks, we discovered Allie Pettway standing on her steps, waving. I approached her with her quilt piece held up and she responded just as her sister predicted, "You bought my piece; well bless you, thank you for coming by." Her 1930s home has been improved with gas, electricity, indoor plumbing, and new interior wallboard, but otherwise it is a classic of the Farm Security Administration period with linoleum floor and three bedrooms around a central kitchen. When we arrived she had been sitting on her screened porch where she likes to sit and sew. The light is good, the air is fresh, and the bugs don't get in. She was working on some small bright quilted samples like the one I had just bought. After greeting hugs, she told us she's lived in this spot all her life. She repeated, "All my life. My husband, his name was John the Baptist Pettway. That's his name and most called him by that; he was a good man."

The first and oldest quilter of Gees Bend had piercing brown eyes that held a steady gaze. What all she had seen since she was born in 1916 was beyond my knowing. She was at the age of living fully in the present, her movements and plans directed by the dictates of her body. Her daughter, who lives nearby, visited daily. She and other relatives looked out for Mrs. Pettway, allowing her to remain in her home. During our visit she complained of her lower back hurting, so without thinking, I put my hand on the small of her back. She said, "Oh that feels good. That feels so good. Bless you." I kept my warm hand on her lower back as much as I could during our short visit; it gave me as much comfort as it did her. It calmed me to be connected to the quiet strength that emanated from Allie Pettway's frail body.

She asked where we were from and was excited when I said California. She said she's been there many times to visit her three daughters and "I don't know how many grands." When I asked if she recalled housing civil rights workers, she drew a blank. A while later she said, "We didn't let any stay here. We were active in the movement but we didn't keep any workers. They'd come after you for that."

We admired her quilts. Before we left, she pressed me to take a second small sample that she painstakingly signed with arthritic hands. "Don't be tellin' my sister, Nancy. We're not supposed to give any out except through the co-op." When I went to use her bathroom, I slipped some bills under her house keys on the kitchen counter, hoping she wouldn't remember where they came from. We drove away waving, leaving one of Gees Bend's living treasures sitting on her sun porch.[31]

Return to Boiling Springs and Millers Ferry, 2008

After our successful visit in Gees Bend, I wanted to try to find Boiling Springs—or where Boiling Springs used to be—since everyone said it was deserted. We had to drive a long way around the bend in the river, way up in the northwest corner of the county on Highway 28, far away from any other community. My heart sank as we drove past ancient abandoned houses overgrown with mounds of kudzu and other weeds. We didn't even see any trailers, at least not on the main road. We passed tree-lined, red dirt lanes where I had spent many days walking for miles with local youth pointing out houses of potential voters, knocking on weathered cabin doors. I wondered what happened to those kids, Robert, James, and Mae. Were they still alive? Where did they live now? Did they remember that summer? Would anyone remember me, not as a name, but as an ally in an important piece of their history, even as another blurry white face? Probably not, there was so much happening during the movement years, everyone was in so much danger all of the time that it's a wonder anyone could remember her own name.

We drove onto a few unpaved roads off of Highway 28 without finding any building other than the nicely maintained but closed Bethel AME Church. The few homes that were visible from Highway 28 had open doors hanging off rusty hinges and porches long ago collapsed. The formerly vital little community seemed abandoned, just like I had been told. As we drove back toward Camden, I felt discouraged. Boiling Springs held so many vivid memories for me that I couldn't believe there was no one left who could talk about those days. More than four years later, after asking dozens of people about the Robinsons and Lawsons, a former resident of Boiling Springs informed me that she knew Mrs. Robinson and that she had told her about me, but that Mrs. Robinson didn't want to be contacted. I briefly spoke with two of the Robinsons' adult children, a son and a daughter who had both moved away. The daughter had changed her name and denied that anyone in her family had ever been active in the movement. She denounced civil rights as a total failure.

The Robinsons' son recalled canvassing for voters together and was more than glad to hear from me, but respected his mother's privacy. "We all wanted to end the way it was, being treated like slaves. We couldn't even buy a soda in a white store. Before you came, I went to a mass meeting in Selma, and we began canvassing for voters. But even after we got the vote, I still couldn't get a decent job in the South, so I came up here and got a good job in the North."[32]

Through a former Boiling Springs resident, Mrs. Robinson finally agreed to speak with me. I thanked her for the courage and kindness she showed when I stayed at her home. She said, "I'm glad to hear from you. They dropped the copy of your letter to me. It's the right address. There is no reason why they didn't deliver it to me back then except they didn't want me to get it. Yes, you shared the bed with my daughter and my son took you around canvassing. I remember you but not your name." She laughed when I recounted the time when she insisted on scrubbing me in their washtub before she would let me leave the house. "I hope I wasn't too hard on you! We were strict with our all our children but they grew up all right; they all had jobs and none got in trouble." I assured her that she was more than kind and that I was relieved to hear that they did not suffer from my stay in their home.

"I let you stay with us because my two oldest sons were very involved, and I wanted to let them know I was with them, that we were in it together. I had all these children, twelve kids altogether, and wanted something better for them than how it was then. I am proud of what we all did but, *Please, keep me anonymous.* There are still some hateful people here. If they knew I was involved [in the movement] they could do me harm, mess with my social security check or some such."[33] I told her that it broke my heart to hear that she was afraid but that there are enough Robinsons in Wilcox County that I could honor her request and still tell part of her story.

Other former Boiling Springs residents were happy to share their memories with me. Deborah Burrell Tucker and Voncille Burrell Spencer were proud that their mother, Virginia Boykin Burrell, was trained by SCLC to teach voter literacy and that their father, Eddie, was also active in the movement. Voncille told me that she began canvassing for voters at age thirteen and that she remembered walking around with me in Boiling Springs.

Voncille recalled a terrifying time when her father was working on voter registration. "He went to a little club one Saturday night to get his whiskey. I was very worried because he was wearing a white shirt that could make him an easy target. I prayed so hard that he would get home safe that I hardly slept, and we didn't see him until the next day. What happened was he got his liquor and was driving back home when he saw headlights and knew that they were following him. Shot out the back of his blue and white Fairlane with buckshot, completely wrecked that car. He also got shot in his cap; you could see the holes. He ditched the car and ran up into the woods to the Kings house where they let him hide for the night. The next day he called the Department of Justice and they sent someone out to take a report. Of course, nothing happened," she said with a sigh.[34]

I was overjoyed when the Burrell sisters connected me with the daughter of Mary and A. V. Lawson. Betty Lawson Henderson told me that her family maintained a civil rights safe house for years so she didn't recall me specifically, but she believed it was her home where the Robinsons brought me to share in their memorable meals. Her family is proud that they have held onto the land they acquired when slaves were freed, even though white landowners, who first tried to force them out and more recently to buy them out, surround them. "But we have held onto it and kept it in the family. We have family reunions out there most Thanksgivings and had 56 people attending in 2011."[35]

While the Burrells, Lawsons, and some of Robinsons proudly claimed their place in history, it is sad, but understandable, that others did not. It is hard for many people to recognize that continued unprovoked white on black violence gives tragic credence to lingering fears among a significant portion of African Americans. The NAACP continues to call for massive economic, social policy, and educational change that taken to their fullest measure could fulfill the dream of the historic Civil Rights Movement.[36] It is a crime that we live in country where people still have to fear being targeted for the color of their skin or for their commitment to racial justice. The courageous heroes of Wilcox County risked their lives and property to be active in the movement. They deserve to live in peace and comfort and to be honored for their contribution to the progress that has been made, most especially the right to vote.

As Luke and I drove south toward Camden from Boiling Springs, I insisted that we try to find the new ferry to Gees Bend that everyone was so proud of. We turned off at Millers Ferry Landing, the site of the old Henderson Plantation where the overseer chased Robert and me off back in 1965 and where the old Gees Bend ferry had launched before it was shut down. The late afternoon was warm and pleasantly muggy, slightly overcast. Our car windows were down and the mosquitoes were biting. The grass was green, and the earth in some places was rich black and in others deep orange-red, just the way I remembered. The only people we saw were a middle-aged man and woman with their feet dangling over the bank, fishing as peaceful as could be. I rolled down the window to ask where the ferry landing was and the woman explained that the new ferry landing was down the road, closer to Camden, but it was too late for us to search further.

Return to Camden, 2008

On our second day, we drove through Camden in overcast daylight. It was a thrill to get out of the car and just walk around. Instead of being intimidated by the stately courthouse and terrorized by the likelihood of being arrested, the town had shrunk into its real size and age. The buildings no longer seemed grand except for the refurbished courthouse, which now houses a library and government offices. Although there is a new courthouse and some other public buildings, the construction of the Camden bypass has left downtown nearly empty, and blessedly free of fast food places. We were pleased to see African American–owned businesses, Miz Kitty's Café and Reflections Boutique, on Union Street where forty years ago black people were forced off the sidewalk and rudely served in the white-owned stores. Before our visit, Reflections owner and community leader Alma Moton King had called to offer to show us around Camden. She also graciously invited me to make some remarks at the upcoming National Council of Negro Women (NCNW) Black and Pink Gala. "I guess we're the pink," Luke quipped when he showed me the new pink shirt and black-and-pink tie his wife had helped him pick out for the occasion. The NCNW gala is the biggest "do" in the black community, and nearly everyone I wanted to meet would be there.

After a successful career in New York City, Alma King returned committed to the revitalization of downtown Camden and to improving the county where her family has lived for generations. Over the next few days, we popped in and out of Alma's store, the site of much good conversation, as well as the only place to purchase dressy clothes in Wilcox County. She showed us around when she could, working her cell phone all the while.

Alma drove us around to see some of the advances made in Camden: a new nursing home and two developments with nice homes where blacks and whites live side by side, although she agreed with others that there is seldom cross-racial socializing between neighbors. "Some progress has been made. There is a long way to go, but things are better and getting better all the time," she said. Alma, and later others I spoke with, wondered aloud if the many who enjoy the benefits of these advances have any idea of the decades of sacrifice that have brought the community this far. They believe that there would be much greater progress if everyone banded together as they did in the past.

Back then there had been two attached buildings, one they called "the jail" and the other "the old jail," or "courthouse annex," where we were booked before being put into cells in the adjacent jail. Locals now refer to them as the "old jail," meaning the one used to house prisoners from the 1950s to the1980s, and the "old, old jail" that had served as courthouse annex, booking center, and voter registration location for black people in 1965. As we stood in the heat staring at the red dirt lot where the old jail had been torn down, shivers went through me as I pictured our dank, dirty cell and remembered listening helplessly to Mike Farley's screams as he was being beaten.

The courthouse annex, or "old, old jail," is falling down and boarded up, though we were told they are trying to get it saved as a historic site. Luke stood staring at the collapsing building wishing it could talk. He still couldn't remember anything beyond what Charles Bonner had told him of his time in the Camden jail. Whatever trauma took place during those two days remained locked inside.

As we stood there gazing at the decrepit building where so many people suffered so unjustly, both by incarceration and by being forced to register there instead of at the courthouse where white residents could go, a black deputy pulled up and leaned out of his truck window. "Y'all all right?" he asked. Luke told him we'd been in jail there, right there. The young deputy smiled blankly and waved as he drove off.

When I asked Alma about historic preservation and the potential for civil rights tourism, she told us that they were working to develop designated sites similar to the ones in Selma but that they hadn't considered keeping the old jail where so many civil rights activists and locals suffered. "That was an evil place," she said, "It was torn down as soon as we could." I agreed about that jail being vile. The foul smell of the place caused me to burn my dress when we were released; just thirty hours in that cell permeated my dress with pure evil.

After some shopping in the afternoon at Black Belt Treasures, an artists' cooperative in Camden, I carefully laid my batik tote bag on the chair in my dingy room at the Southern Inn motel. As I sat down to prepare my remarks I thought: Life has been damn unfair for people with darker skin, not only in the United States but also worldwide. If you are a straight white American with any money at all, you most likely have not lived with the threat of being denied your legal rights, endangered and debased, or even murdered, based on something you have absolutely no control over. Now that I was worked up into a proper stew, I rewrote my two-minute talk.

Even though I speak publicly for a living, a few hours later, as I stood in the crowded Wilcox Central High School auditorium at the podium, I shook as I tried to figure out how the microphone worked. Folks shouted out directions to me from the audience, "Turn it around, turn it around!"

I did as they suggested and then quipped, "Thank you so much. They told us when we came down here in '65 to listen to local leaders and I guess that still is the best strategy." Their kind laughter eased my nerves.

"Thank you NCNW and Alma King for allowing me to say a few words and for making us feel so welcome. I want to begin by saying what an honor it was to serve in the movement with folks like Dan and Juanita Harrell, Major Johns, Rev. and Mrs. Threadgill, the teachers and students at Camden Academy. . . ."

I continued with as many names as I could in the short time I had and quoted James Baldwin before my concluding remarks:

> The sea rises, the light fails, lovers cling to each other, and children cling to us. The moment we cease to hold each other, the moment we break faith with one another, the sea engulfs us and the light goes out.

"We had a vision of the Beloved Community. We tried to live our lives in a circle of trust, the essential, life saving faith we had in each other to put the movement first, ourselves second, and to always look out for each other. Most of us white students from that time miss that closeness more than anything.

"I'd say more black people saved more of us whites the summer I was here than the other way around. We put each other's lives in danger, wittingly at times in order to get the work done, sometimes to prove our point that integration won't kill you—although it might—and sometimes, just to have fun.

"Martin Luther King Jr. was one of many nonviolent leaders who spoke of the Beloved Community as a transracial community of brother- and sisterhood. In 1957, writing in the newsletter of the newly formed Southern Christian Leadership Conference, he described the purpose and goal of that organization as follows:

The ultimate aim of SCLC is to foster and create the "beloved community" in America where brotherhood is a reality. . . . SCLC works
for integration. Our ultimate goal is genuine intergroup and interpersonal living.

"And in his last book he declared, 'Our loyalties must transcend our race,
our tribe, our class, and our nation.'[37]
"In 1965 in the small African American churches in Wilcox County,
the circle of trust had only recently begun to expand to include white civil
rights workers, and then, with sensibly mixed feelings based on mixed results. Your openness to us and to our naïveté may have been perceived by
some to be due to our whiteness and our acceptance of you, but my own experience was that you were just good people. 'Spectacular folk,' as my friend
Luke, who is here with me tonight, always says. You all had been through
so much, heard so many broken promises, and yet you kept opening you
hearts and homes to us. It was one of the greatest privileges of my life to
stand by your side and be of service in your struggle for justice. For that, I
can never thank you enough."

After a full program of moving speeches and entertainment, our eyes
brimming with tears, we stood to sing "This Little Light of Mine" as candles
were lit and passed among high-spirited high school students, determined
parents and strong elders.

We *Shall* Remember Them

At the rising of the sun and at its going down, We remember them.
At the blowing of the wind and the chill of winter, We remember them.
When we are weary and in need of strength, We remember them. . . .
As long as we live, they too will live; for they are now a part of us, as we
remember them.

Traditional prayer said at graveside by Reform Jews

After the Voting Rights Act became law on August 6, 1965, we imagined that things would improve dramatically for African Americans throughout the South. We left thinking that the battle had been won, or at least that the freedom fighters were on the road to victory. National media informed us that progress was slow, but I was ignorant of the ongoing terrorism, lost jobs and stolen land, and even murder of activists that continued in Wilcox County. Movement teachers were fired from their decent paying school positions and blacklisted from other jobs. Tenant farmers lost their homes as well as their income from farming.

As I continued talking with folks, I learned how deeply people were scarred by the continued backlash they suffered due to their own and their parents' work in the movement. Some former student protesters bear permanent physical and emotional scars. A few who live in the county still feel so unsafe in their own community that they requested anonymity. Others moved away and cannot bear to return, even to visit family or to attend school reunions. Interestingly, activists over sixty-five years old tended to have a more optimistic view of both the past and the present than most of those who were younger than I am.

In Memory of Major Johns

One of the leaders who inspired optimism in others was our beloved SCLC field director Major Johns. I never got to tell him how much he taught me about courage and discipline. Born and raised in Plaquemines, Louisiana, Rev. Major Johns was instrumental in the Civil Rights Movement in Mississippi, Alabama, and Louisiana for at least a decade, yet he is scarcely mentioned in books written to date. It was difficult to find people who knew him personally, although his importance as a student civil rights leader in Baton Rouge has been documented in the global nonviolent database at Swarthmore University.[1] In 1960, five years before we met him in Camden, Major Johns was arrested along with other Southern University students for sitting-in at a Kress lunch counter in Baton Rouge as part of a multistate Congress of Racial Equality (CORE) integration drive. When they got out of jail, Major Johns and two classmates stood on a school bus while he made a rousing speech.[2] He and other CORE members organized a march of more than three thousand Southern University students to the state capitol to protest segregation and the arrests of students participating in sit-ins at segregated drugstore soda fountains and bus terminals. All of the arrested student leaders were expelled from Southern University and barred from all public colleges and universities in the state. In 2004, long after Major's death, the student civil rights workers were awarded honorary degrees and the state legislature passed a resolution in their honor, sadly Major Johns did not live to see that day.[3]

Jesse Smith, who had shown Luke and me around Lower Peachtree in 1965, remembers Major spending time at his home and at his father Rev. Smith's church. "Major Johns, once in while he would talk about the black history of America—Crispus Attucks and all that. He was so inspiring. He'd quote from the Constitution about the right of the people to form or abolish this kind of government. There was so much power in his words; that man could speak!"[4]

From others, I heard that Major became an ordained minister after his time in the movement. He was always a man of great faith and he was able to graduate from Louisiana State University as well at New Orleans Baptist Theological Seminary where he received master of divinity in 1979. Johns died in Baton Rouge at age forty-six, from a brain aneurism, while working at a school for troubled boys in New Orleans. Major Johns had a big heart and really understood young people. Although Major Johns didn't live to receive his honorary degree from Southern University, which had expelled him for standing up for his rights, he succeeded with both his education and vocation.

According to his younger brother, William Johns, "After Major was arrested and expelled, the judge gave the expelled students the choice to go to jail or join the Army. So, they forced him into the Army, but true to his beliefs, he served as a Conscientious Objector. He got out of the Army in 1962 the same year I went in. He was stationed out in California at Ft. Ord for a while. When he got out, he joined the movement full time.

"We were always proud of him. A lot of people were afraid to say or do anything, afraid of losing their jobs, but some people were supportive. The high school principal used to keep him in clothes; lots of time you had to do it [give support] in silence. Couldn't let them know.

"One night I got home to Plaquemines and heard Major was here. My mom was kinda concerned because he got arrested downtown. I went down there and was just standing on the sidewalk lookin' for him. Suddenly it was all cattle prods and tear gas; I just happened to be there so took my blows. I was only there to see him. They were all involved, my younger sisters, marching and everything. I like the way people have grown out of that prejudice, segregation. Some of them have anyway. I think things are better. I have seen a miracle in my lifetime with President Obama getting elected. I never thought I'd live to see that.

"They were living in New Orleans when Major died. I went to see him every weekend; it was so hard. The year before he died, he was having headaches and he wouldn't see any medical professionals and he kept working. He believed that God would heal him. Major was supposed to get the full-time director position at the boys' school where he was chaplain when the head guy retired, but he died before that happened. For his funeral they gave a day off from the school so the boys could attend."[5]

Return to Pine Apple and Stories from the Crawfords

While Luke and I commiserated over the loss of Major, I focused on trying to find our other old friends and coworkers. Early on in my search, I was happy for Luke but a bit jealous that I had been able to help him find his host families, the Crawfords and Smiths, while the families I stayed with remained elusive. Then I recalled from the book of Ruth the words that I recited at my Jewish conversion ceremony: "Wherever you go I will go with you, and where you stay I will stay. Your people will be my people." I realized that all the freedom fighters of Wilcox County were my people; I had taken that vow when I came here to join their struggle long ago. As I reached out, I discovered that movement connections stretched across both time and distance. So I spoke with whomever wanted to tell their story, all who were connected in any way with the voting rights movement of Wilcox County. These became *my* people.

From my uncomfortable bed in a roadside motel in Camden, an unrelenting ringing sound jarred me back to the present. Luke was phoning from his room next door, "Hey! Rise and shine sunshine, I got some coffee goin' over here." It was 7:30 A.M., time to get ready to meet Bob Crawford Jr. at the old family home in Pine Apple, where Luke canvassed tirelessly that summer long ago. We climbed into the rental car and headed southeast on Highway 28 and soon connected with Highway 10, which took us to Pine Apple. After a few U-turns on wrong but scenic side roads, we found the Crawford homestead we remembered so well.

A tenant in a trailer out front let us know that Bob Crawford Jr. would be there shortly. The Crawfords' big old house was in total disrepair, its pole roof sagging, and its windows mostly boarded up. Where the brick chimneys had collapsed into the kitchen and front room, there were jagged spaces big enough to crawl through.

As I walked around the property, I heard Luke shouting from inside the house, "You won't believe this! This is incredible! All these antiques, man! Somebody would pay a fortune for this pie safe, these utensils, this flour sifter." I crawled in over broken fireplace bricks into the kitchen. There was Georgia Crawford's old wood-fire stove with pots still on it, several wooden cabinets, and lots of vintage cookware, all in extremely used condition. This was where Mrs. Crawford heated her irons, kept coffee going all hours for tired workers, and made her incredible peach pie. Despite the gloom and dirt, warmth still emanated from her kitchen. Some rooms in the old house were sealed off or doors shut. We had to be careful not to fall through the rotting floorboards. There were desiccated canned fruits and jams on the shelves, and open magazines and schoolbooks, along with a pile of letters, spilled onto the floor in the front room. In a back bedroom, a bed covered with dust was still made up. Stacks of homemade quilts, some of them not yet finished, were stored in an open chest by the bed. The entire home looked as if the owners had gone for a walk and forgotten to come back. We later found out that Bob Crawford Jr. could not bear to change anything in the house from the day his beloved mother died, and as we toured the county, we discovered other homes in similar condition, although none as full of old furnishings, books, and linens.

While we were waiting for Bob Jr., we walked down to Mt. Olive AME church adjacent to the Crawfords' property. The church had been lovingly restored and the doors were open. I told Luke he should go stand at the lectern, the way he had at the mass meetings long ago. "I don't think I said anything, I left that to Dan Harrell or someone to preach. I just got the folks to the meetings," Luke said modestly. He started thinking about Eric Jones again. It still weighed on his mind how Eric, who stayed at the Crawfords with Chuck Bonner and him, had made an antiwhite speech at a mass meeting Luke had organized. Eric said it was time for blacks to get rid of the "honkys." Being eighteen, Luke heard this one voice louder than all the others, louder than all the people who thanked him for helping them get registered, louder than Dan Harrell who valued him so much that he asked him to stay on. Besides being our peers, back then the SNCC *guys* seemed so cool compared to the serious, religious SCLC *men*. So what if their philosophy counted us out? That was part of this racial revolution, wasn't it? Luke had returned to the intersection of his memories and his current view of life, looking for truth and hoping for healing. "You know I oughta find Eric and thank him," he said. "If he hadn't made me feel like I didn't belong here, I probably would have stayed and got killed."

After a while, Bob Crawford Jr. pulled up in a truck towing a box trailer. At the time, Bob Jr. was seventy-two years old, powerfully built, and partially disabled. Bob Jr. greeted us with a huge grin and big hugs, and then began telling stories in his deep gravelly voice. He asked Luke to haul out a couple of comfortable folding chairs and set them up in the grass beside his truck, ready to reminisce. The retired teacher, truck driver, and US Army veteran knew that his family had been one of Luke's favorite families and was delighted that we had found him.

"We had been workin' tryin' to get folks organized for a long time, but we couldn't get any support," he said. "We couldn't get any help until you showed up. Then we got cars, material, plans; you all made a huge difference. It never would have happened without you. There was just too much goin' against us."[6] Bob Jr. went on to tell the stories Luke had been pining to hear. Luke was especially pleased when Bob Jr. admitted that despite all their grindingly hard work—farming cows, raising chickens, selling corn and other vegetables and fruit, Georgia taking in ironing, and Bob Sr. working at the sawmill for thirty cents a day—the real money that had bought the farm and eventually enabled Bob Sr. to quit the sawmill was from moonshine, just as Luke had always guessed. Even though the county had been technically "dry," most men in the county relaxed with some liquor on Saturday nights, just as sure as they attended church on Sunday mornings. Drinking was not only a way to unwind from hard labor, there was also an element of economic independence in getting back at "The Man" by buying from a bootlegging neighbor.

Bob Jr. said, "I have to say, I can't believe you came all this way. Not just now, but back then. You left your comfortable homes in California and came all the way down here just to help us. You didn't have to do that. I didn't think much of it at the time, but now that I think about it, it's just incredible!" These were the words that both of us had longed to hear; we had often wondered if we had been more of a hindrance than a help to the Wilcox movement.

Near the end of our visit, after Bob Jr. and Luke swapped many memories, Luke told the Dew Drop Inn story, about the time when Bob Sr. and the SNCC guys were up all night with shotguns at the windows while Luke went to sleep in the back. Bob Jr. remembered the Dew Drop nightclub though he hadn't been around when the incident with Luke and the white guy with the tire iron took place. He had been teaching school over in Monroe County where he lived with his wife, Jessie, and their infant daughter, Joy. Bob Jr. said that in his heart he believed in nonviolence, but in his spirit he was more of a Deacons for Defense kind of man, the militant defenders of civil rights workers.[7] He knew if he had been around the movement in Pine Apple, so close to his family, he would have gotten them in some kind of trouble. "So I stayed over there and just sent money and such. I taught my students about their rights and got in plenty of trouble with the school board over that," he said.

Before we left, Luke helped Bob Jr. break into the house through the front door where a board had gotten jammed. Bob Jr. said due to his bad leg, he couldn't crawl though the spaces we had earlier, so he hadn't been able to get in there for nearly ten years, even though the place became his after his parents passed away. Once Luke unstuck the doorjamb, Bob Jr. walked straight into the front bedroom. As if no time had passed, he pulled back the quilt, lifted up a pillow, and pulled out a half-empty bottle of moonshine. He laughed, "I thought I left this here." He took a big swig, offered Luke one, and put the bottle in his pants pocket. "Damn, my daddy made the best stuff!"

The three of us poked around inside for a while. Bob Jr. said he needed to get his daughters over here to decide what they wanted. Luke bent over a pile of letters on the floor and, unbelievably, he immediately discovered one postmarked August 1965. The envelope had his old name, Bob Block, with his father's San Francisco return address typed on it. He eyes watered as he read aloud:

> I'm really sorry about the way I left in such a hurry but my friend was getting out of the service in Louisiana and he was my only ride home. I'll never be able to thank you enough for all the things you did for me and the movement. I can only tell you that I will be back as soon as possible and that my thoughts are always with you. For that matter, there is a good movement going on here and we're fight-

ing the school system, which arranges boundaries so that most of the Negroes go to the same school.[8] Enclosed is a typical handbill that we use. Well, that's about all that there is to say except keep fighting for freedom and don't let nobody turn you 'round!!

Uhuru, Bob[9]

Luke and I looked at each other wordlessly, with tears in our eyes. Meanwhile, Bob Jr. was rummaging around looking for something to give us. He opened a trunk of quilt tops that his mother had been working on and urged me to take one. I protested that they were his daughters' inheritance. He pointed out that they could come out here any time to claim them and that there were plenty, so I happily selected a bright triangle pattern made from synthetic cloth but carefully hand stitched by Mrs. Crawford. Luke then asked for that old blue cardboard sign with white sparkly letters inscribed with the simple quote: Do unto others as you would have them do unto you. As he untacked it from the wall, Luke said, "That's what your folks lived by all right; I learned a lot about the kind of person I wanted to become from them."

Bob Jr. said, "Before you go I gotta tell you, you know my daddy agreed with Dr. King. He said we all need to work together, black and white. This separate thing wasn't going to work. So long as you are good people it don't matter if you are black or white. Just treat ever' body like they treat you. You remember, that's how my daddy was, a fair man."[10] Bob Jr. swept Luke and me into a big sweaty hug. He could have talked all day and we would have gladly listened, but we hoped to see a few more people in the short time we had to revisit Wilcox County.

A few months later, I called Bob Jr. to fill in some of the Crawford family stories. Both SCLC and SNCC workers stayed there during the movement. There might have been divisions in Selma and Atlanta, but in Wilcox County, there was no room for that kind of foolishness—you were either a movement man or woman or not. The Crawfords were solid movement folks and protective parents to the young civil rights workers they housed.

From the Crawfords' granddaughter, Joy Crawford-Washington, I learned that Bob Sr. had spent some time in the state penitentiary shortly after we left. So I asked Bob Jr. whether they set his father up because of civil rights? Bob Jr. told me, "My father went to the penitentiary because of moonshine, but he was stigmatized, targeted because of his involvement in the Civil Rights Movement. There were three or four men in that business making moonshine. They had all been caught any number of times, but the sheriff only went after my father. Sheriff Lummie Jenkins said that Daddy was goin' to get some time because of what he did with the movement. Lummie didn't like those 'smart niggers.'"[11]

One of the many times Bob Crawford Sr. demonstrated his intelligence, tenacity, and commitment to civil rights was in the spring 1966 elections when black residents of Pine Apple were able to vote for the first time. Bob Sr. was a poll watcher, a volunteer citizen who assured that the voting officials didn't violate any rules and that all qualified people got to cast their ballot. But when he reported for duty at the Sugar Shack polling place, Alabama state election inspectors forced him to leave. He persevered and drove around until he found the federal election observers who overruled the state officials and said he had a right to monitor the voting for irregularities.[12]

Bob Jr. explained, "Before you were here, Daddy was banned from other people's properties for soliciting people to vote. Landowners of sharecroppers' places let Lummie Jenkins charge the voter education folks with trespassing on private property so that they couldn't organize. Somehow some of the tenants had the grit to meet my father anyway, in a public place to learn about registering. But if they were found out, they would be put off their places for speaking with us.

"Lummie told my daddy, 'People like you who participate in the Civil Rights Movement is good prospects for fish bait in the Alabama River.' I never would have thought my daddy would die a natural death. He wasn't scared of nobody. He was arrested right after you all left, must have been fall of 1965. He was sentenced to the state pen for year and a day; he served nine months of that. It didn't change him a bit; he came out and went on in his same way. In fact, he must have barely been out a month when he was out there being a poll watcher; that's my daddy all right."[13]

A few years after our reunion with Bob Jr., I met his daughter, Joy Crawford-Washington, who has become a dear friend. She once wrote to me: "I'm so grateful and proud of the work that you did along with so many other brave soldiers of the Civil Rights Movement in Wilcox County. You were just a young couple, yet you and Bob (Luke) fought side by side for peace, justice and equality. My beloved grandparents knew they were destined to be involved in the movement. They sacrificed to serve others and make the future brighter for us."

On a more colloquial note Joy shared this memory, "I remember when granddaddy and I were coming home one evening, we saw my grandmother standing in front of my older sister Debbie with my granddaddy's rifle and a pitchfork, in the backyard near the house. My grandfather asked, 'What

are you all doing?,' and my grandmother responded that some man was calling his name, and she was not going to let them take her and my sister by
surprise."[14] Joy speaks of her grandparents with deep feeling. "Their courage inspires my sisters and me every day, and we will continue to share their
story with generations to come. Talking with you has brought them back
to life and renewed my commitment to their memory and their vision for
equality. I speak often to young people about how the movement involved
more than just Dr. King or Rosa Parks."[15]

Return to Lower Peachtree and Stories from the Smiths

While I wrote up my notes, Luke went out to Lower Peachtree to visit
Carolyn Smith Taylor and her brother, Jesse Smith, in Lower Peachtree.
When he had called earlier, for the first time in forty-three years, Carolyn
shouted so loud I could hear "Bob! Bob Block! You are Luke, now? All right,
but you'll always be Bob to us. Of course I remember you! Come on out!"

Luke returned from Lower Peachtree bubbling over with enthusiasm.
"It is so incredible! Carolyn has a real nice home right next to their folks'
place. Jesse comes out from Montgomery and stays there some weekends.
They preserved the house and the church. They have a real nice grave for
Rev. Smith; it's a talking grave. You press a button and some of his speeches
and sermons come on over a speaker. Really amazing! They have a whole
wall of photos in the house. Carolyn made me feel right at home, just like
it was yesterday." I asked Luke endless questions, but he was living in the
moment of the visit so he just told me they said they'd be glad to talk with
me anytime. Over the next four years I spoke with three of the Smiths'
now-adult children, and met both Carolyn and Jesse. We learned that Rev.
Frank Smith and other teachers lost their jobs, in part because white students stayed with them. Stories of their family's perseverance in the face of
injustice reconfirmed the high esteem in which we had held them, as did
the stories of so many Wilcox County activists.

When we met Rev. Smith, we had no idea that he was in the midst of
what would become a lengthy legal battle for his livelihood, his principles,
and ultimately, his ability to support his family in Wilcox County. In the fall
of 1965, right after we left Wilcox County, the county board of education
terminated Rev. Frank Smith from his teaching position at Lower Peachtree
High School because of his participation in the Civil Rights Movement. I
knew that he had graduated from two-year Selma University, but I didn't
learn until I spoke with his daughter, Carolyn Smith Taylor, that he had received both a BA and a master's in education from Alabama State. He was

one of many stalwart leaders who believed that education is an essential element of liberation for oppressed people.

Rev. Smith and his family suffered greatly for his commitment to telling the truth inside and outside the classroom. From the time he first joined Gees Bend activists in 1963 and attended SCLC organizing and voter education training in Selma and Birmingham, white school officials scrutinized him. After he allowed students, including his teenage son Jesse, to meet at his own church and to organize a Freedom School there, he was warned many times to shut down the school, or else. The "or else" that finally drove him out of Wilcox County for many years was termination and being blacklisted from teaching anywhere else in the region. Rev. Smith and many other teachers who filed unjust firing and elimination of pension claims did receive some compensation many years after their original complaints, but a significant period of their professional life was denied them.

White people's anger over the prospect of integration was so intense that one of the most dangerous actions the Smiths took was allowing two white female civil rights workers, who were passing through on their way to Clark County, to stay at their home for a couple of nights. The white girls went with the Smith kids to a dance at all black Lower Peachtree High and danced with the young men there. Word spread like wildfire through the white community. After this incident, threats to the Smiths increased, including a shot-out mailbox and threatening telephone calls in the middle of the night. It seemed that white people could always find a way to justify their hostility, and often it was blamed on some trumped-up story about black men and white women, as if that could justify mistreatment, even murder.[16]

Despite all that, the Smiths welcomed Bob Block as a frequent guest in their home and never hinted at the pressure they faced. In fact it was the opposite. Bob said he not only felt treated like part of the family, but safer out there with the Smiths. We had wondered why Rev. Smith was so somber back then; now we knew.

I asked the Smiths' youngest daughter about her family housing white civil rights workers besides Luke. Now a retired middle school guidance counselor, Carolyn recalled the incident that caused quite a stir in the area. "My brother Jesse remembers them well: Noni and Joni were the girls' names. They must have come before or after you were there. Anyway, what I remember most is those girls were dropped off at our place at night. As soon as they got in the house, they asked my mother if they could wash their hair, so we knew they had been out doing civil rights fieldwork. There was some dance at the school. We were wondering if they were going to dance with the black boys. They did; they danced with everyone who asked. Daddy told us he heard the sheriff was going to come and so he told us, 'If he does, you go outside just sit in the car and wait.' But nothing happened right away. Later, we got threats because of that."[17]

When I told Carolyn that she was one of the girls I was jealous of because everyone said the Smith girls were the prettiest ones in Peachtree, she just laughed. "You didn't meet us because my sister Geral and I only came on weekends. We were over at Alabama State in Montgomery. But, I remember Bob. We were so excited to have him in the neighborhood. Because you know that was our first time interacting with white people on an equal basis. It was exciting! Maybe we didn't have the sense to be scared, but it was a real exciting time. Everybody was so active and willing to sacrifice. When he visited recently, I told him, 'Here you are Bob, a white kid, this is a black neighborhood and anyone could have picked you off. And you came here, to be with us.' He worked hard. Almost anytime we'd look down the road we'd see him coming and we'd say, 'Here comes Bob.'

"My sister Geral said to be sure to tell you what a difference it made to us that you came." Carolyn read from a letter by Geral (Gwendolyn Geraldine Smith): "'Your participation offered guidance and allowed the world to see the plight of the folks in Wilcox County. It allowed us to know what was available from the federal, state and local governments—so much was out there that we were unaware of.'"[18]

During our conversation, I told her that it was amazing now to think that back then I sat there with her mother, waiting for Bob and Jesse to come in from canvassing, shelling pecans on the porch just as relaxed as could be, never thinking that racists could have pulled the trigger on us at any moment. The Smiths were among the bravest people I ever met.

When I spoke with Carolyn's brother, Jesse Smith, whom I recalled as a highly articulate and effective teen leader, it was no surprise to learn that he became a minister like his father. He now preaches at a Baptist church in Montgomery. "I was about fifteen or sixteen years old that summer you were here. At Lower Peachtree High everybody was doing something in civil rights. My dad being a history teacher, he told us, 'The best thing that you can do now for the Civil Rights Movement is to get your lessons, be a good student of history.' Lots of the kids had been going to Pleasant View Church for meetings. Stokely Carmichael from SNCC came down and spoke; we were very impressed. He might even have come up to the house and ate some watermelon with us before they went back to Lowndes County. They sure stirred us up about the freedom movement. This was during the school year, before you came.

"One night Daddy wrote out the complaints of the students at the high school: No running water, no library, gym or science lab. The student body signed it. Someone from the Board of Education came and we gave the letter to him.

"We began to become militant, the students and even the teachers who we had thought were Uncle Toms. One day some young SCLC workers, nineteen- or twenty-year-old black youth, came around and began singing freedom songs outside the window. When we heard that, we just got up and walked out of class. We began to organize ourselves into a student group right there on the grass; they elected me as president.

"The marches were starting to happen in Camden, which was thirty-five miles away. The students came to Pleasant View Church right below our house—yes, my daddy was the minister there—everybody would come at night to make plans, like who would drive, we'd collect gas money. We went in to Camden to the marches from Antioch Baptist Church up to the courthouse. I was never afraid; I was trying to keep my buddies from throwing bricks, staying nonviolent. That was my job. And I made sure the little girlfriends and boyfriends didn't go off into the bushes.

"I remember Bob Block real well. We were sort of like brothers then. It felt real good. One day I was cutting Larry's hair and Bob asked me to cut his. He had great faith in me; I had never cut white hair before, but I went ahead and tried. It looked real bad on the sides. He looked at it in the mirror for a long while and then he said, 'It'll grow back.'

"I admired Bob's 'never give up' attitude. Somewhere in Pine Hill he asked this man was he a registered voter. He said, 'Son, that ain't none of your business.' We made a U-turn—no use talking to him—but we kept on goin'. In Lower Peachtree where I lived, we had been trying to get the people to go over to sign up for commodities. Bob got Mr. Campbell and his wife to sign up after he wouldn't listen to me or other black students. They needed that food for their family. Then after Mr. Campbell signed up, a bunch of other folks went over and got signed up. You helped us a lot."[19]

Jesse said that every time he goes to vote and puts on that little button, "I have voted, have you?" he feels proud to know his family was right in the front lines of making it possible for black people to vote. "This past election, I went with a lady who had never voted before but she wanted to vote for Barack Obama. I helped her through the whole process. She was so happy.

"Another time from back then that I'll never forget is that a whole lot of us went over to Montgomery to join the end of the march from Selma to Montgomery. When they came around Dexter Curve we stepped in and walked up to the capitol together to welcome the marchers. I'll always remember that day."[20]

When Jesse graduated from Lower Peachtree High School in 1967, it was an all-black public high school. As part of the dismantling of historically black schools, the white Wilcox County school board closed the school the next year. Despite the family being harassed, the Smiths enrolled their youngest son, Larry, as one of the first black students to integrate Pine Hill Elementary School.

I was fortunate to reach Larry at his home in Tampa, Florida, where he lives and works as a commercial airline pilot. Speaking of his early years in Lower Peachtree, Larry recalled, "We moved away to Ohio in 1968, so I was still quite young. I went to all the mass meetings at the church almost every Friday night," he said. "Mostly I remember the Kool-Aid and the singing. Lots of people were coming and going from the house all the time. I don't remember you specifically but there were always white people around our house.[21]

"When they decided to send me to integrate Pine Hill Elementary, my parents actually sat down and asked me about it, explained it to me. I was there for second and third grades, school years 1966–67 and 1967–68. I remember Daddy telling me that the school wasn't accepting seniors into Pine Hill High for the first year of integration. That's why Jesse didn't attend. Although my father didn't say so, I'm sure he would have preferred that Jesse, his seventeen-year old son, be the first of our family to test school integration rather than his seven-year old son!! I had been attending the all black school in Pine Hill. On the first day of school we met at the all black school for prayer and support from some of the students and teachers. Then Daddy drove the three of us: me in second grade, Ruby Tate in eighth grade, and Elijah Clifton in the ninth about three miles on the other side of the railroad tracks to the all-white Pine Hill High School. The first day, we arrived after school had started. After going to the office, I was escorted to my second grade classroom already in session.

"By the time Daddy drove us to the school that day, he had already been fired from his teaching job. As best I can recall, he drove us to school every day during that school year. He drove up, sat, and watched us as we walked into the school building. Each day he stayed there until we walked out of view. In fact, when I felt lonely, I would go to the bathroom and look out the window hoping he would still be sitting there in the car. Although he wasn't there then, he was always there when school was over.[22]

"That first year, I was the only one in my classroom. In third grade there were three of us: Ethel Carlton, James Collier, and myself. The summer after third grade we moved to Dayton, Ohio, because Daddy was fired.

"At that school, you had to line up to do everything. When I got in line, the other students would rub my arm to see if the black would come off.

That first school year a teacher allowed some older kids to drag me across the football field during the lunch recess. When they published our yearbook photos, we were arranged off in a corner of the page to separate the black and white students, as if to make sure you didn't miss the point. I keep the yearbook and show it to people when I give talks.

"There were a couple of white kids who may not have been from around there who played with me sometimes. There was a white kid I knew from class who I saw in town once, in the backseat of his parents' car. I waved to him but he had to sneak a wave because his parents wouldn't have approved."[23]

The entire Smith family was deeply affected by a tragic car accident in 1973 in which the Smith's eldest son, Frank M. Smith, his wife and child, as well as his sister-in-law, brother-in-law, and their child, were all killed. The pain of that loss can never be erased. Surviving family members find strength in their faith and each other, and in preserving the blessed memory of their courageous parents.

Camden Academy and Thomas L. and Mildred Threadgill

Before returning to Wilcox County in 2008, I heard from several Camden residents about the shocking destruction of Camden Academy, the historic mission school where Chaplain Rev. Threadgill had let some of us white civil rights workers stay despite constant pressure from the school board to get us out. When I read more about the Academy's fate in Cynthia Griggs Fleming's book, *In the Shadow of Selma*, I wept. Griggs Fleming wrote, "On December 23, 1965, Wilcox County's superintendent sent a letter to Threadgill informing him that he and his family would have to vacate their house on Camden Academy campus. Only Threadgill and the white civil rights workers who had been staying in the school dormitories were evicted."[24] After reading that, I spoke with other former students who explained that the entire school wasn't torn down right away, but that the chapel and chaplain's home were removed. By 1975, no trace of the historic buildings was left.

The white authorities had been after the Threadgill family for a long time, looking for a way to punish them and to stop the Academy students from organizing on campus. White civil rights workers staying there was the final straw. The school board proceeded with condemnation procedures against the Presbyterian Church–owned school. They used federally mandated school integration as an excuse on paper, but they never had any intention of integrating the schools, only of keeping a separate and unequal system in place. After speaking with Sheryl Threadgill, I wept again at the realization that I was part of the destruction of her home and the security she had enjoyed living on campus. She was only thirteen when they were

16. Top row: Mrs. Theola Gordon, Donna Gordon, Mrs. Mildred Threadgill, and Sheryl Threadgill. Front row: Herbert Cole and his sister, Luraleen Cole, and John Cunningham in the Gordons' front yard in Camden. These children were among the first to attempt to integrate Wilcox County schools. (Copyright © 1966 by Bob Fitch.)

evicted. Then I reminded myself that white guilt has never done any good for people of color, so I stepped up my determination to tell the story of the brave souls of Wilcox County and to bring attention to their ongoing need for greater resources.

Rev. Threadgill and his wife supported families and students in their courageous attempts to integrate the white public schools, setting the example by encouraging their own young daughter to lead the way in the dangerous desegregation of the white Camden high school. As a freshman in 1967, Sheryl Threadgill was one of the earliest students to attend white Wilcox High. No local, state, or federal protections were given to these students or their families. After one year, Sheryl returned to Camden Academy due to the incessant cruelty of her classmates and mistreatment by teachers. However, she continued to be a leader in school integration marches and demonstrations.

When I called to ask Sheryl about the Academy, she sighed and replied, "The Academy? Our home and the chapel were torn down immediately after you left in August 1965. The Board of Education definitely initiated the tear down because the white ministers/seminarians [and students] stayed there. My dad had come down with a chronic lung disease from which he eventually died. He was getting treatment in the hospital in Tuskegee when they served the eviction notice. So he left the hospital to come home and move us. We had to move out to a vacant faculty home at Millers Ferry Mission School [another Presbyterian mission school]. Our house and the church were torn down completely. The next year my dad built our house where I still live, using some of the materials from that chapel."[25]

After their eviction and the loss of his job, Rev. Threadgill was one of the earliest African Americans to run for the Wilcox county commission. He lost by one vote, so he demanded a recount, which was denied. Ever one to seek justice, he filed a federal discrimination suit against Wilcox County election officials in 1974 but did not prevail. He did receive some compensation along with other fired teachers after a lengthy court battle with the Wilcox County Board of Education, but nothing that could come close to making up for the losses he and his family suffered. Rev. Threadgill died when he was only sixty-six years old.[26]

"My mother doesn't get mentioned enough, Mrs. Mildred Locke Threadgill," Sheryl told me. "She was quiet and soft spoken. She taught home economics and Bible studies at the Academy until she passed in 1977. It wasn't easy for her to be an educator; she had to manage the household while my father was out being a community pastor. He was a dominant figure, but she was brilliant in her own right. She worked through the U.S. Department of Agriculture food commodities to get food to the county. At first, even though they needed the food, people didn't want to accept the commodities. My mother taught people how to improve those dry white beans, season them up into a real nice dish. She worked with Presbyterian Church youth on campus. She did all that while raising us, and maintaining the household with my father gone a lot. And she was under constant pressure for our family's activism."[27]

Sheryl converted the injustice of her family's mistreatment into the fuel that has sustained her lifelong fight to bring social services to the county of her birth. She reminded me of the classic movement song she and her classmates used to sing as they lined up for marches from the Academy and headed down hill to the inevitable confrontation with the police and sheriff. It was the same song that Charles Bonner and his companions sang in Selma and that demonstrators all over the South modified with local lyrics. The Wilcox County version as I heard it went like this:

Oh, Lummie, you never can jail us all, all, all
Oh Wallace, segregation's bound to fall . . .
I read in the paper
just the other day
that the Freedom Fighters
Are on their way[28]

Protesters made up new choruses to suit the situation at the moment. In Camden, school demonstrations continued for nearly a decade, but the schools never actually integrated. Sheryl explained that there really were two major movements in Wilcox, the voting rights movement that we were part of and the school desegregation movement that she and many of her classmates were deeply committed to from their early teen years.

After a career in human services, in what could be her retirement years, she is the full-time volunteer director of BAMA Kids—an acronym for Better Activities Make All Around Kids—in Camden, which provides summer programs, after school tutoring, recreation, and arts education with an emphasis on African American culture and values.

Many residents credit Sheryl Threadgill for getting running water out into parts of the county that still lacked this basic service in the 1980s. Sheryl explained how the water project came about through her position with the Department of Human Resources. "Our initial program was to support the elderly, train family members to take care of their own, and teach students to build steps and ramps. The project director was interviewing people and learned that the rural communities didn't have water. So the Kellogg Foundation got interested, we wrote private and public grants and got the water. That really paved the way to get this program, BAMA Kids off the ground, too. Many more resources became available to us."[29]

A committed activist, Sheryl served as campaign manager for her adopted cousin, David Colston, the nephew of David Colston Sr., who was slain in the church parking lot when Sheryl was a young girl. In 2010, David Colston of Haneyville, Alabama, was elected as the first African American Wilcox County native to become a representative in the Alabama legislature.[30]

Sheryl continued, "My family made the ultimate sacrifice; they lived and maintained that sense of community and responsibility that I have been able to continue. People tell me that they remember my folks and some of the things they worked for so hard that we have been able to carry forward, so they didn't fall by the wayside."[31]

There is no way to overstate the importance of Camden Academy and its indisputably greatest spiritual and community leader, Rev. Thomas L.

Threadgill, his courageous wife, Mildred Locke Threadgill, and their children, Sheryl, Larry, Harold, and Anthony. The Threadgills sacrificed their home, their livelihood, and their health in service for the Wilcox County freedom movement. Rev. Threadgill was a community leader and a defender of the students who left campus to march for their parents' voting rights and for their own rights to an equal education. He had often intervened on behalf of the students with fearful teachers and reluctant Principal Hobbs.

Several times each night during my first journey back to Wilcox, I woke from nightmares, dripping in sweat, and wondering where I was. By day, Luke and I kept busy visiting the people and places that had meant so much to us. I tried to live in the moment, but at night my mind attempted to integrate these new encounters into old memories that included terror as well as joy. Luke said he had nightmares too. As we drove those old familiar roads we kept saying, "I can't believe we are back here. We are so lucky to be here. Together. Alive."

As Luke and I drove up the steep campus hill to the site of the old Camden Academy, I warned him that there was nothing left that we would recognize. The new J. E. Hobbs Elementary School, all brick and metal, stands where the lovely historic wooden buildings once were, and behind the new buildings, decayed temporary classrooms lay tipped over with partially completed workbooks scattered in the weeds. Gone was the boys' dormitory where we first made love and the auditorium where students rallied to plan demonstrations and boycotts. It was here where I learned to ignore the adult staff arguments; their voices going at it long after we kids were dismissed. It was on that top floor porch that ran the whole length of the building where I sat out on the old wooden swing, looking at the moon through the pecan tree, praying that some day everyone who lived here could enjoy peace and justice. Back then, as teenagers ourselves, we had wondered out loud if we'd live to tell our children about this summer, this place. Even though the buildings that held the hopes of that summer were gone, here we were, forty-three years later.

Kids still hear the scary true stories about the back of campus being "Hangman's Hill" where the KKK used to lynch "Negroes" who violated their insane beliefs about how black people ought to behave, the place where I saw my first burned cross and blurted out my story to the *Washington Post* reporter. We couldn't find the old pecan tree. Luke wandered off into the kudzu. After a while he came back saying he thought he saw some of the foundation of the old boys' dormitory, but I thought it was closer to the front of the campus and pointed out some old steps near a paved playground as a more likely spot. I stared into the thicket of sycamore and oak but all-invasive vegetation covered every trace of the vibrant past of Camden Academy. Although the Camden Academy buildings were destroyed, the legacy of the school lives on. Many community leaders in Camden today credit the strict but broad education they received at the Academy for their ability to succeed in college and in life, and as one of the main reasons some of them returned after careers elsewhere, to give back to the community. One of them said to me, "I can almost tell when I meet someone in my age group today, whether or not they went to the Academy. There is a graciousness and confidence that we learned from our teachers who always told us that we had potential but that we owed it to our community to give back." Although the school that had given us civil rights workers shelter was destroyed, the community that had taken us in at their peril welcomed us back.

Snow Hill Institute

Before we left Wilcox County, we had time to stop briefly to pay homage to Snow Hill Institute, the oldest historically black school in Wilcox County, founded by Tuskegee graduate William James Edwards for freed slaves and their children in 1893. With good fortune we found Edwards's grandson, Donald P. Stone, living on the campus of Snow Hill. We visited with the seventy-three-year-old activist and author on the porch of his grandfather's 115-year-old home over the last bites of Kate Charley's coconut pie. The historic Edwards home is next to one maintained by filmmaker Spike Lee's aunt and uncle. Bill and Jacquelyn Lee used to bring Spike and his siblings to spend time in Wilcox County with their grandparents, and the cousins played together during the long hot summers, right here on this ancient porch.

Donald left Wilcox for thirty years, graduated from Morehouse College in 1957, and stayed in Atlanta until recently. He worked with SNCC there during the movement years. In his book *Fallen Prince: William James Edwards, Black Education, and the Quest for Afro-American Nationality*, he documents his grandfather's tremendous struggles and achievements toward African American education and independence after Edwards graduated from Tuskegee University. Asked how it is living here now, Donald said, "In one way, the livin' is easy, low cost, and comfortable in a predominantly black community, but we are still highly segregated."

When I mentioned my diversity-training partner Charles R. Stephens from Atlanta, Donald said he knew him well and that they shared a love of jazz along with their early sit-in arrest records. "When you get down to people who are doing the right thing, it's a small world isn't' it?" he said.[32]

Before we left, I stood for a moment at William James Edwards's grave beside the house. Edwards was born in 1868 and died in 1950. After Dr. Edwards's independent school was shuttered, it served as an all-black public school for many years. The Wilcox County Board of Education then closed it permanently in 1973, along with most historic black schools, when the trustees were finally forced to comply with federal injunctions to integrate. Like Camden Academy, Snow Hill represented African Americans who wanted to improve opportunity for their children, something the all-white school board could not abide. Dr. Edwards and his descendants had a vision and tenacity that are deeply needed today, that's for sure.

As Luke drove us back through Mississippi to Memphis we didn't talk much. We were each lost in our own thoughts, much as we had been four decades ago, when we looked back on Selma through the dirty windows of a Trailways bus. For myself, I felt immense gratitude for a renewed connection to some of the bravest and best people I had ever had the honor to know and for the new friends we made this week. I also understood that my search for the stories of Wilcox County freedom fighters was far from over.

18

We Honor Them

I am here and so are you.
And we matter.
We can change things.

Ella Baker, founder of the Student Nonviolent Coordinating Committee

Stories of heroism in the face of violent mistreatment during the Civil Rights Movement in Wilcox County could fill volumes, and yet few of these stories have been told, with the exception of Fleming's *In the Shadow of Selma*. Many who moved away cannot bear to return. Some want to forget the horror of southern racism. Other residents are trying to improve the county and believe that dredging up the past will do more harm than good. But the statute of limitations has not passed on the memories of the brave freedom fighters of the 1960s. Small, grassroots bands of people were the heart and soul of the movement, and their stories should be heard and remembered.

Sim Pettway Sr. and the Wilson Family

When I arrived in Camden in 1965, I heard that the mayor had beaten a young boy for participating in a large peaceful march to the courthouse a few weeks earlier. Forty-five years later, I dug deeper into this story.

On May 6, 1965, the *Chicago Daily Defender* ran an article titled "Claim Camden Mayor Kicked Negro Teenager" that included the following description: "The ruthless image of operation segregation in Alabama's Black Belt was reflected when a 13-year old Negro boy charged in a complaint with the Department of Justice that the mayor of Camden, Ala. threatened his life with a pistol and kicked him for participating in racial demonstrations there several weeks ago. The victim, Walter Wilson Jr. who was a 7th grade student at Camden Academy at the time of the incident, said the incident occurred April 6. The boy's parents have since moved to Prichard, Ala, having fled from their Wilcox home in fear of reprisals."[1]

The child and his family suffered repercussions, but not Mayor Reginald Albritton, who went on to be reelected and later served as probate judge until his retirement in 1988. I eventually located Walter Wilson's brother, Sim Pettway Sr., in Mobile. About the incident, he told me, "My brother Walter has passed, but it was me, not Walter, that the gang of so-called white community leaders were after that day."

After I heard Sim Pettway's powerful story, I asked the planning committee to include him as a speaker at a commemorative mass meeting in Camden that was being planned for March 1, 2010. Sim told me some of what he planned to say that night: "I am the brother of Walter Wilson. In 1965, I and another young man, Ralph Eggleston, started a movement to change things in Camden, Alabama. We were tired of getting worn-out books, broken furniture, everything the white schools were throwing away; that's what they gave us at Camden Academy. We were just sixteen years old and had enough of this abusive treatment. We asked for assistance from our teachers Mr. Albert Gordon, Reverend Threadgill and others who we could confide in. We were advised that we were too young to take on such tasks but we decided to organize a march anyway.

"We had some rallies in the old auditorium at school, and we started a couple of marches. On our first demonstration we marched up to the Wilcox County courthouse where Sheriff Lummie Jenkins met us with his deputies, and we were told that we better get our N-tails back in school. He stated to me, 'Boy, I know your mother and father and we are going to see about this.'

"We led one or two more marches, but we were turned back by police each time so it was suggested to us kids that we needed assistance from other leaders. Before the help could arrive and as we were preparing for another march, Reverend Threadgill came to our classrooms to get my sister Izora Pettway and me. He told us to get in the car quickly because our mother and brother were hurt. He took us home. We found our brother Walter Wilson had been beaten and my mother Bernice Pettway Wilson was struck and manhandled because of me leading in the marches. Walter had stayed home that day because he had a cold; it was actually me this mob came looking for. They found my brother Walter and my mother. After they beat them, they warned her that her boy [Sim] better stop what he was doing.

"My mother called my sister Josephine Jasper in Prichard, Alabama, outside Mobile and told her that we had to leave Camden or that they would be coming back that evening if we didn't go. My mother was frightened, so my uncle Bizell Pettway carried us hidden in a truck to Jackson, Alabama, where my sister Josephine picked us up at the Alabama River Bridge.

"But that didn't stop me from working in the movement. I worked on many voter registration drives at the Nazarene Baptist Church, was president of the SCLC in Prichard, and am active with the NAACP today."[2]

17. Rosetta Anderson identifies herself and Sim Pettway Sr. in a photograph taken at a 1966 Camden voting rights rally addressed by Martin Luther King Jr. (Photograph by Roy Hoffman, copyright © Mobile Press Register and the Alabama Media Group 2010.)

Sim told me more of the story than he shared during the mass meeting. "It was so hard on my mother, a young woman being torn away from her sisters, her own mother, the only life and home she had ever known. I was so angry that they had hurt mother and beat my brother that I wanted to go get a gun and kill those white men. Getting out of town that night probably saved my life. The Department of Justice did an investigation, but the only one outside our family who witnessed the attack was a black man who was too afraid to testify so no one was prosecuted. That man later worked for the sheriff's department in Wilcox."[3]

When I was speaking at University of South Alabama in 2012, Sim and his wife, Minerva, and other Wilcox County freedom fighters were invited to sit in the front row. I accompanied my talk with slides. One was a photo featuring Dr. King standing in a doorway outside Antioch Baptist Church in Camden, preaching to a crowd of hundreds of worried-looking locals in April 1966.

When this slide came on the screen, Sim's cousin, Rosetta Anderson, shouted out, "That's Sim! That's Sim, right there in front in the white shirt!"

It caused quite a stir. Sim shrugged his shoulders. When I asked him later he said he thought it could be him but he'd have to send the photo to his sister. A month later, he called to tell me the rest of the story.

"Although the Pettway Wilson family was forced to leave Camden to save our lives, I periodically snuck back into the county to visit my other relatives and to show *them* they couldn't scare me. So yes that is me, right in front. I didn't recognize myself at first; I don't recall being that good looking!

"My oldest sister Izora returned to Camden Academy. She was in her senior year and said, 'I don't care if they kill me; I am going back to graduate with my class.' Another sister, Bernice Wilson, was one of the first black students to attend and to graduate from the all-white Wilcox High School. An uncle was run out of town because his little son used the whites-only drinking fountain downtown."[4]

Sim explained that all the students wanted were better school supplies and an equal education instead of tattered, marked-up books and broken desks under falling plaster in segregated schools. They weren't trying to date white girls. But the insane disease of racism infected the white authorities so that they could not see that these were just kids who wanted a good education. While appearing benign on the surface, Mayor Reginald Albritton was one of the most insidious racists because he was in a respected position yet was extremely cruel and violent.

Sim continued, "A few years ago, I went back to Camden with my sister Josephine and you will never guess who invited us in for tea, as nice as could be. Mrs. Albritton, the mayor's wife. Can you imagine? She was a nice lady, married to a horrible man—now she's a widow. We didn't talk about that day that my family was chased out of town by her husband."[5]

"Despite all that happened to my family, I never allowed myself to carry the anger. All this mistreatment only increased the commitment of our family to overcoming racism and injustice not only for ourselves but for all. I passed on to my children what my mother taught me. My mother always said, 'Son if you do carry that anger, you are just lowering yourself to their level. You have to rise above their ignorance,' and so I did."[6]

The Boys in the Church

Almost everyone in Wilcox County remembers two things about the summer of 1965: the passage of the Civil Rights Act and the attack on the boys at Antioch Baptist Church. The last time I saw Frank Connor and Emmanuel Hardley, who were beaten the worst, they were in Major Johns's car heading to Good Samaritan Hospital with Frank bleeding to death in the backseat. Robert Powell and the Nettles brothers escaped but were shaken and angered by the attack. At the time, the boys told both Major Johns and Bob that they knew the men: they could see their faces through stocking masks. Major Johns told us the names as well. That same night, Don Green, who was still in jail in the solitary confinement bullpen, was beaten again, more severely than before.

On July 1, 1965, the *New York Times* published this account of the attack in the church:

> Two Negro youths were hospitalized today with injuries inflicted by a group of white men who broke into a church after a civil rights rally last night. The Federal Bureau of Investigation has entered the case. The youths said that they were beaten in Antioch Baptist Church by white men wielding blackjacks. One victim, 18 year old Frank Connor, had a 2–1/2" gash in his head. He and the other youth, Emanuel Hardy [*sic*] were reported in good condition. The church has been headquarters for the Negro voter registration drive since early March when the Rev. Dr. Martin Luther King Jr., had the Alabama civil rights drive in full swing. More than 30 white persons have joined the drive in recent weeks here.[7]

Riddled with misinformation, no doubt received from Sheriff Jenkins who endorsed the attack, the *New York Times* article sharply contrasted with a press release by the Rev. Ralph D. Abernathy, vice president and treasurer of SCLC, issued July 1, 1965. The mistreatment of our SCOPE group in Wilcox was cited as yet another reason to hasten the passage of the Voting Rights Act:

> Field workers of the Southern Christian Leadership Conference and local Negro citizens engaged in voter registration projects throughout The South are being subjected to sinister harassments and brutal intimidations. . . . Wilcox County is one of the most infamous of the state's Black Belt counties, where until recently not a single Negro was registered to vote.
>
> In Camden, the county seat, local whites Tuesday night broke into a house of God, Antioch Baptist Church, fired a shot gun blast against the wall and brutally beat seven Negro teenagers, two of them so badly they had to be hospitalized.

Earlier Tuesday, an 18-year old white SCOPE worker was released from jail so badly beaten that he had to be hospitalized. The brutally beaten youth was one of 18 persons arrested by the Camden Mayor, Sheriff and posse men when SCOPE workers protested against local merchants by distributing boycott materials.

We firmly believe that the vicious treatment of the local Negroes and our voter registration workers is symptomatic of a sick society in which Negro citizens are denied the right to vote for elected officials.[8]

Contrary to the *New York Times* report, the young men were hardly in good condition. Frank Connor nearly died. Emmanuel Hardley was severely beaten, and Grady Nettles was injured as well. Frank was only seventeen years old and most of the boys were even younger. We may have seemed like a group of thirty as reported by the *New York Times*, but there were fewer than a dozen white civil rights workers in Wilcox at the time. Some left the same week that we were arrested and the young men were attacked, so by July we were down to eight, counting the "White Revs," and by August, there were only five of us. From the beginning of my search, I was determined to find as many of the "boys in the church" as possible. It wasn't easy and took several years. Because everyone in Camden recalled the attack vividly, and because relatives of the attackers still live there, most people were initially reluctant to give me names and numbers.

When first I located Frank Connor in Pensacola, Florida, he told me that he barely survived. He was in the hospital in Selma for months. His parents separated during that time, and he had to return to live with his father near the church where he was beaten, which was very hard for him. Frank suffered permanent traumatic brain damage and was unable to graduate with his class at the Academy. Despite this horror, he later married, had children, and earned a good living as a truck driver before his retirement. After I mailed him the *New York Times* article, he called me back and said, "It was as scary as I never knew what. I didn't know if I was going to get killed. They didn't want blacks and whites to be together but that was no cause to try to kill us. That took us completely by surprise, to come in a church like that. A certain part of my body holds that always. I put my hand on my head and I thank the Lord I didn't die. I was bleeding all over. The doctor said I only had a 50 percent chance to live.

"I had revenge in my mind for many years. When I visited, I didn't even want to walk up through town. I'd just go to my brother's house and stay there. There are some low-down white people there. If they could get the power again, they'd do the same thing over again. They don't think we are people. But they'd be surprised this time. Not me, I wouldn't take up arms against them, but there are some that would, for sure. I was losing blood like you know what. But I made it. My mind is not like it used to be. I had fear in my mind for a long time but the Lord helped me through"[9]

Frank called me back a few weeks later. Our conversations had brought that terrible night back vividly. I apologized. He said, "No, it is always there in the back of my mind. There is no way to forget it completely. I felt like I woke to find the shadow of death was hovering over me. Just before the man began to beat me with a lead pipe, I instinctively put my arm over my eyes; I didn't want them to blind me. Two men hit me over and over and over, like they would never stop. The Lord must have been protecting me; otherwise I could be blind. Or dead.

"Me and a bunch of other guys went to a class reunion a few years back and they talked about that like we were heroes or something. I tried to block it out of my mind. I left to go to New York in 1968. Living in Camden, it was a nightmare . . . a real nightmare, I tell you."[10]

All three of the men the survivors identified are dead: Bob Lane of the Lane Butane Company; Bob Spencer, who worked for Lane and was still wearing his blue uniform that night; and Francis Gregory, the gas station owner who was witnessed trying to run over student marchers and who was suspected of burning down two black competitors' businesses. Everyone clearly recalled Gregory as being one of the most vicious attackers that night, savagely beating the boys with lead pipes. John Golden also recalled that one young man told him that one of the attackers was a deacon in a local white church. An older woman told me: "You know it is a small area. Everyone knew who they were, but there was nothing we could do or say. The FBI wasn't going to do anything about it." But there is no statue of limitations on attempted murder, and murder was clearly what the attackers intended that night. In addition to the three who are now dead, there were at least five more attackers. Who knows where they are today?

Alma King's cousin, Emmanuel Hardley, was one of the young men who was attacked. He had died of diabetes in his early forties, but when we visited Camden in 2008, Alma took me to meet his son, Bo Hardley, who had a small shop that offered soft drinks and a pool table in addition to one barber chair, where I found him cutting a young boy's hair. After Alma introduced me to Bo, I showed him the article from the *New York Times*.

He stared at me with his scissors midair as I rattled on, "Your father was a student who worked with us many, many years ago, here in Camden. He helped register voters and protect our church office at night. One night he and some other young men were beaten up by the Klan and nearly killed." Bo didn't say anything. I asked him, "Do you remember that scar your father had on his forehead?" He replied, "No, I never knew anything about it. He never talked about none of that." I told Bo that his father was a brave young man. He continued staring at the article in disbelief as I handed him a copy. Before we left I blurted out, "I don't know what kind of father Emmanuel was or how his life turned out, but I just want you to know he was a hero to us, even though he was just a young boy. He was so brave." Bo shook his head side to side. I gave him a big hug and told him that I was glad we met.

Also in the church the night of the attack were brothers Charles and Grady Nettles. Charles lived with his father, Sylvester, in a home across from Antioch Baptist Church, while Grady lived farther out of town with his mother, Mattie, and younger siblings. Both Charles and Grady were active with our SCOPE project, and the entire family was deeply and publicly involved in the movement for many years. Mrs. Nettles and her ten children participated in meetings, marches, and the boycott. Mr. Nettles courageously housed civil rights workers until he was forced at gunpoint to stop.

When I caught him by surprise on his mobile phone in Florida, Charles Nettles said that he remembered that attack but that he doesn't like to talk about it. He then spoke briefly with me about his father's sacrifices during that time. "My father was a custodian at the school [Camden Academy]. Years later, I found out that he used to sit up at night with a shotgun. They had threatened him that they'd kill us if I didn't stop working in the movement. He sat up all night in the window to protect us. He worked hard all day and then he didn't get any sleep at all."[11]

When I called Charles's younger brother, Grady, at first he was reluctant, but after I told him that his brother and others from Camden had shared their stories, he told me about a traumatic incident that affected him far more than the attack in the church, even though he was among those injured that night: "They firebombed my mother's house while all us children were inside sleeping. She got us out in time all right but they killed a lot of the farm animals. Everyone knows who did it, but nothing happened. But she didn't give up; she didn't quit the movement. She died peacefully and I was right at her side."

The Nettles's home fire was reported as an accident, even though a gas can was found on the site. No charges were ever filed. After two years of harassment and isolation her son Larry was the first black male to graduate from the previously all-white Wilcox High School. It is widely speculated that their house was targeted because of Larry's attendance at the high school.[12]

Robert Powell

After an emotional reunion in Selma in 2010, I heard the story of my canvassing partner Robert Powell, who escaped shaken but unharmed from the attack in the church. Forty-five years later, Robert's memory of that night was vivid. "To think they could come into a church like that and attack children! When the Klan came for us they wore hoods, had baseball bats, tire irons, guns, and all kinds of weapons. We heard gunfire. They started beating people. Everyone was looking for someplace to run. A couple of us leaped out the side window. It was complete panic. We split up; some were hiding up in trees. Behind the church there was a pipe about six inches wide across the gully. That was our secret escape route. We knew it so well that we could run across it in the dark. They didn't know about that, we kept it to ourselves. Henry Robertson, William Truss, and I took across that pipe and hid out by the Mason Hall. Then we kept out of sight, out of downtown, for a while.

"When I was running away they [the Klan] still had their hoods on so I didn't recognize any of them. For sure, that was one of the most scary moments, but it was one in the line of many."[13]

"Years later when I was working in the North, sometimes I'd find myself deep in thought about the past. I used to avoid coming back to Camden until after my father George died at age seventy-seven. That part of the country killed my father. He used to work part time for McDonald's Grocery on the highway near our house. McDonald had a young son, younger than any of my brothers. My father had to say 'Yes sir' and 'No sir' to him, just to keep his little part time job. If my father hadn't done that they would have fired him. It really stuck in my craw."

I asked Robert if he could ever imagine moving back to Wilcox County. "Only if I was absolutely destitute would I consider such a thing. Even then, I don't know—there are just too many bitter memories. A lot of us left Camden with broken spirits, because of all of the years of fighting for our rights and integrated schools; the school equality fight was long and discouraging. But we had something that made us persevere. You persevere through so much, you wonder how you can overcome it. How could people be so cruel? We were determined to leave two-dollar days behind and go on to bigger and better things."

He recalled, "I wasn't that active until we were attacked in the church that night. I had gone out on the school marches, but for them to come into a church and beat children; that really lit a fire under me. After that, I told the leaders: just tell me what to do and I'll do it. I guess I got assigned to you. Yes, we rode my father's mule sometimes; I remember that was hard, your legs being short and my daddy needed the mule for work some of the time. We sure walked a lot, didn't we?

"I first met you at Camden Academy. Over lunch I remember telling you and Major Johns that we used to live on Whiskey Run where there was a house on top of the hill behind us with a poor white family. We visited at each other's houses as kids. The Daleys were one white family where I knew the kids. We wrassled and fought like any kids. Feeling equal with whites wasn't so strange to me as to some others. I think that is part of why you and I got along. The way we were mistreated by local whites, I knew they couldn't be better than us.

"I had already been canvassing before you came, even before Dan Harrell came. Our teacher Mr. Albert Gordon used to take us around to various towns in Wilcox and Monroe counties and pair us with locals there to get them to register. Mr. Gordon came down and talked with my parents. My father was a mill worker at Rider's Saw Mill. Mr. Gordon explained that if we got involved he could put us in areas outside of Camden where we would not be recognized, so that Dad would not lose his job.

"In 1970, when I was a college junior in Birmingham, I came to a mass meeting in Camden at Antioch Baptist Church with some friends. When we were leaving, someone tried to cut us off the highway. They put their car right in the middle of the road with the headlights on bright, right in our faces so we couldn't see. We had to drive off the road and flip the car to avoid hitting them. I told the state trooper it was the Klan but they didn't do anything. Grady Nettles was in the car with me, we were all banged up, but nobody was killed."[14]

Robert was one of the many students from Camden Academy who were able to improve their lives through higher education. Robert earned a degree in mechanical engineering and enjoyed a successful career in Connecticut before his retirement. A few years ago, Robert moved to North Carolina in order to be closer to his mother without having to live in the South. I remembered Mrs. Powell, Rosanelle (also known as Ducca Mae), as a powerful, beautiful woman who loved her children fiercely and defended their right to participate in the movement against criticism from neighbors. Their family home on Whiskey Run was mysteriously burned to the ground while Robert was a senior in high school. Every photo and family keepsake was lost, although they rebuilt and still own the family property. Until his mother died at age ninety-six, Robert came to Camden regularly to share caregiving responsibilities with his siblings, but he told me that he could never live full time in the South again. "To think all we went through, all those years of marches, and the kids still don't go to school together."[15]

As for colorful, courageous Don Green, he was unavailable to speak with me, but former classmates said that he lives in South Carolina and has a successful business. As a teenager, he had been arrested, beaten, and set up for crimes he didn't commit, but he always bounced back. Robert Powell agreed that Don Green was our local Stokely Carmichael. Don had an in-your-face attitude and rock-solid determination. He never let the authorities grind him down, which made him a constant target for abuse. What I remember most about Don is that even after all the arrests and assaults, he was still singing "I Love Everybody" at the next mass meeting, singing like he really meant it.

Rosetta Marsh Anderson

In 1965, I didn't get to know her, but Rosetta Anderson was an active, behind-the-scenes local leader for many years. When I met Mrs. Anderson in 2008, it was impossible to believe that this attractive, energetic woman was several years older than I. She organized mass meetings, transportation, food, supplies, and strategies so that demonstrations, boycotts, and registration projects worked as successfully and safely as possible. After we met, Mrs. Anderson sought me out to tell me more about how the local movement was organized. Everyone in the community knew she was involved, but Mrs. Anderson said she kept a low profile with the white people she knew at that time.

She said, "I was the first secretary of the first NAACP and for SCLC here. The Wilcox Civic Progressive League, I was secretary of that, one of our most important early organizations. We organized, we filed complaints with the Justice Department; we learned our rights and taught them to others.

"When the unrest began, Rev. Freeman was pastor at St. Francis Baptist Church. He helped organize and lead one of the first small marches along Route 221 until the police turned them around. The church deacons there were fearful so they fired him, but our congregation at Antioch Baptist Church took him on and supported his effort to use the church as a headquarters for the movement.

"For voter registration in Camden, we had adult leaders and student leaders. Rev. Threadgill, Jesse Brooks, Albert Gordon, and I were the four adult leaders. If we wanted to get a crew in from Coy we'd tell them what time we'd have a mass meeting or when to meet to march. I was a designated driver and organized others to drive those risky old roads. We had threatening calls to our home regularly. My sons had to watch over our house because I had to leave them there alone. Maybe I didn't realize how dangerous it was then, but I know I didn't let myself fear for them. I could see the hatred in people's faces when we went up to the courthouse, but I couldn't dwell on it."[16]

Mrs. Anderson began her early working life doing housekeeping and child care in white homes. She was among many women in Camden who used their access to both races to benefit the movement. She learned how things were viewed inside white families and then used her knowledge to develop strategies for the freedom fight.

She recalled, "I got started working in the movement young and have never stopped. The incident that changed my life was this particular Saturday I didn't have to babysit [younger siblings]. My mother and father were going over to the field to hoe some potatoes. My parents said we could go out to play after we cleaned the house. As soon as they were out of sight, I heard a *bump, bump* of car doors. It was Lummie Jenkins and three of his goons. Said they was looking for liquor, even though I knew they weren't going to find any—if there had been any my daddy would have already drunk it up. I asked could I go get my mama and daddy or get my other sisters and they said. 'No. Tell old Chance we was here for the liquor.' They ransacked our home. I was really scared, shaking and crying.

"When they left, it looked like Hurricane Katrina had been through our home. Years later I realized it could have been worse because we were just two girls home alone. I stood on that porch while they wrecked our things and thought, 'they tell me that the Sheriff was elected by the people. If I live, I am going to campaign one day to eliminate him.' It took a whole lot longer than I expected, but we did it!

"The Civil Rights Movement started brewing in the early 1960s at Camden Academy; it started from the children. They came to the Parent Teachers Association meetings where I was Secretary to tell us that they didn't like second hand books the county sent them and that they felt like they were getting a second class education. I had a cousin [Sim Pettway] who was friends with Ralph Eggleston, one of the main student leaders. They started recruiting students to protest. As soon as my cousin got involved, the Sheriff went to my aunt's house, roughed her up, and told her she needed to get out of town."[17]

Asked about organizing the local movement, Mrs. Anderson explained,

"How we organized was pretty amazing, now that I think about it. We came together regularly, met at Antioch Baptist Church, and then other churches got involved. The children were the real leaders though—they got the adults involved. We'd ask the children about which area was ready for action. We also had telephone trees, although very few had telephones back then.

"How did we get word around? Honestly I don't know how we did it—it was a miracle really. The young people carried messages. They had school buses back then so they could organize on the buses. We parents listened to what they told us and then we knew what we had to do to organize for their safety and transportation.

"We worked pretty cooperatively. If anybody disagreed, we had a meeting. We got together as adults and settled it among ourselves. Then we'd say 'this is how it is going to be.' We listened to the children and they listened to us.

"I was busy going from one end of the county for several years. We had precinct meetings until every little community was organized. We had leaders in each of the four ends of the county. We also did a lot of boycotting. Children had to walk the picket line in front of grocery and clothing stores. We used the younger children because they wouldn't jail them and they couldn't lose jobs.

"I was responsible for transportation and seeing that the young people were taken care of as best I could. One day I picked up student Brenda Bussey in Camden and her mother said, 'Rosetta, you came to pick up my little girl. Don't take her out there to get her killed.' That day I prayed so hard my chest hurt. If something happened to her child I don't think I could have lived." Brenda Bussey not only survived, she went on to be one of the first students to integrate Wilcox High School, got a good job and lives in Camden today.

"The boycott against purchasing at white stores that wouldn't hire us, the one when you were there in 1965, was so effective. Lots of folks donated food to families that honored the boycott. Once we had so much extra meat that it spoiled, and we even had to haul some to the city dump below the church. They [the white store owners] could smell it and they were upset. There were a few white folks who contributed to us, believe it or not. They couldn't say anything, everything they did had to be undercover, especially if they were local."[18]

Even with her caution, Mrs. Anderson felt the repercussions of her work in the movement. "Even when things kind of settled down, we were kind of ostracized, not in a way you could put your hand on it, but for sure we could not get jobs. Finally federal agencies came and gave us work. I started with Manpower [a federal employment program] as a field representative and ended up a case manager. It was the only way I could get a job. Later, I worked in an antipoverty program with migrant farmers through the Alabama Economic Opportunity program.

"I had four children; I lost my first daughter, Lena Jo, who was deeply involved in the Civil Rights Movement here. All the sacrifices we made, getting harassing phone calls, worrying about my children. It took its toll, I tell you.

"I am older now, and wiser. Through the years I tried to show my sons ways to get through the bitterness and how not to hate white people. When you came, you all gave us courage. And we felt it was our job to protect you. We could never let ourselves think about how helpless we really were because we knew we had God on our side. The harassment kept on for years. Sometimes they called the house [anonymously] and threatened to kill me. They burned down the government commodity building near us.

"Some of the things we accomplished through the movement? Mainly, things are more relaxed; we can go where we want to go. Right now most of the people hired in Camden are black. Terrorism doesn't bother me now because I lived through that time of terror. There were even my own people who avoided me, crossed the street to show they were not with me, not with the movement. But I still have hope; all of us want the same thing when you sit down and really talk."[19]

A Community Rises to the Challenge

As I continued to trace Wilcox County movement folks, I discovered that there was not one family who did not suffer repercussions for their civil rights activism: lost jobs, lost homes if they rented, and fire-bombed homes if they owned. Children as young as twelve continued to be beaten, tear gassed, and arrested for marching for school integration, for being with white civil rights workers, and for no reason at all. Tenants were put off farms that were not only their sole means of earning a living but also their homes. Students, their parents, and teachers held march after march from 1965 to 1972.

Despite repeated federal injunctions, the Wilcox County Board of Education not only refused to integrate the schools, they also fired all of the teachers active in the movement. Although class action lawsuits filed by some of the fired teachers eventually resulted in reinstatement and compensation, the settlements could never repay the hardships they and their families endured over the years they had to scrape out a living outside their chosen professions.

What strategies did people develop to deal with the constant terror of racism while keeping the hope of liberation alive? A blended approach of accommodation and secret activism was a survival strategy for many. Many parents encouraged their children to go on to college to escape the barbed-wire fence of hatred that limited livelihood and barred opportunity for African Americans in rural Alabama.

When I began to recover some of the personal histories of Wilcox County, I was told many things that I hadn't understood in 1965. Local movement leaders had been organizing for years before we arrived and unfortunately had to continue for years after we left. I knew that summer of 1965 things had heated up primarily due to the Camden Academy student walkouts and marches demanding equal schools, decent jobs, and voting rights for their parents. Because their protests had been met with violence, arrests, and threats, many teenagers were sent away that summer, which particularly accounted for the lack of high school–aged girls. The only teenage girls I recalled by name were Robert Powell's sister, Hulda Ann, who was about twelve in 1965, and the Robinson girl in Boiling Springs. When I met Camden native Betty Anderson, niece of Mrs. Rosetta Anderson, she confirmed that most teenage girls were sent away that summer even if they continued to be active in the movement. Betty explained to me, "With all that had gone down that Spring with our marches, being tear gassed and all, our teacher, Mr. Albert Gordon took a group of six students, mostly girls, over to Mississippi to do voter organizing work that summer because it was too dangerous for us in Camden."[20]

The local leaders knew that white civil rights workers were going to bring on worse violence from the racists and that we would be gone at summer's end. Poverty also played a factor in my working with very few young women. Young black girls, especially if they were the eldest in their family, worked extremely hard year-round, and their load of child care and farming responsibilities increased when school was out for the summer. Few young women were released from chores to participate in our voter registration project in the way that some of the young men were. In the years after the vote was secured and equal education was the primary focus of demonstrations, teenage girls often took the lead in organizing.

In 1965 there were dozens of local families who we celebrated as "Movement Folk" while we mindlessly criticized others as "Uncle Toms"—people who did whatever it took to appease the powerful whites, most especially avoiding any appearance of being involved in the civil rights struggle. Frustrated with the slow pace of progress in Wilcox, all of us from outside the county—black, white, adult, and student workers alike—complained about those who didn't join the struggle. We young white kids hadn't stopped to consider that most of the nonparticipants were terrified. Now I was learning how wrong we had been to judge those who held back, or were held back by their parents. The people who were not with the movement were simply trying to stay alive and give their children a chance at a better life.

As Alma King reflected on her senior year at Camden Academy, "We were out protesting most of our senior school year (1964–65). We'd leave campus by 9:00 or 10:00 A.M. immediately after devotional services. Our teachers Mr. Gardner, Ms. Lymons, and others would go along with us. I didn't go all the way into town because my mother didn't want us to get involved, but I'd go down as far as the bus station at the bottom of the hill. We lived way out in Possum Bend; once that school bus left you didn't have a ride home so I couldn't participate in the marches—you never knew when or how they would end.

"As soon as we graduated, my cousin and I were sent away from there. My mother wanted to protect us, so I had just moved away just as you arrived. I graduated May 27, 1965, and on May 28, my cousin and I boarded a Greyhound bus for New York City." Alma shared a sentiment expressed by several current community leaders, "If I had not gone away, I could never have come back in a position to make contributions to this community. We didn't have advanced education or job opportunities here."[21]

As I listened to the multitude of reasons why parents were unwilling to sacrifice their homes, their jobs, and their children's lives in a battle that looked like it would never end, I erased the word "Uncle Tom" from my vocabulary forever. We zealots for the movement thought that everyone who wasn't with us had been beaten down by the whites. When people refused to answer the door or told us to get away from their homes, we judged them harshly. Now I realized that whether they openly participated in civil rights activities or not, almost everyone was doing the best they could despite enormous barriers to the activities of daily life erected by officially sanctioned segregation.

Parents who allowed their children to be out front paid the price of constant fear as well as criticism from more conservative parents. Hundreds of children and adults were jailed; some were beaten and permanently scarred. Some who were very young during the movement years experienced tremendous anxiety over their parents' activism. Cleo Brooks's wife, Arthurine Kelsaw Brooks, said that her mother's work in the movement made her fearful. "I was just little then but my mother, Martha Kelsaw, was very active. When they went in to the protests in Camden with the others from Coy I got very anxious. My mother came back with the smell of tear gas on her clothes. That smell so frightened me as a young child; that smell stayed with me for years."[22]

Shelly Dallas Dale, Wilcox County tax assessor since 2001, recalled growing up fearing the power of white people. She overcame it by becoming active in the movement when she was just sixteen years old. She said, "I lived all my life in Camden. I was born in an area called Olive. We lived on the Jones's property, on their plantation as tenant farmers. One afternoon my brother Essie was opening the gate because they would throw us a dime or a nickel. At that time, it was a big amount for us. Old Jones complained that my brother closed the gate in his face, which wasn't true. He told my mother if my brother ever closed the gate on him again, he would kill him.

"That very night, my mother packed all seven of us up and moved us to another place seven or eight miles up the road onto some rental property until she got us a self-help government house.[23] Leaving the Jones's plantation meant the end of farming for us. We had been sharecroppers, so we lost our home and livelihood at the same time."[24]

Gloria Jean McDole, director of the E. M. Parrish day care center (named for one of the unfairly fired teachers, Mrs. Elizabeth M. Parrish) recalls, "I was in high school at Camden Academy and graduated in 1967. Our teachers let us leave school without holding it against us. I marched and was tear gassed. We were coming from the campus uphill to the little community center, and they tear gassed us there. I never went to jail though.

"My aunt, Mamie McDole, went to the all the meetings and organized—you likely met her. Our family had our own home place in the Highway 265 area so she didn't need to be worried about being put off the place. I lived with my aunt from the time I was fourteen until she died of complications of Alzheimer's in July 2009. Years earlier she told me some stories, and now I wish I had written them down. She did so much to help the movement here. Those were some times.

"You remember—they used to have that siren that blew every Saturday night at 8:00 P.M. that meant all blacks had to get out of town? You are young, just comin' up, hearing that, knowing that is meant for you, it made us stop and think."[25]

Although on the surface it may have appeared that progress was slow, the constant oppression fueled continuous action toward justice. Along with strategies to improve and integrate schools, boycotts of local stores continued to be a bold and effective tactic. Shelly Dallas Dale recalls, "After you left, other outside civil rights workers came from time to time to helps us locals organize, decide which stores to picket. They tried to rotate us so that folks who lived in Camden went over to Selma to picket there and folks from there demonstrated in our downtown, so they couldn't be so easily targeted. We were trained in strict nonviolence according to Dr. King.

"We were nonviolent, but that didn't mean we didn't use every peaceful tactic available. For example, if someone black went into a white store that we were boycotting, if they broke the boycott, one of our men who was dressed as a woman would grab that person's bag of purchases when they came out of the store and take off running. They'd go off in the woods and change out of the dress and wig, and come back to the picket line dressed as a man. That way the shopper trying to report the incident was describing a woman, and no woman dressed like that could be found. We had one young man who had a thin face and was a fast runner, so he was very good at disguising himself that way. Making sure no one got home with purchases from a boycotted store won people over to participating. Pretty soon the stores were suffering financially and had to admit defeat, so we won."[26]

Mrs. Rosetta Angion

Mrs. Angion's neat white home in the highly active community of Coy had been one of the places where we met our rides and picked up or dropped off flyers and voter information. Mrs. Angion was only too happy to reminisce about her involvement in the movement.

"I had sixteen children altogether and was pregnant when I got involved in the movement. I went to meetings in Selma; people picked up information here at my home. My daughters Mary and Edna were hurt in the Bloody Sunday march, so when we got them back home safely I didn't send them out anymore. But a whole lot of us went over from Coy; we were there to greet the marchers in Montgomery. Later that night, when our buses were stopped for hours, we didn't know why. It turned out that was the night they killed Mrs. Viola Luizzo.

"It was dangerous in Wilcox because they were always after us, but it was fun, too. I remember one day we was marching, from St. Francis Church on Highway 221 to town. I was pregnant at the time, but nothing could have kept me away that day. The cows were inside the wire fence and were marching right beside us. It was fun I tell you! I enjoyed doing that; I always felt like we would reap the benefit from doing that. I wanted to do all I could to make it a better place to live for all black people. Some of my children died, but the ones that lived all did well in life. My son is a minister with programs that help the community and children's activities over to Mt. Gilead Church."[27]

Despite the intense and unrelenting challenges of that time, many of the activists I spoke with echoed Mrs. Angion's sentiments when she recalled

18. Rosetta Angion, Wilcox County freedom fighter, Coy, Alabama, 2008.
(Courtesy of the author.)

the joy of being part of the movement and the thrill of the victories during
the long struggle. "One of the best days I will always remember is the day
we marched with John Lewis. He walked with us right up to the courthouse
and then he walked in—we could see him walking around inside where none
of us had gotten inside before. That gave us a lot of courage, let me tell you.
We were so proud that day! Now you go up there and there is black people
working in the courthouse, some of them are my relations. That I lived to
see the day: yes, yes, yes!"[28]

19

Keep Your Eyes on the Prize

Keep your eyes on the prize
Hold on
Traditional song, "Keep Your Hands on the Plow"

Dr. Martin Luther King Jr. in Wilcox County

Without a doubt, the Wilcox County freedom fight from start to finish was homegrown and locally led. Oppressive racism coupled with firm faith in justice fueled the movement year after year. Outside civil rights workers came and went. John Lewis, Bernard and Colia Lafayette, and many others were noted, but no one inspired the community and validated their struggle like Dr. Martin Luther King Jr.

King scholar and Camden native Lewis V. Baldwin vividly recalled a talk in early 1965 during which Dr. King exhorted a large crowd standing outside Antioch Baptist Church to keep working on voter registration in spite of unrelenting attacks on the potential registrants and demonstrators: "Don't let anybody make you feel that you don't count. You may be poor. You may not have had the opportunity to rise to great academic heights. You may not know the difference between you does and you don't. You may not have opportunities that many other people have, but I want you to know that you are *some*body and that you are as good as any white person in Wilcox County, You gotta believe that!"[1]

Lewis and his brother, David, were in the back of the crowd, but they both remembered the gist of King's message: You are somebody and you matter in this world, you matter to God and He is on our side. Stories of what King said, how he looked, and how he made people feel circulated around and around the community until they took on a legendary tone that continues to be expressed today.

The entire Civil Rights Movement was a grassroots uprising of black folks who were fed up with being denied their rights and had taken action into their own hands, and a visit from Martin Luther King Jr. was tremendously important. Nationally, Dr. King was the most public face and most celebrated leader of this great nonviolent social revolution. He was an inspired preacher and teacher whose appearances both encouraged and validated local efforts. His visits also brought media attention and the much-needed visibility that influenced northern political opinion.

Whenever King's visits were public, large crowds assembled to welcome him, and when he joined their marches, locals were grateful for the more subdued police reaction his visits prompted. After asking many people about their memories of Dr. King, it became clear that he came to Wilcox County on several occasions and each time made multiple appearances in different locations, causing memories to blend together. Various residents recall him at Antioch Baptist Church, the Bessie W. Munden "Negro" Playground, Camden Academy, and Gees Bend with dates ranging from 1963 to 1966. Dr. King came to Gees Bend to meet with Rev. Lonnie Brown, Monroe Pettway, and others to encourage them in their voting rights march as early as 1963. Lewis Baldwin and other residents recalled whirlwind visits by King from February through April. What is certain is that by the summer of 1965 King had made at least three public appearances in Wilcox County and had held additional private meetings with Rev. Threadgill in the chaplain's home at Camden Academy. On April 9 King gave an inspirational speech when, for the first time, Wilcox County demonstrators were able to secure a permit to march. Six hundred marchers marched from the church to the courthouse while Dr. King was whisked away by his aides after giving a rousing speech.[2]

Mrs. Rosetta Angion remembered marching with him to the courthouse in March 1965. Mrs. Angion recalled, "I'll never forget sitting up watching TV, seeing Dr. King in other places marching, and whatever they tried to do they accomplished because he came there. I remember saying, 'Lord I wish he would come to Wilcox County,' and he did. I will never forget him coming here. We were tear gassed and beaten with sticks just because we wanted to vote. And then he was standing there with us, in the rain, right on the jailhouse steps.

"I was deeply involved long before that. I remember marching in Camden, going to meetings, and then the great day when we stood in the rain to get registered, the day Dr. King was there. He stood on the jailhouse steps and spoke. It was such an amazing time for me, to do something we had never done before. Earlier, I found out that if we weren't registered voters, we weren't even citizens. The only way you become a real citizen is to vote. I decided I'd do anything to help black folks get what we were supposed to have but were denied. After that I did everything I could to improve the lives of my community."[3]

Some former students at Camden Academy were unsure whether they met King in February or in April of 1965, or later, but the common thread to all of their memories was that the students were thrilled to meet the famous leader. Alma King recalled, "I remember him coming to the school when I was a senior, so it was 1965. It was cold weather when Dr. King came so it could have been February. One of our instructors prepared us for his visit. She taught us how to greet people in power; I can't remember which teacher, but she had traveled to Europe and met dignitaries. She showed us a film of meeting one of the presidents in Europe so we would know how to behave properly.

"Dr. King came and spoke to us, and we all shook his hand. When I got home I put my hand in a plastic bag and my mother couldn't understand why I wouldn't take it off. I remember he had the softest hands I had ever touched on a man, really soft."[4] Apparently the idea of preserving the great leader's handshake caught fire among the young women students. Lewis Baldwin describes in the forward to his book, *There Is a Balm in Gilead*, how King's touch affected his cousin, Vera Moody. She declared, with some exaggeration, that she would "never wash her hands again."[5]

Sheryl Threadgill recalled that King was on campus both before and after her family was evicted and uprooted. "My father knew Dr. King well, and he visited several times. They had a lot of meetings between our house and the principal Mr. Hobbs's house on campus at The Academy."[6] Sheryl and others suspect that King not only supported but also leaned on Principal Hobbs to stand up to the Wilcox County school board, which Hobbs had initially been reluctant to do.

Clarence Blackman was in elementary school, but he remembers King coming to the Camden Academy where he and Mary Baldwin (Lewis and David Baldwin's sister who would later become Blackman's wife) were young students. "My first recollection of Dr. King is when he came on campus; I would have been in fifth grade. I remember he was in a station wagon with Reverend Threadgill. Mr. Hobbs, our principal, was the one who actually invited him to come to the school to talk to us about the value of education because he, Principal Hobbs, had taken so much criticism for not being supportive of the students participating in the movement.

"Dr. King came with his whole entourage. My recollection is being surprised that he was so short. As a kid, I was thinking, 'Oh this little man; He is so little, what can he do?' He spoke outside the building. They may have built something for him to stand on, a platform. He was pretty much telling us how to organize and to stay in school. His pitch was all about nonviolence and the importance of education. There was long reception line and his people were controlling who met him. The older guys tried to chase me and the other little boys away, but I kept sneaking forward. Finally, by dodging in like that, I was able to greet him and shake his hand. I'll never forget that.

"Before he came we had several big marches. The third time, they got a permit. I was mostly hiding away back in the crowd because my parents would have been upset. Me and Jimmy Washington would sneak off campus and try to get over to the church for the marches. One time I remember a big march from school; we marched down the hill singing. When we got to where you go up to the courthouse, they came right at us with billy clubs, tear gas, even guns pointed at us—the city police and the sheriff, Lummie Jenkins.

"I still have flashbacks in that area where they tear gassed us. Before the march, at school they had provided us with wet towels. I remember lying on the ground, feeling that sting in my eye, even with the wet towel. I'm not ashamed to say most of us were crying as we headed back up to the school."[7]

In January of 1966, immediately after the murder of David Colston, King came to Wilcox County with SCLC photographer Bob Fitch, who took photos of the body for the media and the justice department.[8] On this visit, King came into town quietly, called on and prayed with the Colston family, and then met with a small group of student leaders on campus but did not march with them the next day.[9]

Dr. King understood that there were those in the community who held back because they feared loss of property and even life. These were well-founded fears, so he used the strongest terms possible to inspire them to join the freedom fight. King called upon people of faith to rise up against oppression. King's position, as Lewis Baldwin interpreted it, "affirms the moral obligation of every rational person to challenge and overcome the forces of injustice and retrogression. This means that it is essentially immoral for victims of oppression to willingly accept oppressive systems and conditions. King knew that it is never oppression that destroys a people, but the acceptance of oppression without protest."[10]

Two Brothers: Lewis V. Baldwin and David L. Baldwin

Two Camden youth who were heavily influenced by Dr. King's visits to Camden, as well as by their family upbringing, faith, and attendance at Camden Academy, were Lewis and David Baldwin. They were the oldest two of ten

KEEP YOUR EYES ON THE PRIZE / 253

children of Rev. L. V. Baldwin, the charismatic pastor who served the Boiling Springs Baptist Church for thirty years, and his wife, Flora Bell Baldwin. The family lived in the Sawmill Quarter during the summer of our SCOPE project, but the brothers were away the summer that I met their father so I did not get to know them until many years later. Lewis Baldwin generously shared his memories and introduced me to his brother, David, whose memories were even more detailed. Their complementary stories illustrate how views of oppression and the fight for freedom can vary not only inside a community but also even inside a family.

Rev. L. V. Baldwin worked in a sawmill as a laborer and also "worked the circuit" as a preacher in Wilcox County. During the student protests, their stern father kept his sons busy because he was always concerned for their safety. Nonetheless, they marched from the school with other students whenever they had the opportunity. Lewis recalled, "In 1965, I was a sophomore at Camden Academy, just sixteen years old. Ralph Eggleston, a boarding student, led a demonstration from campus. He was a main leader. There was a white kid hit so hard by the police that you could see the skin peel from his head."[11]

The young man Lewis saw beaten could have been SNCC worker Strider "Arkansas" Jim Benson, who was brutally beaten in both the Bloody Sunday march in Selma and in Camden in April 1965, or he might have seen a young reporter who several students saw attacked with a knife and nearly scalped. Viciously attacking white civil rights activists served the dual purpose of trying to scare the white kids away from Camden and of warning the black activists that these white demonstrators were not going to bring any protections, unlike they had in some cities.

Lewis explained his level of involvement: "Camden Academy had boarding students who were freer to be active since their parents didn't live in town. When we marched, my brother and I tried to stay in the back of the line and not get hit. At first, we thought it was fun; we didn't take it so seriously. But in February 1966, I was at Antioch Baptist Church right after David Colston was killed. His wife Cassie Colston was one of our teachers at the Academy. She and her son had to see that, see him murdered in cold blood. We went on a protest the next day; that was a very serious march. That has stuck in my mind for a long time."[12]

Like many other Camden youth, the Baldwin brothers went away some summers to have different experiences from what they were able to have in repressive Camden, and they left for college right after high school. Families who sent their children to the Academy or the other mission schools like Anniemanie, Prairie, Millers Ferry, or to the independent Snow Hill Academy, had high hopes for their children. Hard-working, underpaid teachers at these schools told stories of their own experiences in college at Tuscaloosa, Tuskegee, Talladega, and other historically black colleges, to inspire their students to strive to escape grinding poverty and racism through higher education.

Lewis Baldwin credits his Camden Academy teachers, his college education, and his success as a scholar with helping to transcend some of his early life's harsh experiences. Even so, he says there are definitely lasting effects. "The scars are there. I have experienced a lot of difficulty at times, trying to release some of the anger that lingers in my heart. I have the will, but the painful memories remain."[13]

Lewis viewed his father's commitment to his ministry as not only religious service but also as a way to rise above the daily torment of mistreatment. Lewis noted that Rev. L. V. Baldwin practiced a black church tradition: "Preachers often opened services with a segment they called 'the warming-up time' during which they spoke of the week's many 'trials and tribulations.' My father knew and could identify with what his people had gone through the previous week, so he always began the Sunday sermon by recalling the many struggles people had faced in order to highlight the power of God's blessings in their lives. The trials and tribulations were both personal and communal, but some preachers ingeniously used cryptic language when addressing issues like racism and oppression. They often talked about the evils and the destructive power of hate without actually mentioning racism, knowing that being more specific could place them in danger. Even with a white sheriff or constable present, the preacher could attack hatred and highlight the importance of love.

"My father's trials and tribulations were real. He had a hard time feeding, clothing, and educating the ten of us in a society that threatened his body and insulted his spirit daily. I remember him buying shoes for half of us, and promising, with the others weeping around him, that he would have to get theirs later. It was hard for some of us children to understand at that time. My father was struggling to make it in a hostile world.

"Called and treated like a 'nigger' six days a week, Sunday was his day to be reaffirmed as a child of God and to be lifted into a transcendent moment. He could then endure another week. I never felt that my father's 'warming up' moment was used openly and/or publicly to energize, inspire, or motivate people around the need to protest. Preachers knew the danger of this. Even so, the message was clear to the community—'keep on keeping on, and God will stand and march with you.' In other words, the message of inspiration and hope was there, but certainly not detectable to the powers that be."

Lewis said it took him years to realize that his cautious yet courageous father took an amazing stand when he began to drive voters to the polls in 1965 and 1966. Just giving someone a ride to exercise his or her legal rights was still considered an act of defiance—"being 'uppity,' as the mayor would have called it."[14]

Lewis kindly advised me about collecting stories from Wilcox County, "You have the difficult task of talking about the physical and emotional scars. But I hope you will also take into account the joy and the bright side of black life in Camden, which arose out of a sense of community and of being children of the universe despite the pain and oppression. In other words, it was an experience in which pain and affirmation existed side-by-side, and this was expressed in powerful ways in religion and art, music and folktales. There are many experiences in my childhood that I am grateful for, experiences that helped form the man I am today."[15]

Lewis is fully aware that as a coping mechanism, he has blocked out many painful memories from his youth. Lewis's response to the mistreatment his family and community faced daily was to engage in rigorous study and to devote his life to interpreting and teaching the philosophy of that great nonviolent preacher, Martin Luther King Jr., who impressed him so much when he was a young man standing in the crowd outside Antioch Baptist Church.

After Lewis Baldwin graduated from Alabama's Talladega College in 1971, he continued his studies, earning a master of arts degree and also a master of divinity degree from Colgate-Rochester Divinity School in New York and a PhD in American Christianity from Northwestern University. Lewis Baldwin is widely recognized as a foremost scholar of religious history with a primary focus on the life, thought, and legacy of Martin Luther King Jr. Baldwin is a professor at Vanderbilt University and lives in Nashville, Tennessee, with his wife, Jacqueline Laws-Baldwin.

Lewis Baldwin's brother, David Baldwin, graduated from Talladega with a BS in mathematics and physics and from Embry-Riddle Aeronautical University with a master's degree. He served for seventeen years in the US Air Force before retiring as a major. David Baldwin has taught middle and high school math and science, and is the author of two math textbooks.[16] David Baldwin is also an ordained Baptist minister in the tradition of his grandfather, father, and brother Lewis. In June 2011, Rev. Baldwin returned to Wilcox County with his wife, Linda F. Baldwin, to serve as pastor to the 122-year-old Mt. Zion Missionary Baptist Church in the Sedan area of Coy. As with most Wilcox County residents who moved away from home for decades, speaking of the time and place of his youth brought back strong feelings as well as the dialect and expressions unique to Wilcox County. Lewis was correct about David's nearly photographic memory of his youth, which became evident during our multiple lengthy telephone conversations between 2009 and 2011.

David recalled, "The summer of 1965? I was fourteen years old then and we were away working in Birmingham. Our father tried to keep us insulated from the Civil Rights Movement, other than when we went to school at Camden Academy." Even though his sons were only covertly involved in the student movement at the Academy, the sheriff especially pursued Rev. L. V. Baldwin because, as his sons believe, their father strove to better himself. Sheriff Jenkins was rabid on the topic of "uppity" black people. However, as David reminded me, "you did not have to be involved with the Civil Rights Movement to be harassed by authorities; just being black was their only basic criterion for abuse."[17]

Lewis concurred with his younger brother's memories of the economic and racial mistreatment, "My father dealt with racism daily at the sawmill. He sometimes spoke of the verbal insults and the lack of respect whites showed for blacks. Mr. Frank McGraw owned the Commissary on the sawmill grounds, and we would go down with Daddy on Wednesdays to get groceries. We often got groceries on credit. I remember my father and grandmother speaking of what they called bill padding, meaning that Mr. McGraw was cheating them out of hard earned money. Other blacks made the same accusation, but they knew not to approach Mr. McGraw with such thoughts."[18] Being cheated out of wages, low as they were, was so common that most of the men I interviewed said they considered the few honest white people they interacted with to be exceptions.

Besides working in the sawmill and preaching, Rev. L. V. Baldwin did some farming. David remembered, "Most of us had a garden, some corn— my paternal grandparents had an eighty-eight acre lot fifteen to twenty miles out in The Hills, they called it. Some summers we helped our uncles in the fields. They kept us busy working collards, corn, and cotton but I liked the hard work.

"Dad always had a work ethic. He had a little side business in cucumbers. We'd sell them to make pickles, the little tiny ones. The factory was very particular about the size, so the ones the factory didn't take my daddy would sell. He had his regular customers on a route. But when he was away, we'd get our uncle John Henry to drive us around. We'd sell them and collect the money. We swore our customers to secrecy and Uncle John Henry never said anything. Sometime we'd give them a break on the price, a little lower than Daddy's. So when Daddy returned he'd take another round of cucumbers to the customers. Only when he came back they didn't want any but the customers kept our secret. So we enjoyed our farming. Yes, indeed!"[19]

Lewis later added, "David is right in saying that we enjoyed the farm work, but it also inspired us to strive for something better. We saw all of the blisters on daddy's hands and on our own hands, and our teachers at Camden Academy taught us that education was the way out of that kind of existence." Lewis clarified that the reason the young men siphoned off cash was that they had to turn over all their earnings to their father as long as they lived at home and were given little or nothing back. That made it very hard to leave home, which both boys longed to do.[20]

Despite encouragement about his potential at school, Lewis also recalls daily experiences of racism from his youth. "The way it was, it was constant terrorism perpetrated by white men. We grew up hearing about 'luminary' white professionals like Dr. Paul Jones, who was rumored to sterilize black men. Dad often said he needed to insulate us from whites.

"I began driving the car for my father before I was even old enough, so he wouldn't fall asleep and crash the car. He worked hard at the sawmill all week and then preached at Boiling Springs, Arkadelphia, Macedonia, and other Baptist churches—'worked the circuit'—as they called it. He was very popular around the region, and he even preached in the North sometimes.

"Sometimes when I was driving, as we were coming back through Pine Apple we'd pick up a trace of police. They'd get behind us, and start following real close. What saved us was that my daddy knocked down trees and built a makeshift road to our house. In preparation for when they got behind him, he would speed up and then cut his lights and dash down into this ravine that cut through the drive to the house. Then we were home, safe one more time. That was after we'd moved out of the Sawmill over to an area called Estelle. He got a little place that they kept until they died."[21]

David's memories of his father's mistreatment by the white establishment in Camden are still vivid. He recounted, "They called my father 'Boy,' all his life. His psychology was totally subjected to white domination. As you can imagine, after we got out and saw the world, we viewed things quite differently. After college, I was in the military. We'd come back and see how he acted in front of the whites. Once I brought him a thousand dollars to pay all his debts so he could be free and clear of them. We went to the appliance store in Camden to pay everything off. On the way out, he was looking for something else because he wanted to appease the white guy, to get back in debt. Many years ago, when my father owed the last payment on a car, he went to pay it off. They were still open; they weren't going to close for a couple of hours. They took the payment and took the car both! Told him he was late. Weren't nothing he could do.

"Our family had five boys and five girls, and two children that died. The four oldest had the hardest time. Our dad misplaced his oppression and put it on us. As we got older we began to understand the pressure he was under; some of the younger ones didn't know what he had gone through.

"Sheriff Jenkins had a posse that constantly terrorized us. I can't see how any of us recovered, really. In the last ten to fifteen years I finally got past breaking out in a sweat when I see a policeman behind me. I always ponder what my life would be like if I had not gone through that experience of being constantly terrorized. Pure terror was what it was, big things, and little things, just constant.

"You couldn't just walk up to the counter at the drugstore. Whites walked in and got waited on right away. But we had to wait in a separate line and couldn't go up until no more whites were in the store. One time I waited two hours while someone was just chatting with the clerk about their family and such. It wasn't just our family; it was how they treated everyone who wasn't white.

"My father did a radio station spot advertising for the Great American Homes so they would give him a new house. Those new developments like Westgate were ones my daddy helped promote so that blacks got into contracts with the company. They were supposed to give him a home, but they never did. Nor did they ever remunerate him in any way."

David continued with a torrent of memories: "The civil rights workers would come to school. They told us to leave all our identification before we marched, so if they arrested you they wouldn't know who your parents were. If your kids were arrested they would put the parents out of the house. Very few [black people in Camden] owned their own homes. The only reason I was in any of the student marches was because the teachers let us out of class. Our father didn't know about it. The principal Mr. Hobbs initially didn't support us but then when his own life was threatened, he started wearing guns to school. He had a long ride into town so he protected himself.

"One time we were marching and Mr. Gregory who owned the filling station near the Academy drove straight through us. He could easily have hurt someone, killed somebody even. But blacks still gave him all our business.

"When Mr. Albert Gordon and Mr. Lawrence Parrish were fired from their jobs as teachers at the Academy for their involvement in civil rights, they opened P&G Filling Station. But as soon as they opened, they [the Klan] burned it down—it may not even have gotten open before they torched it."

David believes that committed adults saved him and other children from Camden by offering them encouragement to get out and get an education. "The Bessie W. Munden Playground was the only place for recreation. We had some kind of solace there. Mrs. Bessie Munden was a great teacher; she helped us a lot. Our third grade teacher Mrs. Mamie Smith got us started on getting out of there. Mrs. Smith lived on a hill at Westgate where her family had owned land for a long time. She was very light-skinned and had connections in Great Barrington, Massachusetts, the birthplace of W.E.B. Du Bois. Lewis and I went up there several summers, and it was so different [so much better] I didn't want to come back.

"Mr. Wendell Edwards, my high school math teacher, was the son of the Snow Hill Institute founder; he helped us get into his alma mater, Talladega College, by writing us strong letters of recommendation. We used to call him 'Rock Jaw';[22] he was so determined. 'You guys are going to college,' he told me. He took me and Lewis up there in his car. You had to have someone to get you out of Camden.

"When I was in eleventh grade my teachers said they couldn't teach me anymore, that I was college material. Talladega College gave me the admissions test and accepted me on the spot. I guess I was advanced for my age. This was April 1968, three or four days after Dr. King was assassinated. Going there to go to an all-black college like that was quite an experience. We had a few mixed faculty but all the students except one teacher's son were black. After I returned from college, I felt a release, a new lease on life. My parents were not highly educated; they didn't have a chance.

"Another thing that broadened my horizons was responding to a bulletin board advertisement at Talladega College that led me to Atlanta, where I worked at the Community of Hope Lutheran Church teaching math and shepherding vesper services. This storefront church had a young white pastor. During my work at Community of Hope, Dr. King's mother, Miz Alberta, would come by every Wednesday to bring the children some teacakes. I didn't know she was a celebrity, I just thought she was a nice lady. During that time, I also worked on Andrew Young's campaign for Fifth District congressman against a known racist, Wyman C. Lowe. Rev. Young and I had numerous conversations about strategies for getting white support and votes for his campaign. I believe that Andrew Young won in the primary but lost in the general election that year."[23]

David remembered instances when local youth fought back forcefully: "Not too long ago, my brother Charles and I went into the Piggly Wiggly supermarket in Camden and recognized Charley Davis Jr., whose family had lived near us. Lummie Jenkins and his vigilantes had tagged Charley Jr. and his brother as being two of the worst blacks in Camden, meaning they weren't afraid of the sheriff. We were all coming back from our summer work in Massachusetts to where we lived then, out on Whiskey Run. As soon as Daddy saw that Lummie and them had Leroy and Charley Davis Jr., and was harassing them, he rushed us into the house. They weren't doing anything at all but when they were attacked, Charley Jr. and his brother wrestled the policeman to the ground and Leroy took his gun. As I recall, both of them got away. The last time I heard, neither of them was ever caught, even though they scoured the place looking for them.

"I did not let my experiences outside—in college, the military, teaching, and the ministry—wipe out what I experienced coming up. I want to always be able to see and understand Camden in contrast to those other experiences. I'd still like to find some way to improve things there, help the students."[24] In 2011, David Baldwin began to deliver communion to people unable to get to church and was planning to set up a youth mentorship program.

As these stories poured forth from the Baldwin brothers and others my heart was heavy. But people told me that during the movement years, they were bound together by their shared faith that someday the oppression would end. It was a period of excitement and unity. For many years, I shared in a popular belief that black people were held back by their strong Christian faith with its doctrine of endurance. But nearly every one I spoke with credited their strong faith with their ability to survive the trauma of the past and to find some measure of peace and forgiveness today.

Far from keeping people down, many of the churches in Wilcox, particularly Antioch Baptist in Camden, Little Zion in Coy, Pleasant View in Peachtree, and Pleasant Grove in Gees Bend were vital centers of the movement. Congregants could move from a prayer service to a mass meeting in a heartbeat. Despite ongoing attacks and bomb threats, courageous deacons at Antioch Baptist allowed their church to continue to serve as Movement Central for mass meetings, organizing and planning sessions, food distribution, and the starting point for many marches. Armed with strong faith and righteous indignation at daily injustice, community organizers found both the courage and the volunteers they needed to keep on going. Faith, hope, and discipline reigned as the community continued the nonviolent and legal battle toward equity that continues to this day.

Lewis Baldwin stated that the importance of the churches must not be underestimated: "The churches were actually the power base for the movement, especially churches like the Antioch Baptist Church. But even those churches that refused to open their doors to demonstrators were involved. They provided food, marchers, and served as sources of inspiration because of their messages of hope and the certainty of divine deliverance. It was the gospel we got from all the churches that kept us going, even when people like David Colston were beaten or killed. Ministers like daddy and our cousin, the Rev. Sol T. McNeil, were not radical, but their sermons, with their ungrammatical profundity, gave us hope and courage. They reminded us that God had not left us alone; that the promises of God for His abused and downtrodden people would ultimately come to pass—the promise of deliverance from evil and suffering."[25]

On March 1, 2010, when Lewis Baldwin appeared at Antioch Baptist Church as keynote speaker for the forty-fifth anniversary commemoration of a march Dr. King led, he opened the gathering with inspirational remarks echoing the style of his father, Rev. L. V. Baldwin, and of Dr. King himself: "We have come to this historic church at this particular moment in history, to remember the struggle that took place forty-five years ago. We are here to remember Martin Luther King Jr., who gave us his physical support, and whose presence still lingers in the far corners of this place . . . we gather here tonight to remember the events as they unfolded in this little town of Camden, Alabama. But this is not merely an occasion to look back and to recall the struggles of the past, it is also a time to look ahead and to keep dreaming, because God is the God of both the dream and the dreamer. It is time to take the struggle to the next level, to continue to fight the fight, because we do not live in a post-racial society. The forces of racism are still active across vast stretches of this land, so the struggle must go on. We have no choice but to keep moving, knowing that one day we will reach the promised land. And when that day comes, we can all unite our voices in echoing the immortal words of Dr. King—words that come down from our forebears: 'Free at Last, Free at Last, Thank God Almighty, We are free at last.'"[26]

A Change Is Gonna Come

Oh there been times I thought I couldn't last for long
But now I think I'm able to carry on
It's been a long, long time coming
But I know a change is gonna come, yes it will
"A Change Is Gonna Come," Sam Cooke, 1965

Progress and Potential

Through faith and nonviolent and legal activism the black majority ended government-sanctioned segregation in Wilcox County. However, with limited employment opportunities, underfunded public schools, and continued social segregation, many residents believe a new movement is needed—one that involves the entire community and that requires both government and business investment.

Shortly after President Obama was first elected, Pebble Hill resident John Matthews told me, "I think change is coming to Wilcox County and the Black Belt. It all boils down to one thing: People have to get together. We could benefit from something like they had when Nelson Mandela got out of prison in South Africa, a Truth and Reconciliation Commission. Not just to talk about the past, but it would help even more if they would admit they have stood in the way of improvements ever since. Talk is good, but we need action; we have to work together on the economy in this county."[1]

A few former residents who have moved away feared their Camden relatives would suffer if they told stories of the horrors they suffered as young people. Many current residents stated that racial tension still underlies every community concern, from contentious elections to a divided school board and city council, to a continually declining population. One longtime resident told me that over the years, a few white women have privately told her how bad they felt when they were young. "They knew what their parents were doing was wrong, but they couldn't say anything. They would have been disowned or worse. Of course, they could do something now, something along the lines of economic reparations and cooperation to build a strong public school system."

Another Camden native said, "If they would just get over themselves and see that we all need to work together, we could bring prosperity to this county, but I don't have much hope of that happening."[2] Others are optimistic that the ongoing worldwide economic crisis and greater focus on the particular challenges of poverty will finally draw all Wilcox residents together. After the Great Recession of 2008, nearly everyone was struggling, even those who had felt comfortable until then. However, most everyone agreed that some kind of honest conversation about race relations must precede any in-depth cooperative efforts.

Black residents reported that they are not knocking on doors to become closer to the white community in Camden because they have not heard from their white neighbors that they regret past mistreatment. Despite common knowledge of the names of the perpetrators of civil rights murders and attempted murders in Wilcox County, no new lawsuits have been filed and no old cases reopened. No amends have been offered or recompense paid.

Many people suspect that open hostilities have quieted only due to a change in political power, not a genuine change of mindset. Potential for dialogue might develop if some of those unnamed white families who were supportive of the movement would come forward to claim their place by the side of today's black leaders. Their own grandchildren and great-grandchildren are not getting the education and opportunities they could get if everyone pulled together to uplift the public school system.

In discussing progress and potential, locals accept their own responsibility to make change. Despite the advances brought about by the right to vote, some residents told me that elections are still corrupt and that bribery is common. With her customary candor, Kate Charley explained, "Elections are bought by alcohol. It flows like the Alabama River around election time. Everyone is bribed here, that's how it still works. The color has changed but that's about all."

Kate also reflected, "I am African, Caucasian, and Indian, with all those races coursing through my blood, I claim all of them. Sometimes I get disgusted with 'us,' by which I mean mostly blacks. As great as the Civil Rights Movement was, it encouraged us to become independent and seek a better life, but there are some ways we didn't grasp at all. Years later some of us look like we are still waiting for a handout, like the world owes us something, but it doesn't. We are not supposed to just wait for our 'forty acres and a mule' like we read about in school. That's not gonna happen. We are supposed to have the opportunity, not the handouts. It made some too dependent; some of us are weak in that way. I tell people to their face, they need to stop talkin' about 'y'all' and 'them,' and say 'we' sometimes. We have to do it for ourselves."[3]

Sadly, Wilcox County is still the poorest county in the state of Alabama.

Today, as in the past, most Camden young people cannot find jobs even if they go away to college. Shelly Dale believes that Wilcox County could be revitalized under the right conditions. She told me, "First and foremost, we need good jobs, some kind of industry. Second, we need to develop a skilled labor force so that more businesses would be interested in coming here. Third, people who have left need to return and invest in whatever is here. There are a lot of great, wonderful people here. Many people leave here and do well in life—professionals, doctors, professors, and business people. Young people want bigger cities. But if there were good jobs, some would come back here for the quiet life. Our crime rate is very, very low."[4]

Rosetta Anderson said hopefully, "We are trying to come together, all nationalities to build our community but it seems we are more divided now than ever. I regret it very much, but I don't think in my lifetime that I will see as much unity as we had back then. But, the economy could bring a lot of us back together. Out of the blue somebody could stand up tomorrow and take up where we left off, declare a new war on poverty."[5]

Gloria Jean McDole observed, "Relationships are somewhat better, but you can still feel that prejudice. Some of the younger people don't pay attention, but we older folks, we still feel it." When asked about interracial dating or marriage, Gloria Jean McDole and Sheryl Threadgill both agreed that there was little, if any, because youth don't go to school or have after school jobs or attend church together, so there is no way for them to get to know each other in natural settings. "If you sit and listen to them [whites] talk they say they don't care about being with blacks, but somebody has to make the first move" Sheryl explained, "Like with the children in sports, they could have better sports. The youth come to black games because our school teams play well and we're publicly supported. But we don't go over there, to their private [white] school. There is no interracial dating unless the youth are from outside the area, no locals would."[6]

Although the Wilcox County freedom fight was grassroots from start to finish, most of those who were involved agreed that outside civil rights workers made a difference. Gloria Jean McDole explained, "Back then there was no vote. Now people can vote. It made you feel good to be part of something that helped some kind of way. We schoolchildren led the way with the marching, the parents were afraid. They had no place to go and didn't want to get thrown out of their houses. We welcomed your help from outside, yes we did."[7]

Mrs. Rosetta Angion says that she can rest easier, knowing that she did all she could to bring about change. "There has been a *big* change since black people became citizens, able to vote, to have a voice altogether like it should be. I am able to go to the polls. Those that are able to work can get a job. We are able to go in the courthouse. I feel a lot safer. Now we know that black people have rights just like white people, not everything belongs to them. Now what really needs to happen, people need to come together, work together and don't be fighting against each other [within the black community]. I'm one of the few left that was there, remembers it all. They should learn about our history. Keep working, it's not over with. Keep tryin' to help each other."[8]

An active community member at age seventy, Mrs. Arzula Johnson of Pine Apple explained to me why she did not participate in the voting rights movement but got involved after the act was passed. She said, "Lots of people were too afraid. I didn't protest; I couldn't. I was married at the time and my husband held me back. Once the law passed, I was right there. I registered to vote August 30, 1965. I'll never forget sitting on that hot pavement for hours in a line of hundreds of folks. It is important for our young people to know our history, to know about you being here. Just you being here meant a lot, even if we weren't all active. But because of you, we got more courage and made some of the advances that we did. Near every one elected is black now. Things are almost reversed."[9]

When Barack Obama was inaugurated in 2009, John Matthews called to tell me, "Yesterday I drove a car full of the BAMA Kids down to Montgomery to see a film. I was listening to the We Are One inauguration concert for President Obama in the car and crying. When we got there, I turned around and told those kids 'Lincoln said we all were free, but it took another one hundred years for Rosa Parks to sit down and not take it any more. Hundreds of other people worked and sacrificed to get us to this point where a black man is about to become President. The fact that you guys are riding right now through that very city where our great march took place shows that this country can be free from the top to the bottom. You will remember this day.'"[10]

A groundswell of support from youth, women, labor and diverse people elevated Barack Obama to become the first African American US president. He ran not on the basis of his race but on a desire for change. The movement to elect him was comprised of millions of individuals, many of them too young to recall the Civil Rights Movement but old enough to recognize that big changes still needed to be made. During his first term, a well-funded conservative minority led the charge to defeat his economic and social policies at any cost and to prevent his reelection. But in November 2012, the majority again voted for the president and against the old establishment. Progressives actually have the numbers to fulfill the dream of true equality, to end poverty, and to ensure justice for all. The question remains: Will we ever join across race, economic class, and generations to sacrifice short-term, personal gain for the collective future good?

Forty-Fifth Anniversary Commemoration and Mass Meeting

By the time I returned to Wilcox County again to commemorate the voting rights march that Dr. Martin Luther King Jr. led on March 1, 1965, I had spoken with dozens of area residents, made some strong long-distance friendships, and was invited to be one of the speakers at the Forty-Fifth Anniversary Commemorative March and Mass Meeting at Historical Antioch Baptist Church.[11] The event was held the same week the Bloody Sunday march was commemorated, which provided an opportunity to fulfill the pledge that my old friends Charles Bonner, Luke Block, and I had made—that someday we would walk over the Edmund Pettus Bridge in Selma together. With the encouragement of Sam Walker, program director for the National Voting Rights Museum, Wilcox County leaders held their own event for the first time at the beginning of the Selma Jubilee week. Joy Crawford-Washington of Mobile and I served on the planning committee along with local leaders Sheryl Threadgill, Rosetta Anderson, and others.

My husband, Samuel Torres Jr., and I spent a week in Camden, visiting with many of the people who had shared their stories with me. We met some new folks and revisited those who had become friends. Former police chief and Wilcox County commissioner John Matthews reminded me of a day when he had rescued my coworkers and me, a day I had forgotten, given that most of our summer of 1965 days were filled with long treks through wooded rural roads with potential danger on every side. John took us to his family's old cornfield in Pebble Hill and retold the story in his eloquent baritone. John explained that he, his father, and brothers were working in this very cornfield when their father saw me, Luke, and a black youth walking deeper into the woods around sunset, instead of toward the highway and our ride back to town.

John recalled, "Evening was upon us and night was not long in coming. You were heading into the community where the roadway and trails lead to a large wooded area. Daddy knew you didn't have a clue where you were or what direction you were going. The young black man with you was not local and didn't know the way either. Daddy told me, 'Son, go get the truck and get those civil rights workers off the road before something happens to them.'"[12]

As we looked across the now weedy field, I remembered how this tall,

19. Maria Gitin and former Camden chief of police and Wilcox County commissioner John Matthews revisit Pine Hill, Alabama. (Copyright © 2010 by Samuel Torres Jr.)

skinny-but-muscular sixteen-year-old pulled up in an old truck and asked where we were headed. When we said Antioch Baptist, he told us to get in. We did what John recommended. The first principle of our field worker training was: follow the locals' lead.

John laughed, "I was glad you all jammed into the cab with me because there was just a flatbed in back and it would have been obvious who you were. So we four piled in the cab of that old '56 green Chevrolet pickup and off we went. It was my first contact with civil rights workers.

"Looking back, I don't think Daddy gave a second thought about using his truck or putting me in danger to give a hand to you. Although we were fortunate enough to have our own land and farm it, on that day we were working a field we share farmed with a white family. There could have been consequences. To the best of my knowledge, nothing was ever said to Daddy about that day."[13] How many other unknown benefactors made it possible for me and other Wilcox County civil rights workers to be alive today? I will never know but extend my gratitude to each and every one.

Today, John Matthews, a tall handsome man with a shaved head, is a respected community leader who returned from what could have been a comfortable retirement in the North to lend a hand to his still-struggling community and to raise cows and corn on his father's land.

John added, "What I remember about the white civil rights workers was that our parents and we young people had been doing this for a long time, but when you came we believed the cavalry was coming—that everything would change. It did, but it took longer than anyone imagined it would back then.

"The Civil Rights Movement freed us all to be better, a better people. It definitely helped. They realized they couldn't kill us all so the establishment came to terms with what it was. The movement definitely helped step up progress: things moved faster than they would have on our own."[14]

Before the mass meeting, community members convened at Antioch Baptist Church for a short march to the courthouse to reenact the march led by Martin Luther King Jr. forty-five years earlier to the day. A small group participated, mostly older folks with some BAMA Kids carrying the Wilcox County freedom fighters banner. When we took our places in the line of a few dozen families to march from the church to the courthouse where so many had once been turned away, I was one of four white people. No residents lined the street to cheer on their neighbors. The city council held a meeting that conflicted with the event timing, and there was no media presence despite outreach by the planning committee. Someone may have been trying to send a clearer message: a rock was thrown through the window of a BAMA Kids van after they left the march. Fortunately, the adult driver was alone at the time and was not injured.

As I walked with my husband, Kate Charley, Jessie and Joy Crawford, Sim and Minerva Pettway, and others singing to the nonexistent crowds, I marveled that we could do this safely, and with a seemingly unneeded police escort. At the old courthouse, Rev. Patricia Kimmons-Pettway gave a moving tribute to the lives lost on the road to freedom. We wept for our departed friends as we embraced in a prayer circle. Then, Sheryl Threadgill and some of her former classmates began singing their old protest song, "Lummie, you never can jail us all," and our tears turned to laughter before we headed back to the church.

Once back at Antioch, I was nervous when my speech followed eloquent Lewis Baldwin and other respected local leaders. I planned to speak about my dear friend, Ethel Brooks. Although Ethel may have been gone a long time in their minds, I was still grieving and wanted to commemorate her properly. As I stood before the nearly full church I began:

In 1965 at age nineteen, I was one of the smallest foot soldiers in the nonviolent freedom fight in Wilcox County. The first night I spent in Wilcox County was right here, under these pews, while the Klan fired off shots outside this church. Most people know that the spring and summer of 1965 turned the tide for voting rights for African Americans and changed history forever, but few people know how much of that change occurred right here in Camden.

Before I arrived in June, students had led demonstrations to the courthouse where you were met with violence, beatings, tear gas and arrest. Adults organized, demonstrated, marched from this very church. Hundreds of Wilcox County residents were on the Edmund Pettus Bridge in Selma on Bloody Sunday—some of you were injured in the attacks on the marchers. Dozens of you were at Dexter Curve when the marchers made their finally victorious entry into Montgomery three weeks later. Although the famous five-day Selma to Montgomery March ended in tragedy as it had begun with death, arrests, and beatings, fearless freedom fighters continued on here in Camden as you did in communities throughout the South, out of the limelight and without federal protections.

In my three months in Wilcox County, as I walked your red dirt roads doing voter education and registration work, ran from the Klan, was arrested, attended mass meetings, and supported local leaders, I met dozens of people who I have never forgotten. Many people could and should be honored tonight, but it is with a heavy heart I am here to honor someone who died too young, someone who should be here with us, her clear alto voice singing the freedom songs she loved so much, my friend and hero, Ethel Lenora Brooks of Coy, daughter of Julia and Jesse Brooks.

I could barely choke back my tears but continued to tell them what many may have forgotten, or never known.

When I met Ethel she was only twenty-four years old. She lived in Coy, one of the most active areas in the county. Ethel organized carloads of students to participate in the Selma marches. She was fearless and tireless, impatient with those who were not ready to join the movement. She taught me how to act, what to do, and even how to sing Freedom songs with the right spirit. She was always there for us. It is still nearly impossible to accept that she isn't right here with us tonight.

I started to choke up again but continued telling them about Ethel's jail pants, about her trying to outrun the Klan, and even about the strawberry wine on the Fourth of July. I wanted to bring her back to life—the real Ethel, not a fantasy Ethel.

> There were many leaders, both well known and unknown in this county. As far as I'm concerned, Ethel was one of the very finest. Thank you for giving me the honor of sharing just a few memories of my dear friend and yours, Ethel Brooks.

Several others spoke movingly of their family's contributions before we concluded with fifty or more of us standing in a friendship circle, arms crossed in the old tradition. Everyone and everything felt so familiar to me, it felt like coming home.

Later that week, when I had a chance to speak with a few folks over at the house where we were staying, I tried to explain how Wilcox County changed my life, what I learned as we worked side by side that long ago summer. I could never again ignore racism, bigotry, and bias. My experience in Wilcox County helped me develop a core belief in the ultimate goodness of people as well as the potential for evil in all of us. I learned that wisdom doesn't always come from schooling, but that education is the surest way out of poverty. I learned that you don't have to be perfect and you don't have to have everything figured out in order to be of real help to a cause. I experienced the deep joy of belonging to a movement of the people. In the midst of their own battles, the people of Wilcox County offered me love and acceptance that I had never before known.

One evening over dinner, Alma King and I shared early memories about some of the things that may have had an influence on the fact that we now have friends of other races. Alma told me about a little doll she had, "You know, I don't know where I got it, but I had a little doll that was white." I expected her to say that it made her feel bad that the doll didn't look like her, but she continued, "I loved that doll. And now, I have some white friends, I have some good white friends."[15] I told Alma about an early memory of being frightened when I saw a black person for the first time—a dark-skinned nurse's aide—leaning over my hospital crib when I had eye surgery in San Francisco at age two and a half. My aunt Ruth gave me a little black doll because she said I had hurt the lady's feelings when I cried and she wanted to make sure I didn't grow up prejudiced. Alma and I mused about how sometimes it is the small as much as the large events in life that leave a lasting impression.

Despite ongoing socioeconomic and political challenges to racial justice and equality, Lewis Baldwin summed up what he believes people can learn from the Civil Rights Movement. He wrote, "I feel that the Civil Rights Movement in Alabama made a lot of difference, and one can see this only if he/she realizes what actually existed before that period of activism in our history. . . . Every generation must take its place in this endless struggle for freedom and equality of opportunity. . . . The Civil Rights Movement teaches us that the struggle against oppression and victimization is always a moral imperative, and that it must be launched through moral means. It reminds us that violence, which has become increasingly evident in epidemic proportions at all levels of our society and world, can never be the best route to a truly free and just human situation. Youth should look to the Civil Rights Movement for lessons and for inspiration, but not necessarily to duplicate everything that the freedom fighters of the past did. The freedom fighters of yesterday become in many ways models, but the youth must find their own paths to freedom. The answer to today's problems of grinding poverty, neglect, and injustice rests with them, for those who fought a half century or more ago have already made their contributions."[16]

At the end of the week Luke Block and his wife, Willow, joined Samuel and me in Camden. I prepared a sage bundle, took a copy of a photo of Ethel, and we drove out to the old Canton Bend bridge where Ethel's car had crashed. In our own private ceremony, we sang "This Little Light of Mine," I read the *Kaddish*, the Jewish prayer for the dead, and Luke said a few words. We tied a Wilcox County freedom fighter ribbon with Ethel's name on it to the concrete piling with fishing twine and Willow tucked in some wildflowers. The wind blew tears across my face as I said a silent prayer, "Rest in peace, sweet woman warrior." Ethel was a passionate, committed woman and I only hope that she found any part of the love and peace that she deserved before she died.

Return to Selma with Wilcox County Freedom Fighters

That weekend, Luke, Willow, Samuel, and I joined Charles Bonner for the Selma Jubilee—just as we had promised each other we would. It was Luke's first time back to Selma since the original march to Montgomery, while Charles had made the trek annually. We were thrilled to read Charles's name on the monument in front of Brown Chapel as one of the civil rights heroes.

We spent the evening before the bridge reenactment march with some of Charles's high school buddies, including the mayor of Selma, George Evans, and Judge Nathaniel Walker, at a reception for Alabama black mayors. Before the reception, we were invited to join a small group to motor under the Selma bridge on a new tour boat. At sunset, the arch of the empty, infamous bridge looked beautiful, but not as beautiful as our company: a small riverboat filled with African American elected officials and students from the Selma Mayor's Youth Council. After introductions all around, as we looked up at the historic bridge, Charles Bonner reflected poetically, "We were just teenagers marching toward a blue sea of police, armed with guns, tear gas, billy clubs. Those on horseback had long leather whips. But we were at peace with our fear, our courage, and our hope, that as the song we were singing, a 'change is gonna come.'"[17]

Back at the St. James Hotel, we joined city and state officials in a reception to honor the thirteen black mayors of Alabama to celebrate the slow but steady progress that had been made, and to kick off current campaigns. As I washed my hands in the ladies' room, my eyes met those of a younger woman with lovely braids and an African textile dress, mayor of Gainesville, Alabama, Carrie F. Fulghum, who I had spoken with earlier on the boat. We walked together into the hotel foyer, where she turned and said, "If it weren't for people like you, I wouldn't be here, in this position today." We embraced with tears in our eyes, feeling the moment was bigger than either of us and yet intimately personal. Many individuals formed many groups to fight for one goal: one person, one vote. And we won!

On Sunday morning in the warm sun outside Brown Chapel, I worked my cell phone to coordinate three separate groups of Wilcox County participants amid thousands of people trying to find each other along MLK Avenue in anticipation of the big march, the bridge reenactment ceremony, which is the highlight of the weekend observance. As the dignitaries completed their service inside Brown Chapel, Wilcox County's BAMA Kids began singing "Ain't Gonna Let Nobody Turn Me 'Round," which spread through the clapping and singing crowd. Vivacious Betty Anderson tapped me on the shoulder and said, "Look who's here!" I turned to look up at the familiar smiling face of Robert Powell, the sixteen-year-old who had taken me out canvassing the rural roads of Wilcox County. Despite forty-five years' passage since we had seen each other, we shouted out, "Joyce!" "Robert!"

Robert's smile and hugs bridged the years as we caught up on family and our mutual friends in the Wilcox movement, talked about those who had died, and lamented those who suffered so deeply that they couldn't bear to join us today. Here we were: alive, healthy, and standing together in a sea of eight thousand others who still believe that We *Shall* Overcome. We marched together under the Wilcox County freedom fighters banner. Robert proudly picked up one end of the banner and carried it all the way across the bridge while Phillip Young, director of the Bessie W. Munden Playground, held up the other.

20. Maria Gitin reunites with voting rights canvassing partner Robert Powell, Selma Jubilee. (Copyright © 2010 by Samuel Torres Jr.)

Walking with Charles, Luke, and me, with our spouses, were new and renewed Wilcox County friends: three generations of Crawfords descended from Bob and Georgia Crawford of Pine Apple; Sheryl Threadgill with her BAMA Kids; Alma Moton King and Mary Alice Robinson with the National Council of Negro Women banner; Rev. and Mrs. Frank Smith's daughter, Carolyn Smith Taylor from Lower Peachtree. Rev. John Davis was there in his wheelchair with a sign about his having gone all the way to the White House to confront President Roosevelt about his denied voting rights. We were one small band among the thousands of marchers as we headed for the Edmund Pettus Bridge not only to commemorate Bloody Sunday but also to call attention to the ongoing fight for equal education and economic opportunity, still in short supply in this nation.

On this sunny day, we elders knew how fortunate we were to have lived, to be here. Meanwhile, the young people with us were in high spirits from their "Steppin' Out the Vote" concert the night before. They kept singing as we walked forward in amazement that we could cross this bridge in safety. It was my first time on the bridge, and I was thrilled to be with so many

21. Wilcox County freedom fighters cross the Edmund Pettus Bridge during the Selma Jubilee forty-fifth anniversary of the Bloody Sunday march, Selma, Alabama. (Copyright © 2010 by Samuel Torres Jr.)

who had done so much more than I to bring about a world where we could walk—black and white together.

For the first time in forty-five years Mary Alice Robinson bravely revisited the scene of her attack on Bloody Sunday. This time she and all marchers were escorted by police and surrounded by a warm, welcoming crowd. When I placed my hand on Mary Alice's back, I could feel her heart racing as she pointed to the spot where she feared her life might end. Together, we looked over the steep embankment where she had been forced to fall into the brambles. Now there is a small playground in that spot along the peaceful bank of the Selma River. As we walked back across the bridge, she expressed gratitude that she had come. She had known about the bridge crossing re-enactment for decades, but couldn't bring herself to face it until this year.[18]

It was here on this bloodied bridge that some of the most vivid images of the Civil Rights Movement were stamped on the conscience of America. Only recently have people begun to learn about the countless other small

Selmas, and the thousands of unknown heroes who stood up to racism all over the South. The Beloved Community was broad, wide, and deep. Out of the backwoods of Wilcox County, Alabama, rose up a people who risked their lives for the rights of all. A fortunate few of us shared in their struggle for a while. We can best show our gratitude by listening to and telling their stories—our stories.

We won many—but not all—legal battles. There is still policy to be changed, and legal, social, and grassroots action that needs to be taken to achieve economic justice and to preserve and expand voting rights. We must eliminate racism in this country. If we work together across the generations, take our lead from the youth while lending them the benefit of our experience, we can change hearts and minds as well as discriminatory institutions and practices. Deep in my heart, I still *do* believe.

Notes

Chapter 1

1. Jeff Freed became a leader of the historic 1968 San Francisco State student-led strike.

2. *Williams v. Wallace*, 240 F. Supp. 100 (1965), and SCOPE orientation materials, Morris Brown College, Atlanta, Georgia, June 1965.

3. Leventhal, *SCOPE*, 330.

4. "SNCC Looking for Volunteers," *SF Gator*, San Francisco State College, spring 1965.

5. Leventhal, *SCOPE*, 53.

6. Carson, *In Struggle*, 23.

Chapter 2

1. Ludwig van Beethoven, words by Friedrich Schiller. "Ode to Joy," Ninth Symphony.

2. N. J. Demerath et al., *The Dynamics of Idealism*. Participants have raised questions regarding the researchers' motivations for extensive pre- and postquestions about interracial relationships and Communism.

3. During the orientation, Julian Bond was elected to the Georgia legislature on a vote of 2,320 to 48, becoming the second black elected state office holder.

4. Joseph Ruah, SCOPE orientation, Morris Brown College, Atlanta, Georgia, June 1965.

5. James Lawson, SCOPE orientation.

6. C. Vann Woodward, SCOPE orientation.

7. James Bevel, SCOPE orientation.

8. Randolph Blackwell, SCOPE orientation.

9. Albert Turner, SCOPE orientation.

10. Lester Hankerson, SCOPE orientation.

11. Golden Frinks, SCOPE orientation.
12. Hosea Williams, SCOPE orientation.
13. Daniel Harrell, SCOPE orientation.

Chapter 3

1. Carson, *The Autobiography of Martin Luther King Jr.*
2. www.crmvet.org: Civil Rights Movement Veterans—History and Timeline, 1964, accessed April 17, 2013; and Bruce Hartford conversations, 2005–12.
3. John Davis, presentation, Camden, Alabama, March 1, 2010.
4. Walter F. Murphy, "The South Counterattacks."
5. *South Carolina v. Katzenbach*, 383 US 301, 310–12 (1966).
6. Douglas A. Blackmon, *Slavery by Another Name.*
7. *Williams v. Wallace*, 240 F. Supp. 100 (1965).
8. *U.S. v. Bruce*, 353 F. 2d. 474 (1965).
9. *U.S. v. Logue*, 344 F. 2d. 290 (1965).

Chapter 4

1. Negro was the term of respect that African American leaders told us to use. In part I, Negro is used in my letters and quotations from this time. In part II, black and African American are used in deference to the preference of those quoted. Terms change and there never will be one definition accepted by all people of color, a term that likely will be outmoded in a few years as the US population shifts from seeing white as the norm to seeing diverse, biracial, and multicultural as the norm.

Chapter 5

1. Voter fraud was rampant throughout the Black Belt at that time; however, reported numbers also varied from source to source.
2. The N-word is used in this book only when used in a direct quote, and for two reasons: (1) to preserve the integrity and the precision of quoted material from those who were involved on some level in the struggle in Wilcox County, and (2) to convey a sense of the spirit of those times as related to race relations. This author never uses it.
3. Robert Powell, telephone conversation, April 10, 2011.

Chapter 7

1. Later the denomination changed its name to American Methodist Episcopal.
2. Paul Good, "600 Students," *Washington Post.*

Chapter 8

1. David M. Gordon, "Threats Don't Stop Camden Pair," *Southern Courier*. Reynolds is quoted as saying that he only closed the café to us for one day, but our leaders told us to stay away all summer in order not to cause him trouble.

Chapter 9

1. SCOPE records and news articles state eighteen were arrested.

2. SCLC staff encouraged us to view ourselves as leaders, but the locals saw their own community youth as leaders. Their arrest generated greater concern in the community than ours did.

3. William Truss went on to be one of the first students to integrate white Wilcox High School in 1967.

4. Roy Reed, "Say Whites Broke into Church to Beat Negro," *Chicago Daily Defender*.

5. Roy Reed, "Alabama Sheriff Locks Church," *New York Times*.

Chapter 10

1. SCLC's Voter Education Project: see www.crmvet.org, under History and Timeline.

Chapter 11

1. Leventhal, *SCOPE*, 200. Reporter Paul Good signed in at the SCOPE Atlanta orientation as a freelance journalist and listed a local telephone number in Atlanta, not as a *Washington Post* reporter.

2. According to locals, the original ferry was taken out in 1962, but there was another one upstream for hauling logs that white drivers could use.

Chapter 13

1. Roy Reed, "Re-Open SCOPE Headquarters," *Chicago Daily Defender*.
2. Paul Good, "600 Students," *Washington Post*.

Chapter 14

1. Branch, *At Caanan's Edge*, 210.

2. Jimmy Rogers, conversations; and Faith Holsaert et al., eds., *Hands on the Freedom Plow*, 506–8.

3. Other authors have erroneously spelled Colston as Colson.

4. Bob Fitch, SCLC photographer, conversation. Fitch accompanied King and took photos that were printed without attribution in *Jet Magazine* (February 10, 1966), 8–9.

5. *U.S. v. Wilcox County Board of Education*, 494 F. 2d 575 (1974).

6. Bob Fitch's spring 1966 Citizenship Education Project photo archives picture Anelle Ponder and Septima Clark as leaders and Albert Gordon as a leader in training. In a 2012 conversation, Rosetta Anderson stated that she was trained by CEP. Voncille Burrell Spencer and Deborah Tucker Burrell stated in May 2012 telephone conversations that their mother, Virginia Boykin Burrell, was also a trained literacy leader. Burrell was honored for her work posthumously with the 2007 Drum Major for Justice Award at Wilcox Central High School.

7. For further reading on Wilcox County organizing, see Fleming, *In the Shadow of Selma*; and Ashmore, *Carry It On*; and for Lowndes County, see Jeffries, *Civil Rights and Black Power in Alabama's Black Belt*.

8. Hosea Williams, SCLC registration report, October 30, 1965.

9. U.S. Commission on Civil Rights, *Political Participation*, 75/3.

10. State of Alabama Voter Registration Statistics, January 31, 2010. www.sos .alabama.gov/elections/voterreg.aspx, accessed April 17, 2013.

11. U.S. Commission on Civil Rights, *Political Participation*, 224.

12. Ashmore, *Carry It On*, 143–45.

13. *U.S. v. Wilcox County Board of Education*, 494 F. 2d 575 (1974).

14. Sheryl Threadgill, telephone conversation, June 14, 2009.

15. Donald P. Stone, telephone conversation, October 12, 2008. See also Wilcox County Board of Education data 2010. www.wilcox.k12.al.us/, last accessed April 26, 2013.

16. Ashmore, *Carry It On*, 10, 56.

17. Ibid., 186–97

18. Rev. Cleo "Sandy" Brooks, telephone interview, August 21, 2008.

19. Ashmore, *Carry It On*, 148.

20. Sheryl Threadgill, e-mail, October 8, 2011.

21. Demarth et al., *The Dynamics of Idealism*.

22. http://www.ywca.org, last accessed May 13, 2013. The 1970 YWCA National Convention adopted the One Imperative: "To trust our collective power towards the elimination of racism, wherever it exists, by any means necessary."

23. Shaw, *Beyond the Fields*.

Chapter 15

1. Rev. Benet Luchion, DSci Prof. Emeritus (Ret.), SCLC field staff 1963–67. Luchion's quotations were re-created from multiple e-mails and conversations 1993–2012 and approved by him.

2. Leventhal, *SCOPE*.

3. Leventhal, e-mail August 6, 2005, and http://en.wikipedia.org/wiki/SCOPE _Project, accessed April 17, 2013.

4. www.crmvet.org, accessed April 17, 2013.

5. Charles A. "Chuck" Bonner, e-mail, August 17, 2011.

6. For more on the international child sex slave trade, see Charles A. Bonner, *The Bracelet*.

7. Unless otherwise notated, Bonner, Block, Rogers, and Hartford quotes are recreated from personal conversations, December 8–10, 2005, Clear Lake, California, augmented by subsequent e-mails and telephone calls 2005–12.

8. Branch, *At Canaan's Edge*.

9. James "Jimmy" Rogers, personal conversation, Clear Lake, California, December 9, 2005.

10. Bruce Hartford, e-mail, November 5, 2012.

Chapter 16

1. Elsa Barkley Brown, *What Has Happened Here*, 297.

2. John Golden, telephone conversations, June 28, 2008, August 2, 2008.

3. Leventhal, *SCOPE*, 520.

4. Golden, telephone conversations.

5. Ibid.

6. W. Kate Charley, telephone interview, August 4, 2008.

7. Rosetta Angion, telephone interview, June 2, 2009.

8. Mary Alice Robinson, telephone interview, personal conversation, Selma, Alabama, March 7, 2010.

9. W. Kate Charley, conversation, Coy, Alabama, October 10, 2008.

10. Ibid.

11. W. Kate Charley, telephone conversation, August 4, 2008.

12. Leonard Hal, telephone conversation, July 13, 2010.

13. Cleo Brooks, telephone interview, August 21, 2008.

14. Ibid.

15. Leonard Hal, telephone conversation, July 13, 2010.

16. Tommy Hal, telephone conversation, July 27, 2010.

17. Eddie Harrell, telephone conversation, July 19–20, 2010.

18. *Wilcox Progressive Era*, January 10, 1979. Newspaper archives are in bound books in a vault inside the old courthouse (not available electronically).

19. Prince Arnold, brief conversation, Camden, Alabama, March 6, 2010.

20. Cleo Brooks, telephone interview, August 21, 2009.

21. Rosetta Anderson, telephone interview, June 9, 2009. See also Ashmore, *Carry It On*, 186–97.

22. Dan's brother, Leonard Hal, explained that the family name was Hal but that Dan changed his last name because a teacher at Tuskegee told Dan that Hal was a slave name so he changed it to Harrell.

23. W. Kate Charley, telephone conversation.

24. Ibid.

25. Boykin (Gee's Bend), Alabama, demographics based on the 2010 US Census.

26. Fleming, *In the Shadow of Selma*, chapter 6, "Vote."

27. *U.S. v. Logue*, 344 F.2d 290 (5th Cir. 1965)—supporting witness provision overturned.

28. www.smithsonianmag.com/arts-culture/geesbend.html, last accessed May 13, 2013.

29. For a recent history of the Gees Bend quilting organizations, see Linda Hunt Beckman, *Quilt Story*.

30. According to Beckman, "Collective" was a name conferred on the organization by art dealer Matthew Arnett. However, the ladies had experience with cooperatives and they used the term in "quilting cooper" exclusively in my conversations with them on October 8, 2008.

31. Quotes in this section are excerpts from re-created personal conversations with Mary Lee Bendolph, Annie Ross Kennedy, Nancy Ross Pettway, Allie Ross Pettway, and Luke Block, Gees Bend, Alabama, October 8, 2008.

32. Anonymous C, telephone conversation, November 6, 2011.

33. Anonymous B, telephone conversation, January 2, 2011.

34. Voncille Burrell Spencer, telephone conversation, November 6, 2011.

35. Betty Lawson Henderson, telephone conversation, December 29, 2011.

36. For more information, see www.naacp.org.

37. Martin Luther King Jr., *Where Do We Go from Here, Chaos or Community?*

Chapter 17

1. Global nonviolent action database, Swarthmore College, "Baton Rouge Students Sit-In for U.S. Civil Rights" (*Southern University*, 16), 1960.

2. Johns and Moore, "It Happened in Baton Rouge USA."

3. Jevaillier Jefferson, "The Southern University," 16.

4. Jesse Smith, telephone interview, June 8, 2009. Crispus Attucks was the first newly freed slave to die fighting in the American Revolution during the Boston Massacre of 1770. Until recently, his story was often omitted from textbooks.

5. William Johns, telephone interview, May 30, 2009.

6. Bob Crawford, personal conversation, Pine Apple, Alabama, October 10, 2008, followed by telephone conversations 2008–10 to clarify and augment.

7. The Deacons for Defense and Justice taught self-defense methods and offered protection to civil rights workers in areas where attacks came both from individuals and directly from state and county officials. See Hill, *Deacons for Defense*.

8. Block and I demonstrated with NAACP picketers at the San Mateo School Board in fall 1965 as they protested unequal education offered to blacks in East Palo Alto compared to whites in Palo Alto. We weren't arrested, but we were ticketed for blocking the sidewalk and parading without a permit. We had tried to keep the

spirit alive, but the work to be done out West was different and we had not been part of the organizing, so we never really fit in.

9. *Uhuru* is a Swahili word for freedom that was popular during the black power movement.

10. Bob Crawford Jr., personal conversation October 10, 2008.

11. Ibid., June 2, 2009.

12. Ashmore, *Carry It On*, 181–82.

13. Bob Crawford, telephone conversation, December 28, 2009.

14. Joy Crawford-Washington, telephone conversation, March 2012.

15. Joy Crawford-Washington, e-mail, March 24, 2009.

16. Smith, *Why Stand Up*, and multiple conversations with Carolyn Smith Taylor, 2009–10.

17. Carolyn Smith Taylor, telephone interview, April 27, 2009.

18. Ibid.

19. Jesse Smith, telephone interview, June 8, 2009.

20. Ibid.

21. Larry Smith, telephone interview, August 25, 2009.

22. Larry Smith, e-mail, September 7, 2012.

23. Larry Smith, telephone interview.

24. Fleming, *In the Shadow of Selma*, 180–81. On August 17, 1965, the board of education proceeded with condemnation to take over the Academy from the Presbyterian Church in December 1965. However, there were no civil rights workers staying at the Academy after August 1965.

25. Sheryl Threadgill, telephone interview, June 14, 2009.

26. Ibid.

27. Ibid.

28. "Oh Wallace" or "You Never Can Jail Us All," sung to the tune of the pop song "Kidnap" and adapted by civil rights workers to name individual county sheriffs.

29. Sheryl Threadgill, telephone interview, June 14, 2009.

30. Sheryl Threadgill, e-mail, October 13, 2010.

31. Sheryl Threadgill, telephone interview, June 14, 2009.

32. Donald P. Stone, personal conversation, Snow Hill, Alabama, October 12, 2008.

Chapter 18

1. Roy Reed, "Claim Camden Mayor Kicked Negro Teenager," *Chicago Daily Defender*, May 6, 1965.

2. Sim Pettway Sr., telephone interview, February 23, 2010, and written edits by Pettway in e-mail dated February 23 and 24, 2010, and March 2012.

3. Sim Pettway Sr., e-mail.

4. Sim Pettway Sr., telephone conversation, March 2012.

5. Ibid.

6. Sim Pettway Sr., telephone interviews, 2010.

7. Roy Reed, "2 Alabama Negroes Beaten as Whites Invade a Church," *New York Times*, July 1, 1965. Leventhal, *SCOPE*, 520. There were fewer than ten white people in the SCOPE project in Wilcox County.

8. Papers of the Southern Christian Leadership Conference, July 1, 1965, Archives of the Martin Luther King Jr. Center for Non-Violent Social Change, Atlanta, Georgia.

9. Frank Connor, telephone conversations, June 16 and 18, 2009.

10. Ibid.

11. Charles Nettles, telephone conversation, June 9, 2009.

12. Grady Nettles, telephone conversation, June 9, 2009. This incident is recounted in greater depth in Fleming, *In the Shadow of Selma*, 206.

13. Robert Powell, telephone interview, April 11, 2010.

14. Robert Powell, telephone conversations, March–May 2010.

15. Robert Powell, telephone interview.

16. Rosetta Marsh Anderson, telephone interviews, January 22 and June 9, 2009.

17. Rosetta Marsh Anderson, telephone interviews.

18. Ibid.

19. Ibid.

20. Betty Anderson, conversation, Camden, Alabama, March 4, 2010.

21. Alma Moton King, telephone conversation, June 10, 2009.

22. Arthurine Kelsaw Brooks, telephone conversation, September 19, 2008.

23. The federal office of Housing and Urban Development (HUD). "Self-help housing" provides loans to low-income families, www.hud.gov.

24. Shelly Dallas Dale, telephone interview, June 27, 2010.

25. Gloria Jean McDole, telephone interview, May 18, 2009.

26. Shelly Dallas Dale, telephone interview, June 17, 2010.

27. Rosetta Angion, telephone interview, June 2, 2009.

28. Rosetta Angion, telephone interview.

Chapter 19

1. Lewis V. Baldwin paraphrasing King from memory, undated telephone conversation, 2010.

2. Dorothy Walker, Birmingham Civil Rights Museum, Alabama Historical Society, e-mail, June 9, 2009.

3. Rosetta Angion, telephone interview.

4. Alma Moton King, telephone interview.

5. Lewis V. Baldwin, *There Is a Balm in Gilead*, and in an e-mail September 29, 2012.

6. Sheryl Threadgill, interview, Camden, Alabama, May 29, 2009.

7. Clarence Blackman, telephone interview, October 23, 2009.

8. Bob Fitch, conversation, Watsonville, California, Spring 2010.

9. Lewis V. Baldwin, extensive telephone conversations and e-mails, 2009–10, supplemented by telephone calls from 2009 to 2012.

10. Lewis V. Baldwin, e-mail, September 23, 2012.

11. Lewis V. Baldwin, telephone conversations.

12. Ibid.

13. Ibid.

14. Ibid.

15. Ibid.

16. *Eyes for Integers: A Pictorial Representation of Four Mathematical Operatives* and *Eyes for Angles and Polygons.* These books are designed to prepare kindergarten through middle school students for algebra.

17. David L. Baldwin, telephone conversations, May 22, August 3, and September 9, 2009.

18. Ibid.

19. David L. Baldwin, telephone conversation.

20. Lewis Baldwin, e-mail, September 23, 2012.

21. Ibid.

22. While the students thought "Rock Jaw" got his nickname from being so strict, his nephew Donald Stone explained in a November 5, 1012 e-mail that, "My uncles were both nicknamed 'Rock Jaw' because of their football prowess. Wendell Howell Edwards who taught at Camden Academy played a game against his brother William when they were both in college."

23. David L. Baldwin, telephone interview. Andrew Young lost his bid for Congress in 1970 but won in 1972, 1974, and 1976.

24. David L. Baldwin, telephone interview.

25. Lewis Baldwin, e-mail, September 23, 2012.

26. Lewis Baldwin, "Memories of the Struggle in Camden Forty-Five Years Later," keynote address, Commemorative Mass Meeting, Camden, Alabama, March 1, 2010. Typed manuscript provided by Dr. Baldwin.

Chapter 20

1. John Matthews, telephone interview, January 19, 2009.

2. Anonymous C, telephone conversation 2009.

3. W. Kate Charley, multiple telephone conversations 2008–9.

4. Shelly Dale, telephone conversation, June 17, 2010.

5. Rosetta Anderson, telephone interview, January 22, 2009.

6. Sheryl Threadgill, telephone interview.

7. Gloria Jean McDole, telephone interview, May 18, 2009.

8. Rosetta Angion, telephone conversation, June 2, 2009.

9. Arzula Johnson, telephone conversation, September 18, 2008.

10. John L. Matthews, telephone conversation, January 21, 2009.

11. Although my name did not appear on the printed program, I served on the planning committee and was invited to speak.

12. John L. Matthews, conversation, Pine Hill, Alabama, March 3, 2010, and e-mail, April 5, 2010.

13. Ibid.

14. John L. Matthews, e-mail, April 5, 2010.

15. Alma Moton King, conversation, Camden, Alabama, March 3, 2010.

16. Lewis V. Baldwin, e-mail, September 11, 2012.

17. Charles Bonner, conversation, March 6, 2010, Selma, Alabama. Restated in e-mail, September 13, 2012.

18. Mary Alice Robinson, telephone interview, June 2 and 8, 2009, and personal conversation March 7, 2010.

Bibliography

Books

Adelman, Bob, and Susan Hall. *Down Home*. New York: McGraw-Hill, 1972.

Ashmore, Susan Youngblood. *Carry It On: The War on Poverty and the Civil Rights Movement in Alabama, 1964–1972*. Athens: University of Georgia Press, 2008.

Baldwin, Lewis V. *There Is a Balm in Gilead*. Minneapolis, MN: Fortress Press, 1991.

Blackmon, Douglas A. *Slavery by Another Name: The Re-Enslavement of Black Americans from the Civil War to World War II*. New York: Doubleday, 2008.

Branch, Taylor. *At Canaan's Edge: America in the King Years, 1965–68*. New York: Simon and Schuster, 2006.

Carson, Clayborne. *In the Struggle: SNCC and the Black Awakening of the 1960s*. Cambridge, MA: Harvard University Press, 1995.

Carson, Clayborne, ed. *The Autobiography of Martin Luther King, Jr.* New York: Warner, 1998.

Demarth, N. J., Gerald Marwell, and Michael T. Aiken. *The Dynamics of Idealism: White Activists in a Black Movement*. San Francisco: Jossey-Bass, 1971.

Fairclough, Adam. *To Redeem the Soul of America*. Athens: University of Georgia Press, 2001, 233.

Fleming, Cynthia Griggs. *In the Shadow of Selma: The Continuing Struggle for Civil Rights in the Rural South*. Lanham, MD: Rowman and Littlefield, 2004.

Hill, Lance. *The Deacons for Defense: Armed Resistance and the Civil Rights Movement*. Chapel Hill: University of North Carolina Press, 2004.

Holsaert, Faith S., Martha Prescod Norman Noonan, Judy Richardson, Betty Garman Robinson, Jean Smith Young, and Dorothy M. Zellner, eds. *Hands on the Freedom Plow: Personal Accounts by Women in SNCC*. Urbana: University of Illinois Press, 2010.

Jeffries, Hasan Kwame. *Bloody Lowndes: Civil Rights and Black Power in Alabama's Black Belt*. New York: New York University Press, 2009.

King, Martin Luther. *Where Do We Go from Here, Chaos or Community?* Boston: Beacon Press, 1968.

Leventhal, Willy Siegel. *The SCOPE of Freedom: The Leadership of Hosea Williams with Dr. King's Summer '65 Student Volunteers.* Montgomery, AL: Challenge, 2005.

Shaw, Randy. *Beyond the Fields: Cesar Chavez, the UFW, and the Struggle for Justice in the 21st Century.* Berkeley: University of California Press, 2008.

Smith, Gwendolyn G. *Why Stand Up?* Nashville, TN: Choice, 1986.

Stone, Donald P. *Fallen Prince, William James Edwards: Black Education and the Quest for Afro American Nationality.* Snow Hill, AL: Snow Hill Press, 1990.

United States Commission on Civil Rights. *Political Participation: A Study of the Participation of Negroes in the Electoral and Political Process in 10 Southern States since Passage of the Voting Rights Act of 1965.* Washington, DC: Government Printing Office, 1968. Table 4. Data Alabama, Wilcox County as of October 31, 1967.

Journals

Brown, Elsa Barkley. "What Has Happened Here: The Politics of Difference in Women's History and Feminist Politics." *Feminist Studies*, vol. 18 (1972): 297.

Global nonviolent action database, Swarthmore College. "Baton Rouge Students Sit-In for U.S. Civil Rights" *Southern University* (1960): 16.

Murphy, Walter F. "The South Counterattacks: The Anti-NAACP Laws." *Western Political Quarterly* 12, no. 2 (1959): 371–90.

Pamphlets

Johns, Major, and Ronnie Moore. "It Happened in Baton Rouge, USA." New York, CORE, April 1962.

Newspaper Articles

Daniel, Leon. "Camden Cops Grab Banner from Selma." *Chicago Daily Defender*, April 8, 1965.

Feder, James. "King Hit with Ala. Injunction—Stop King from Using Ala. Kids." *Chicago Daily Defender*, April 20, 1965.

Good, Paul. "600 Students Preach Rights Gospel in the South." *Washington Post*, July 12, 1965.

Gordon, David M. "Threats Don't Stop Camden Pair from Serving Whites in Café." *Southern Courier*, July 23, 1965.

Jefferson, Jevaillier. "The Southern University 16: A Tribute to the 16 African-American College Students Whose Sacrifices Improved the Lives of All of Us." *Black*

Collegian Magazine 2005. www.blackcollegian.com/the-southern-university -16-a-tribute-to-16-african-american-college-students, accessed April 26, 2013.

Lynch, John A. "Schedule 'Big Push' for Three Alabama Counties." National edition. *Chicago Daily Defender*, January 30, 1965.

Matchan, Linda. "With These Hands." *Boston Globe*, May 15, 2005.

Nichols, Katie. "Remembering John Reese at Gees Bend." *Selma Times-Journal*, September 21, 2008.

Reed, Roy. "2 Alabama Negroes Beaten as Whites Invade a Church." *New York Times*, July 1, 1965.

———. "60 Negroes Alter Camden's History." Daily edition. *Chicago Daily Defender*, March 4, 1965.

———. "Alabama March by Negroes Fails—Camden Mayor and Officers Halt 200 at City Limits." *New York Times*, March 5, 1965.

———. "Alabama Sheriff Locks Church." *New York Times*, July 2,1965.

———. "Camden Alabama March by Blacks Fails." *Chicago Daily Defender*, March 6, 1965.

———. "Claim Camden Mayor Kicked Negro Teenager." *Chicago Daily Defender*, May 6, 1965.

———. "Dr. King Opens Rights Drive Tuesday." *New York Times*, June 21, 1965.

———. "Re-Open SCOPE Headquarters." Daily edition. *Chicago Daily Defender*, July 14, 1965.

———. "Say Whites Broke into Church to Beat Negro." National edition. *Chicago Daily Defender*, July 3, 1965.

———. "SNCC Looking for Volunteers." *San Francisco State—SF Gator*, spring 1965.

———. "Stymie Negroes' Vote Registration Drive in Camden—Police with Clubs Meet Vote March." Daily edition. *Chicago Daily Defender*, March 3, 1965.

———. "Threaten Daily Protest for Added Voter Days." *Chicago Daily Defender*, April 21, 1965.

———. "Use Smoke, Tear Gas on Ala. Demonstrators." *Chicago Daily Defender*, April 6, 1965.

———. *Wilcox Progressive Era*, January 10, 1979.

Legal Cases

Kennedy v. Bruce, 298 F.2d 860 (5th Cir. 1962).

Reynolds v. Katzenbach, 248 F. Supp. 593 (S.D. Al. 1965).

U.S. v. Bruce, 353 F.2d. 474 (5th Cir. 1965).

U.S. v. Logue, 344 F.2d 290 (5th Cir. 1965).

U.S. v. Wilcox County Board of Ed., 366 F.2d 769 (5th Cir. 1966).

U.S. v. Wilcox County Board of Ed., 494 F.2d 575 (5th Cir. 1974).

Williams v. Wallace, 240 F. Supp 100 (N.D. Alabama 1965).

Interviews/Conversations

Anderson, Betty. Personal conversations, Camden and Selma, Alabama, March 5–7, 2010.

Anderson, Rosetta Marsh. Telephone interviews, January 22, June 9 and 29, 2009; personal conversations, October 11, 2008, and March 3, 2010, Camden; and February 28, 2012, Mobile, Alabama; telephone conversations 2008–10.

Angion, Rosetta. Telephone interview, June 2, 2009.

Baldwin, David L. Telephone interviews, May 18–22, August 3, and September 9, 2009; e-mail and telephone communications, Bell Arthur, North Carolina, 2009.

Baldwin, Lewis V. Extensive conversations and e-mail, December 2010–12.

Blackman, Clarence. Telephone interview, October 23, 2009.

Block, R. Luke (Bob). Extensive in-person, telephone, and e-mail communications, 2005–12.

Bonner, Charles "Chuck" A. Written quotes provided September 10, 2009, Sausalito, California; extensive communications, 2005–12.

Brooks, Arthurine Kelsaw. Telephone interview, September 19, 2008.

Brooks, Cleo "Sandy." Telephone interviews, August 21, 2009, December 28, 2009.

Charley, W. Kate. Personal conversation, October 10, 2008, Coy, Alabama; telephone conversations, August 4, 8, 11, 2008, May 28, 29, 2009, and June 8, 2009, and 2011–12.

Connor, Frank. Telephone conversations, June 16 and 18, 2009.

Crawford, Bob, Jr. Personal conversation, Pine Apple, Alabama, October 10, 2008; telephone interviews, June 2, 2009, December 28, 2009; telephone conversations, 2008–12.

Crawford-Washington, Joy. Extensive personal conversations, Camden, Selma, and Mobile, Alabama, and e-mail, 2008–12.

Dale, Shelley Dallas. Personal conversation, Camden, Alabama, March 3, 2010; telephone interview, June 17, 2010.

Davis, John. Presentation, Camden, Alabama, March 1, 2010.

Golden, John. Telephone conversations, June 28, August 2, 2008.

Hal, Leonard. Telephone conversation, July 13, 2010.

Hal, Tommy. Telephone conversation, July 27, 2010.

Harrell, Eddie. Telephone conversations, July 19–20, 2010.

Hartford, Bruce. Telephone and personal conversations and e-mails, 2005–12.

Henderson, Betty Lawson. Telephone conversations, November 6 and December 29, 2011.

Johns, William J. Telephone interview, May 30, 2009.

Johnson, Arzula. Telephone interview, September 18, 2008.

Kennedy, Annie Ross. Personal conversation, Gees Bend, Alabama, October 9, 2008.

King, Alma Moton. Telephone interview, June 10, 2009; personal and telephone conversations, 2008–12; and e-mail.

Luchion, Benet. Multiple personal and telephone conversations and e-mail, Santa Cruz, California, 2003–12.

Matthews, John L. Personal interviews 2008, January 2009. Extensive e-mail, personal and telephone conversations, Camden, Alabama, 2008–12.

McDole, Gloria. Telephone conversation, May 18, 2009.

Nettles, Charles. Telephone conversation, June 9, 2009.

Nettles, Grady. Telephone conversation, June 9, 2009.

Pettway, Sim, Sr. Telephone interview and email, February 23 and 24, 2010; presentation at Antioch Baptist Church, Camden, Alabama, March 1, 2010; and e-mail and telephone conversations, March 2010–March 2013.

Powell, Robert. Personal conversations, Selma and Camden, Alabama; and telephone conversations, March–May 2010.

Robinson, Mary Alice. Telephone interview, June 2, 8, 2009; and personal conversation, Selma, Alabama, March 7, 2010.

Rogers, James R. "Jimmy." Personal conversations, November 2005, Clear Lake, California; and telephone interview, November 15, 2009.

Smith, Jesse. Telephone interview, June 8, 2009.

Smith, Larry. Telephone interview, August 25, 2009; and e-mail, September 7, 2012.

Smith-Taylor, Carolyn. Telephone interview, April 27, 2009; multiple telephone conversations and e-mails, 2009–12.

Spencer, Voncille Burrell. Telephone conversation, November 6, 2011.

Stone, Donald P. Personal conversation, Snow Hill, Alabama, October 12, 2008; telephone conversations and e-mails, October–November 2012.

Threadgill-Matthews, Sheryl. Personal interviews, Camden, Alabama, May 29, 2009, June 21, 2009; extensive e-mail and telephone conversations, 2008–12.

Tucker, Deborah Burrell. Telephone conversations, November 6 and December 30, 2011.

Songs

"A Change Is Gonna Come." Sam Cooke, 1964.

"Ain't Gonna Let Nobody Turn Me 'Round." Traditional gospel song.

"Don't Look Back." Smokey Robinson and Ronald White. Motown Records, 1965.

"Keep on Pushing." Curtis Mayfield. Warner Timberland Music Company BMI, 1964.

"Keep Your Eye on the Prize." Traditional song.

"Lift Every Voice and Sing." NAACP theme song.

"Murder on the Road in Alabama." Len Chandler Jr. Fall River Music, 1965.

"Never Too Much Love." Curtis Mayfield. Warner Timberland Music Company BMI, 1964.

"Ode to Joy." Ninth Symphony. Ludwig van Beethoven, words by Friedrich Schiller.

"This Little Light of Mine." Traditional song.

"This May Be the Last Time." Traditional spiritual.

Websites

Civil Rights Veterans. www.crmvet.org, last accessed August 5, 2012.

Hunt Beckman, Linda. *Quilt Story: Black Rural Women, White Urban Entrepreneurs, and the American Dream.* The Black Commentator, 456, January 26, 2012. http://www.blackcommentator.com/456/456_quilt_story_beckman_guest_printer_friendly.html, last accessed, August 22, 2012.

National Association for the Advancement of Colored People, NAACP, www.naacp.org, last accessed November 16, 2012.

Smithsonian Institution. http://www.smithsonianmag.com/arts-culture/geesbend.html, last accessed August 23, 2012.

State of Alabama. Alabama State Voter Registration Statistics, January 31, 2010. www.sos.alabama.gov/elections/voterreg.aspx, last accessed July 22, 2012.

U.S. Bureau of the Census. State and County Quick Facts, Wilcox County 2010. www.uscensus.gov/quickfacts, last accessed July 22, 2012.

Wilcox County Historical Society. www.wilcoxwebworks.com, last accessed July 2010.

YWCA. www.ywca.org, last accessed November 13, 2012.

Index